An Important Message to Our Readers

This product provides information and general advice about the law. But laws and procedures change frequently, and they can be interpreted differently by different people. For specific advice geared to your specific situation, consult an expert. No book, software or other published material is a substitute for personalized advice from a knowledgeable lawyer licensed to practice law in your state.

3rd edition

Child Custody

Building Parenting Agreements That Work

by Mimi E. Lyster

Keeping Up to Date

To keep its books up to date, Nolo.com issues new printings and new editions periodically. New printings reflect minor legal changes and technical corrections. New editions contain major legal changes, major text additions or major reorganizations. To find out if a later printing or edition of any Nolo book is available, call Nolo at 510-549-1976 or check our website at http://www.nolo.com.

To stay current, follow the "Update" service at our website: http://www.nolo.com/update. In another effort to help you use Nolo's latest materials, we offer a 35% discount off the purchase of the new edition of your Nolo book when you turn in the cover of an earlier edition. (See the "Special Upgrade Offer" in the back of this book.) This book was last revised in **November 1999**.

Third Edition	NOVEMBER 1999
Editor	SPENCER SHERMAN
Illustrations	MARI STEIN
Cover Design	TONI IHARA
Book Design	TERRI HEARSH
Production	STEPHANIE HAROLDE
Index	JANE MEYERHOFER
Proofreading	JOE SADUSKY
Printing	BERTELSMANN SERVICES, INC.

Lyster, Mimi E.
    Child custody : building parenting agreements that work / by Mimi
E. Lyster. -- 3rd ed.
       p.   cm.
    Includes index.
    ISBN 0-87337-521-1
    1. Custody of children--United States--Popular works.   2. Divorce
settlements--United States--Popular works.   I. Title.
KF547.Z9L97 1999
346.7301'73--dc21

                                                    99-13950
                                                      CIP

For information on bulk purchases or corporate premium sales, please contact the Special Sales Department. For academic sales or textbook adoptions, ask for Academic Sales. Call 800-955-4775 or write to Nolo, Inc., 950 Parker Street, Berkeley, CA 94710.

Dedication

To my daughters, Katelyn, Alysha and Nichelle, who each make my world such a wonderful place to be; and to my new but good friend Ben—I look forward to getting to know you more! And also to you, Steve, for being there as Orcas appeared—and for sharing this journey into unknowing.

Acknowledgments

I continue to owe thanks to:

- Kevin Elkus, John Helie and Steve Elias for helping me cling to the notion that our virtual team will yet pull a rabbit from some hat
- the editing department at Nolo, especially Spencer Sherman, for helping to bring this edition into being, and
- my mediation mentors, peers and clients for helping me to learn with increasing clarity the power of facilitated decision making.

I would also like to thank those that I have come to know and work with in California's family court system for their significant contributions to my understanding of this work and the evolving context within which families are helped to find satisfying and child-focused solutions to their parenting disputes.

Table of Contents

3 Preparing to Build Your Parenting Agreement

4 How to Negotiate a Parenting Agreement

5 Building Your Parenting Agreement

6 Parenting Agreements and Money

7 Making Mediation and Arbitration Work for You

8 Dealing With Changes in Your Existing Agreements

9 Understanding Your Children's Needs

10 Multiracial, Multicultural and International Families

11 Nontraditional Families

12 State and Federal Laws Affecting Child Custody

13 Help Beyond the Book

A Appendix: Tear-Out Forms

Worksheet 1: Describe Your Child

Worksheet 2: Describe Your Relationship With Your Child

Worksheet 3: Adding the Details

Worksheet 4: Checklist of Issues for Your Parenting Agreement

Parenting Agreement

Index

Introduction

This is a book for parents who want to reach the best possible agreement about how they will share and divide their parenting responsibilities during or after a separation or divorce. This book will help you to evaluate your current situation and choose from among a wide range of possible solutions so that you, the other parent and your children can put many, if not all, of your parenting disputes behind you and look to the future with confidence.

This type of agreement can have many names. Most commonly it is called a "Custody Agreement," but increasingly, it is known as a "Parenting Agreement," a term coined by Dr. Isolina Ricci, author of *Mom's House, Dad's House* (Macmillian, 1998), or "Parenting Plan."

Regardless of its label, a parenting agreement typically addresses issues such as:

- taking care of the children
- making necessary decisions on the children's behalf
- making sure the children spend time with both parents, and
- meeting the children's medical, psychological, educational, spiritual, physical and social needs.

This book takes you step by step through the process of creating a parenting agreement. It also explains how your agreement can serve as a blueprint for your future parenting relationship with your children and with their other parent. When thoughtfully prepared, a parenting agreement becomes the centerpiece of a separation or divorce involving children.

A. Make Your Own Custody Decisions If Possible

When parents first turn their attention to custody and parenting issues, they are typically angry, hurt and overwhelmed with both the divorce or separation process and their own feelings. Often a parent's first instinct is to try to gain the upper hand by demanding full custody of the children. All too often the other parent responds in kind. These instinctive reactions create a substantial risk of a long, expensive and emotionally draining journey into the world of child custody litigation, the result of which is likely to please no one.

When parents take parenting issues to court rather than resolve them on their own, they are short-changing themselves. They must rely on a judge or court-appointed evaluator to understand the family's situation and each parent's

position within a few minutes or hours, and then to make wise decisions with the children's best interests in mind. It is very difficult for a judge to "get it right" under these conditions.

Each state has guidelines for its judges to follow when making custody decisions. Nonetheless, judges have considerable discretion in interpreting these guidelines and imposing their own views of what constitutes a good environment for children. The chance that a judge's decision will be ideal for your specific situation is relatively slim.

Most researchers—especially those who study the effects of divorce on children—believe passionately that using the court to resolve custody issues is a mistake in all but a few cases. It is far better for parents to negotiate their own parenting agreement, with the help of outside experts such as mediators, counselors and lawyers on an as-needed basis. Court intervention is appropriate, however, if the children's safety or well-being is at risk and their parents cannot agree on a way to reduce that risk.

B. Parenting Issues and Financial Issues

In addition to parenting issues, separation and divorce often require the parents to deal with financial issues such as dividing property, paying marital debts and providing for support. Although this book focuses only on the parenting issues, by starting with an agreement that serves your children's best interests, you may find that many of the financial issues are easier to tackle and resolve.

For example, if you choose to have one parent take on the majority of the daily parenting responsibilities, you may decide that that parent will live in the family home. But if your children will be spending approximately equal amounts of time with each of you, you reasonably may choose to sell the family home (especially if it is your primary asset) and use the money to rent or buy a home for each parent that can accommodate the children.

Clearly, decisions about financial issues affect parenting issues just as decisions about parenting issues can affect financial issues. This book assumes that, to the greatest possible extent, the "people" issues should come first and your agreement about how to best meet your children's needs should set the stage for deciding the money issues. This is especially true when it comes to child support. Although some parents may stop seeing their children or refuse to pay child support, research shows that the larger the role a parent plays in the lives of his or her children, the more likely that parent is to cheerfully contribute to their support.

C. Why This Book Is Unique

This book has a number of innovative features not generally found in other books addressing separate parenting and related custody issues. To begin, you can use this book whether you are thinking about separation, preparing to negotiate your first agreement or modifying an existing agreement. The six other unique features of this book are described below.

1. This Book Offers Real-World Solutions to Parenting Issues

Parenting encompasses a complex mix of relationships and responsibilities. From the cosmic to the comical, from the monumental to the mundane, the essence of a parent's role is the same—whether or not the parents remain partners.

This book reflects the trials and tribulations of real parents who have encountered and resolved the same is-

sues that you and your children's other parent now face. It presents the research and observations of professionals who help parents resolve separate parenting issues, and describes the solutions that these parents have fashioned for themselves.

2. This Book Is for Married and Unmarried Parents

Many couples in the United States parent without getting married. These parents do not legally separate or divorce, but their needs for parenting plans are just the same as their separated or divorced counterparts. Although most of the examples are written as though a legal marriage had taken place (and the terms "separation" and "divorce" appear throughout the book), parents who were never married can assume that the terms and examples include their relationship.

3. This Book Is for Nontraditional Families and Families With Different Cultural Backgrounds

This book is not just for Caucasian-, middle class- and heterosexual-parented families. Incorporated throughout the text, as well as in chapters devoted to multicultural, multiracial and nontraditional families, is an understanding that all kinds of families need parenting agreements.

4. This Book Is for Families With One Child or Many Children

For convenience, this book is written using the word "children" rather than "child" or "child(ren)." If you have only one child, you can assume that every reference to children includes your child.

5. This Book Can Be Used With or Without Professional Help

This book was written to help you negotiate your own parenting agreement, with or without the help of professionals such as mediators, counselors, attorneys, arbitrators and courts. It includes worksheets you can use for your own negotiations, to record your agreement or to help any outside professional who might become involved. The book helps you assess whether or not your agreement will work, lists resources for getting outside help if necessary and explains how you can finalize your agreement if you are involved in a court proceeding.

You may be surprised to find that this book doesn't sound like what your attorney or divorced friends say is important about separation, divorce and separate parenting. That is because this book is focused on you, your children and their other parent—not on the law.

Many people who have been through divorce, and the lawyers who represent them, focus on terms like "custody" and "visitation" and ask the one question, "Who gets the kids?" While these are certainly important, this book helps parents to first understand their children's needs, and then to structure their agreement accordingly. After you and the other parent have been able to agree about most aspects of your separate parenting relationship, this book will help you to assign the labels which seem to make the most sense.

6. This Book Is a Work in Progress

This book is part of a growing database of real-world solutions to separate parenting problems. If you come up with an issue or a solution we haven't included, let us know on the Reader Contribution Card you will find in the back of the book. If we use your issue or options in future editions, we will acknowledge your contribution (if you wish).

D. A Word to Skeptics

Many parents who go through separation or divorce feel that books like this and processes like mediation won't work for them. This feeling may be based on one or more of the following beliefs:

- The emotional conflict between the parties precludes any approach except all-out legal warfare.
- One or both parents are unwilling to budge on core issues.
- Each parent's bottom line includes the same result (usually sole or primary custody of the children awarded to that parent).

Fortunately, none of these situations is an automatic barrier to negotiating an agreement on your own or to reaching an agreement through mediation or an avenue other than court.

1. If You Think the Conflict Is Too Intense to Negotiate on Your Own

Intense conflict is a natural and normal part of separation, divorce and separate parenting. To presume otherwise would do you, the other parent and your children a disservice. But conflict—even intense conflict—is not reason enough to assume you cannot negotiate a parenting agreement.

Chapters 4 and 7 contain information on how you and the other parent can handle your own negotiations even if your conflict is bitter. Chapter 4 explains how to conduct an effective meeting and improve your communication style, and offers specific strategies for managing conflict. Chapter 7 explains the process of mediation and how it can be used to bring parents together for the benefit of their children.

If your pessimism is especially high as you read these words, skim Chapters 4 and 6 before continuing. Hopefully, you will gain some reassurance from what you find there, and be willing to return here and work through the rest of the book. (See Chapter 13 for more resources.)

2. If the Other Parent Won't Budge

Being adamant about a certain position is not necessarily bad. If the less flexible parent can describe his or her concerns, goals and perceptions of the situation in some detail, you will often have a good list of issues that must be addressed and resolved to reach a lasting agreement.

Perhaps the most effective way to put your discussions on a positive footing is to shift the focus to your children. The worksheets in Chapter 3 help you to identify and describe your concerns, describe your children's needs and acknowledge the unique situations that your family is experiencing. Chapter 9 helps you gain insights into what children need and experience at different ages, and how you might structure your agreement to best meet those needs.

By focusing on your children while negotiating parenting arrangements, you'll probably find that you can adjust your positions enough to produce a good parenting agreement.

E. So, You Just Want to Fight!

There are times when a custody fight appears inevitable. You, of course, may be willing to be reasonable, but you may also believe that the other parent isn't, and that there is really no effective choice other than to fight it out in court.

Many have traveled the adversarial road, and probably for the same reasons you are considering this option. Constant fighting, arguing and blaming in a marriage generally lead to more of the same in the process of dissolving it. Unfortunately, the consequences of continuing this behavior can be dramatic, including protracted litigation, escalating costs, a dramatically reduced standard of living and significant damage to your children's emotional well-being. Jim Melamed, a family law mediator in Oregon, calls these results "the parade of the horribles"—and appropriately so!

1. Custody Litigation Is Unpredictable

While asking a court to resolve differences over custody and visitation is, unfortunately, the traditional approach, it is also highly unpredictable. If you doubt this, ask your attorney to guarantee, in writing, what will happen if you choose to litigate your custody and visitation issues.

Part of this unpredictability stems from the fact that most parents believe their cause to be righteous. This means, of course, that at least half of all litigants are unpleasantly surprised by the judge's decision. More importantly, litigation is unpredictable because judges are human beings who naturally differ in their approach to the kinds of problems that custody and visitation disputes present.

While it is true that judges are supposed to make a decision that favors the best interests of the children, and the laws of every state list factors that judges should consider when determining what these best interests are, the standards themselves leave considerable room for individual interpretation. (See Chapter 12, Section B, for how judges determine what is in the best interests of children.) For example, some judges decide that the conflict between the parents is overblown or unnecessary and order joint custody, thereby requiring cooperation between parents who find the task nearly impossible given their feelings and the realities of their relationship. Other judges, and some states, consider ongoing contact with both parents to be so important that custody is awarded to the parent who is most likely to foster a healthy relationship with the other parent, thus initiating the battle to be declared "most reasonable and accommodating." The parent who gets custody on this basis may or may not be the best parent for the actual job of raising the children. In almost every case, some factors favor one parent and others the other parent. This means that even when two fairly "good" parents face off in court, both are likely to walk away dissatisfied.

2. Custody Litigation Is Usually Costly

If you choose to pursue litigation, the next hurdle will be figuring out how to pay for your court battle. If you decide to represent yourself, you will save on attorney's fees, although the costs and time associated with filing (which includes doing the legal research as well as preparing and serving your court papers) can be significant. If you do hire an attorney, you can expect to pay $3,000 to $15,000 or more in fees for even a "routine" case.

Whether or not you hire an attorney, you may find yourself having to pay for testimony from a counselor or therapist (which generally requires three to five sessions, at an average rate of $75 to $125 per hour, prior to submitting any final report), or a custody evaluation (which generally costs between $2,000 and $7,500 depending on how complicated the issues are, or how much conflict exists in the family). (You can read more about custody evaluations in Chapter 5, issue 12, and in Chapter 13, Section D3.) In addition, you will probably find it necessary to arrange for testimony from friends, relatives, school teachers, clergy members and neighbors.

Funding a child custody battle can be especially difficult in light of the fact that, after separation or divorce, the income you shared must now be used to maintain two separate residences. In addition to separate rent or mortgage payments, telephone service, food and other incidentals, you will be forced to duplicate the furniture, clothes and toys that don't travel with the children, and meet the costs associated with the distance between your homes (such as travel and telephone). Many who separate or divorce are stunned by how quickly their money disappears!

3. Custody Litigation Damages the Children Regardless of the Result

As important as money is, the economic consequences of fighting in court can be dwarfed by the impact it will have on your children. Mental health professionals, the court system, attorneys, mediators and custody evaluators all agree on one thing—ongoing parental conflict is generally the single most damaging stressor for children.

When conflict is obvious and occurs over extended periods of time, children feel torn between loving both parents, hoping someone will magically restore the marriage and wishing that they could be anywhere but where the battle is raging! You may be surprised to note that this is true even when parents have most of their arguments out of their children's presence. Because children have spent all of their lives living with and observing their parents, and because children rely on their parents to provide the basic securities of life, they develop an uncanny ability to "read" them. Children are exquisitely sensitive to each parent's reactions when that parent hears the other parent's name, receives a call from the other parent, receives court papers from the other parent or calls the attorney.

4. Avoid Litigating Your Custody Dispute If At All Possible

Hopefully, all that you've read so far has convinced you that litigation should most definitely be a last resort. The purpose of this book is to give you the tools and information that make it possible to avoid litigation and to resolve your differences with the other parent in as friendly a way as possible. Parenting separately is challenging, but it is a job worth doing well. By making the commitment to put your children's interests first, and by taking the time to educate yourself about your options, you, your children and the other parent may find that you can develop a parenting agreement that each of you feels is essentially fair.

F. Icons Used in This Book

Look for these icons to alert you to certain kinds of information.

 When you see the "fast track" icon, you'll be alerted to a chance to skip some material you may not need to read.

 This icon introduces a family.

 The caution icon warns you of potential problems.

 The briefcase lets you know when you need the advice of an attorney.

 This icon refers you to other books or resources.

■

Taking Stock of Your Situation

Before getting into the nuts and bolts of building an effective parenting plan, you need to understand the context within which your parenting decisions will be made.

A. You Are Not Alone

For the last quarter of a century, the expectation that two people would meet, marry, raise a family and grow old together has changed. Quite a few studies over the past 10 years have confirmed that couples who divorce will be most likely to do so after about seven years of marriage, and that two-thirds of these divorcing families will include at least one child under the age of six. Statistics also show that more than a million children each year for the past 25 years have lived through a divorce.

Other researchers have commented on the changing structure of the family in the 1990s. During the last 30 years, the divorce rate has quadrupled, births outside of marriage have increased by 22% and many families relocate every few years, which deprives these families of the many benefits derived from a geographically close extended family. As this century draws to a close, researchers predict that nearly half of all babies born today will spend some time living in a one-parent family. A family in which biological parents stay together and raise their children is now only true for about one-third of all couples. The reality is that most parents never marry, marry and later divorce or create their families through artificial insemination or adoption.

B. Keep Your Parenting Plan Focused on Your Children

You and your children's other parent are about to undertake a difficult but very important project—making adult decisions that will be the best possible ones for your children to live with. Of course, it may be hard to separate the desire to have nothing more to do with your ex from the task at hand. After all, separation and divorce were not created to meet children's needs but rather to resolve adult problems.

Even if your separation or divorce will be better for your children in the long run, for the short term, most children feel that few things are worse. Divorce or separation can shake a child's confidence that he or she will continue to be loved, cared for and safe. This is true even when children understand the adult reasons behind the decision.

You and the other parent can greatly ease your children's insecurity by using this book to formulate a parenting plan which is focused squarely on meeting your children's individual needs. The more attention you pay to those needs, the more likely you are to build an agreement that works for you as well.

You and the other parent must honestly assess your relationship as parents, as well as your ability to work together. To keep your agreement focused on your children, you must be willing to trust each other and to set aside your anger, frustration and pain. If you've just separated, you may think it will be impossible to trust and cooperate with the other parent. In fact, however, trustful and cooperative separate parenting relationships usually do evolve over time. (See Section C, below.) One of the most effective strategies for moving toward this kind of relationship is to build on points of agreement until you craft a comprehensive parenting plan.

<table>
<tr><td>

DIVORCE AND SEPARATION AREN'T ONLY ABOUT ENDING AN INTIMATE RELATIONSHIP

Some liken the ending of the marriage (or otherwise similarly committed relationship) to a "death." If you accept this premise, or find that this describes your inner state, then you should expect to experience the same progression of feelings that Elizabeth Kubler-Ross, well known for her work in the area of death and dying, describes as the pathway to dealing with physical death. These stages are: denial, anger, bargaining and, finally, acceptance.

Others remind us that separation and divorce occur on many levels, including emotional, financial, legal, social and intimate. Given this somewhat complicated series of relationships, you and your ex (or soon-to-be ex) should plan carefully for how you will manage each of these elements of the separation or divorce. Your children will benefit most when you can distinguish the "adult" issues from the parenting issues, and keep the children out of the negotiations over the adult issues.

As you and the other parent gain an understanding of the full scope of your relationship and the ways in which you will sever your ties or distance yourselves from each other, you will find that you will have an increasing ability to chart your own course, and be pleased with the results of your efforts. In fact, the parents who express the greatest levels of satisfaction with their separate parenting arrangements are those that take the time to negotiate comprehensive, child-focused agreements that both parents can accept and support.

</td></tr>
</table>

C. Know That It Gets Easier Over Time

When parents initially separate or divorce, the process is often traumatic. Many people behave irrationally or are unstable. As time passes, however, many parents can entertain a more rational and dispassionate view of their options.

Let's look more closely at the typical emotional stages parents pass through upon separation, and how these stages might affect each parent's ability to reach an effective, child-focused parenting plan.

1. The First Few Weeks

Just before or just after the initial separation, you are likely to feel confused by a seemingly endless array of decisions, each of which appears the most important. Like most parents, you are probably riding a roller coaster of emotions that includes intense feelings of rage, depression, abandonment, relief, grief, guilt and excitement. In short, deciding to end a relationship, or having one ended for you, can leave you feeling as though you might be going crazy!

Now is not the time to worry about charting a permanent course for your children's future. Instead, try to develop one or more short-term agreements that will allow you, the other parent and your children to settle in to the new arrangements. This will give you time to see what makes the most sense for the long run. For most parents, the keys to success is to separate the adult relationship issues from the parenting issues and developing a clear, child-centered plan that each parent can easily follow. Your own emotional survival—as well as that of your children—is very much at stake and must be your first priority.

GET HELP

A number of books have been written to help parents going through separation or divorce cope at the beginning. (See Chapter 13 for references.)

2. The First Few Months

Several months after the initial separation, your life will probably be a little calmer, but you may still find that your relationship with the other parent can enrage either or both of you. One reason is that while you distance yourself from the other parent, you continue to share your children. They can be a constant reminder of what has gone on (or has gone wrong) and what remains to be done. If you are experimenting with a new partner or approach to how you live your life, you may feel annoyed at the damper on your newfound freedom that you think the other parent's presence introduces.

At the other end of the spectrum, you or the other parent may still feel angry, sad, powerless or abandoned, as you did when you first separated. If so, either of you may suspect that every action or inaction by the other is another ploy to retaliate or undercut your newfound stability.

If you try to negotiate a parenting plan during this phase, you may find it extremely difficult to reach agreement on any but the easiest issues. Many parents, nevertheless, negotiate workable temporary parenting arrangements early on, especially to resolve a particular issue, such as where the children will attend school.

3. One Year Later

A year or more after the initial separation, you may be far more clear-headed about your situation than you were when you first separated. You and the other parent will have firsthand experience with your initial (or temporary) parenting arrangements. You can gauge the effects that these arrangements have had on your life and on your children. You will probably be ready to address most, if not all, of the issues presented in Chapter 5.

4. The Second Year and Beyond

Two years or more following a separation, most families have settled into their first parenting arrangements, and many realize that their arrangements need at least a few changes in order to accommodate the changes in their own or their children's lives. In fact, many mediators report that significant numbers of families renegotiate their first parenting agreements around two years after their separation.

No matter what stage of the separation you are in, remember that the one constant element of separate parenting is change. Neither you, the other parent nor your children can expect the first agreement to be the last. You can never anticipate all of the decisions you will have to make on behalf of your children. Certain provisions will work for the long term while others will need to be revised regularly.

The changes that can trigger the need to modify a parenting agreement are many. One of the most common is the presence of a parent's new partner. Children often have strong opinions about new stepparents, boyfriends or girlfriends. Additionally, when one parent has a new partner—especially if that is the parent with whom the children primarily live—the other parent may need reassurance that he or she will not be replaced by the new partner.

Other changes that tend to trigger the need for a modification of an existing arrangement include:

- a parent's desire to move to change jobs or go back to school
- a parent's desire to move to be closer to relatives
- a child's special needs, or
- a child's desire to live with the other parent.

D. Learn How to Negotiate

Negotiation is the process of reaching an agreement acceptable to the people involved. The more successful the negotiation, the more acceptable the agreement. For the following three major reasons, negotiation is an integral part of separate parenting:

- Most parents tend to be involved with their children, at some level, well into their early adulthood. Parents who stay involved in their children's lives must find a way to work together.
- Children usually want to maintain a relationship with both parents and suffer when their parents constantly fight. The better the parents are at negotiating satisfactory solutions to their differences, the better their relationships will be with their children.
- When parents are unable to agree on basic decisions regarding their children's health, education and welfare, a court will step in and impose decisions. These decisions, though aimed at protecting and preserving the best interests of the children, are often very different from what the parents want or feel is appropriate.

Negotiating your parenting agreement is covered in detail in Chapter 4.

USING MEDIATION TO HELP YOU NEGOTIATE

There are several basic approaches to negotiating a parenting agreement. Some parents resolve the issues on their own. Others ask a counselor to help, work with attorneys or use mediation. Mediation is a process that uses a trained neutral person (someone who has nothing to gain or lose by what you decide) to help you identify the issues to resolve and reach solutions. It offers many advantages because you control the decision-making process.

Mediation is available in all states, either through the court or from private practitioners, and has become popular because it is less adversarial than courtroom litigation. (It is discussed in Chapter 7.)

E. If the Other Parent Is Absent

This book assumes that both parents are at least minimally involved in their children's lives. This, however, is not always true. Some parents leave their families and are never heard from again. Others are around so infrequently that they have abandoned their families in most respects. If this describes your situation, you will probably need the help of an attorney to get a divorce (if you're legally married) and obtain child support.

With respect to daily parenting, consider talking with one of the children's grandparents, a favorite aunt or uncle or a very close friend about sharing the parenting. If it works, you'll have adult help and your children will have the benefit of another adult's influence while growing up.

F. If There Is Violence or Abuse in the Family

Domestic violence, child abuse and child neglect are a feature of family life for many in the United States. For some, these events are unique to the period leading up to and during the actual separation or divorce. For others, a long history of violence, abuse or neglect convinces one or both parents that a separation or divorce is required.

Physical violence, threats of violence, sexual assault and child abuse are illegal. Specific definitions of domestic violence vary from state to state. But federal laws says it is illegal to injure—or threaten to injure—anyone related by blood or marriage, or with whom you are living together or in an intimate relationship. This is true regardless of your cultural or religious heritage, citizenship status or personal beliefs about discipline or the proper relationship between husbands and wives.

If your divorce, separation or co-parenting relationship includes acts or threats of domestic violence, emotional abuse, child abuse, child sexual abuse or child neglect, protecting your and your children's safety must be your first concern. This means getting whatever emotional, legal or other support you need to understand your options. It also means planning for how you will stay safe while you develop a parenting agreement.

The time that one partner chooses to get help, leave an abusive relationship or get a restraining order can be the most dangerous of all. This is because one partner might try to hurt or to scare the other as a way to stop them from leaving or involving "outsiders" in their "family" or "private" matter.

Although each safety plan will be somewhat different, every one should consider:

- where all family members will live
- whether any family member's whereabouts will be kept secret
- whether legal protection (such as civil protection or restraining orders) is necessary
- whether visits with a violent parent will be supervised, and
- how each affected person will get emotional support.

Situations involving violence or abuse usually call for outside help. (See Chapter 13 for more advice and resources.)

Most of the information in this book assumes that your family situation is conducive to negotiating and reaching a parenting agreement. But what about mediation in violent or potentially violent situations? Some professionals actively discourage victims of domestic violence from getting involved in mediation, family counseling or other non-court proceedings where batterers and their victims meet face to face because of the power imbalance that exists between people who have been involved in domestic violence. They worry that a victim might be too intimidated by the batterer to effectively represent his or her own interests, or to be an effective advocate on behalf of the children's interests.

Many experts worry that any type of negotiations regarding custody and visitation with someone who has committed domestic violence is inappropriate because it implies that somehow the violence is excusable. To address these concerns, some states (especially those that require mediation for custody and visitation disputes) allow victims of domestic violence to either skip mediation or to have their meetings with a mediator separate from the batterer, and accompanied by a domestic violence support person. Several states require a judge to deny custody or unsupervised visitation to a batterer unless the judge can say why doing so is safe and in the child's best interests.

You can find more information on how to understand and handle domestic violence or emotional abuse issues in Chapters 4, 5 and 13. After you have found a way to address these issues, you can use this book effectively to build a parenting agreement that can help you now and over time as the situation changes or improves. ■

An Introduction to Parenting Agreements

In the broadest sense, a parenting agreement is the sum total of the arrangements parents make about parenting separately. Common convention and state laws describe these arrangements as "custody." The term "parenting agreement" better reflects the needs and involvement of all concerned, because it implies that the agreement is both comprehensive and tailored to meet each family's needs.

A. What Parenting Agreements Cover

Parenting agreements may be vague or detailed, casual or legalistic. But you should be sure that your parenting agreement meets your state's minimum requirements for these plans, and that it can be enforced by a court or law enforcement agency. At a minimum, a parenting agreement should describe how the parents plan to meet the children's needs and manage parenting responsibilities regarding:

- taking care of the children
- making necessary decisions on the children's behalf
- making sure the children spend time with both parents, and
- meeting the children's medical, psychological, educational, spiritual, physical and social needs.

Increasingly, parenting plans address many more issues, such as transporting the children between parents' houses, the roles of parents' new partners and how parents should communicate when issues arise. Comprehensive agreements offer clarity, anticipate the needs of the parents and children over time and pave the way for better communication and understanding.

B. Advantages of Parent-Negotiated Agreements

Parents are almost always in the best position to know what arrangements are preferable for their children. You know your children's interests, hopes, strengths and weaknesses. You know how your children deal with change and what makes change easier for them to accept. If you can work with the other parent to plan for your children's future, you will provide them the best possible springboard to adjust to your separation or divorce and reassure them that they are loved and cared for.

1. Minimize Court Involvement

Increasingly, state courts are requiring parents to try to resolve custody and visitation issues outside of court. Generally, this means parents with these types of disputes are ordered into mediation as a first step. This is because the law, for all its express protections for children, doesn't know your individual children. This is where your experience as a parent comes to the fore. When you and the other parent focus first on understanding and meeting your children's needs and second on finding ways to cooperate to meet those needs, you pave the way for a successful separate parenting relationship.

Cooperating eliminates the need for an outside person with limited information, such as a judge or court-appointed evaluator, to make decisions for you. This doesn't mean, however, that parent-negotiated agreements are completely independent of the legal system. Rather, they are created in the "shadow of the law." This means that a court retains the authority to review your agreement and make sure it is in your children's best interests. If the court finds that it is not, the court will reject your plan and impose its own.

All states have their own criteria for determining the best interests of the children. Determining what is or is not in your children's best interests is an inexact process. Some of the factors to be considered, however, include:

- age
- temperament
- relationships with each parent
- special needs or activities, and
- religious and social values.

MOST FAMILIES SEPARATE WITHOUT SIGNIFICANT CONFLICT

Dividing the Child, by Eleanor Maccoby and Robert Mnookin (Harvard Press, 1992), studies custody and visitation. The researchers measured conflict levels within divorced families by interviewing both parents at three separate times over a three-year period. The researchers found that 51% of families experienced "negligible" conflict, 24% experienced "mild" conflict, 10% experienced "substantial" conflict and only 15% of families were locked in "intense" conflict.

2. Increase Fairness

Parents, children and professionals all agree that the most successful agreements are those that the parties can describe as fair, meaning that even if they didn't "win" everything, they feel that they have gained something. If your parenting plan is clear and detailed, you will find that day-to-day living is simpler and everyone's responsibilities are well understood. While most children hope for reconciliation, they can probably adapt to almost any plan if they are confident that you believe it to be fair.

C. Goals of a Successful Parenting Agreement

Although every parenting agreement is different, the most successful parenting plans emerge out of a commitment by both parents to:

- reduce the conflict between the parents
- encourage good parent-child relationships between the children and both parents, and
- make the changes inherent in a separation or divorce easier for the children to accept.

1. Reduce Conflict Between Parents

Many parents initially doubt they can negotiate their own parenting agreement. In addition, parents often question whether any plan can transform the anger, pain, confusion and disarray of the break-up into a viable way of parenting. Take heart! The experiences of the vast majority of families who separate or divorce show that conflict, legal or otherwise, is far less than the media—or lawyers—would have us believe. In fact, study after study shows that only about 15% of custody agreements are the product of a full court trial. In most instances, parents negotiate their own agreement, often with the help of an outside professional, such as an attorney, mediator or counselor.

Reducing conflict is undoubtedly your most important goal in separate parenting. Despite this, parents sometimes continue to battle long after their separation or divorce. Often, it is because they:

- cannot accept the reality of a separation or divorce
- want to remain involved with the other parent, at any cost
- have unresolved anger
- have incompatible parenting values

- fear for the well-being of their children when they are with the other parent
- have a history of violence between them, or
- blame the other for the failed relationship.

Having these feelings is perfectly normal, and quite common. If you let negative feelings linger months and even years after a divorce, however, your ability to cooperate in child-rearing will be impaired. Your children will bear the brunt of the anger, blame and acrimony that you display, and will carry the scars for a very long time.

HOW CHILDREN REACT TO CONFLICT IN DIVORCE

In *How It Feels When Parents Divorce*, by Jill Krementz (Alfred A. Knopf, 1998), the author presents the statements of children she interviewed after their parents had divorced.

Zach, aged 13, voiced a common feeling that children share about being fought over when he says, "… if they had fought over us, I know that I would have felt like I was a check in a restaurant—you know, the way it is at the end of a meal when two people are finished eating and they both grab for the check and one says, 'I'll pay for it,' and the other one says, 'No, this one is mine,' and they go back and forth, but secretly neither one wants it, they just go on pretending until someone finally grabs it, and then that one's stuck."

Tracy, aged 16, fears that she may never escape the conflict that already exists in her family. She says, "… the worst thing by far about my parents' divorce is that it's still going on. I mean, my parents don't talk. If they have to talk, it's like screaming. I thought that once the divorce was over, my Mom and Dad could just get on with their lives, but it hasn't worked out that way. I think the fighting will never stop."

2. Encourage Good Parent-Child Relationships

The fear of losing contact or a relationship with one parent usually looms large in the minds of children whose parents are undergoing a separation or divorce. Even well-intentioned parents can inadvertently communicate the idea that their children will hurt them if they show open affection and regard for the other parent.

In *Divorce and Your Child*, by Sonja Goldstein and Albert Solnit (Yale University Press, 1984), the authors present two very compelling arguments against undermining the relationship with the other parent. First, if you succeed in curtailing or preventing visits with the other parent, your children might lose trust in you, fearful of what other harm you might do. Children have relatively little control over how their lives will be structured under any circumstances, let alone after their parents separate or divorce. Your children will watch you very carefully to see if they can trust you to structure their world so that it includes the people they love.

Second, when children are cut off from a parent, they often feel deprived of an important piece of themselves. Many children who are cut off from contact with one parent following a separation or divorce act as adopted children do, searching for their roots by seeking out their biological parents. If you force your children to abandon contact with their other parent, your children may blame you for the lost relationship.

Children will go to great lengths to avoid appearing to "choose" one parent over another. They will often tell you just what they think you want to hear—that the other parent is not as good as, not as well liked as and maybe even more dispensable than are you. While it is certainly preferable "not to say anything if you can't say something nice," if you are not careful, your children will get the message that the other parent's existence is to be denied in your home if they are to remain in your good graces.

This aside, some parents discourage or prevent children's visits with the other parent out of concern over the environment in that parent's home. Knowing when your concerns are justified is not always easy. If you fear for your children's physical or emotional safety, then you may be right to seek supervised, restricted or no visits with the other parent. If the dangers are less obvious and threatening, you will need to examine your own motives very carefully, looking at the situation through your children's eyes whenever possible.

3. Make Changes Easier for Your Children to Accept

The key to helping your children accept the changes that accompany separation and divorce is to work very hard to develop a parenting agreement that everyone feels is fair and workable. Children can adapt to their changed circumstances and to the differences in their parents' living arrangements, house rules and expectations if they see that you are doing your best to be sensitive to their needs. Children can accept that:

- the rules in one household are not necessarily the same as in the other
- each parent is his or her own person and has his or her own style
- each parent has his or her own strengths and weaknesses, and
- their needs can be met even if their parents live in different homes because there will be an expanding world of people who love and support them.

D. Parenting Agreements and Custody

When parents separate or divorce, the term "custody" often serves as shorthand for "who gets the children." Legally, the term has a much broader meaning because it applies to the total relationship parents have with their children. All parents are obligated to provide for their children's physical and emotional needs, and to protect and preserve what is fundamental to their best interests—medical care, education, food, shelter and safety. Custody implies all of these responsibilities.

When parents separate, the custody they jointly exercised over their children must change to accommodate the new living arrangements and the new relationship between the parents. The modification may be minor if the parents live near each other and can communicate well, or profound if ongoing conflict prevents cooperation in parenting. For most parents, it's somewhere in between.

In a divorce or legal separation, courts commonly order either sole custody or shared custody. Under a sole custody arrangement, one parent is the primary caregiver and the other parent's visits are defined by a set schedule. Under a shared custody arrangement, both parents enjoy significant amounts of time with their children and make decisions together.

Some states distinguish between the legal authority to make decisions and providing physical care of the children. In these states, courts can make any of the following orders:

- **Sole legal and physical custody.** In this arrangement, one parent assumes the decision-making responsibility, and children spend most of their time with that parent.
- **Shared legal and sole physical custody.** Parents share decision-making authority, but the children spend most of their time with only one parent.
- **Shared legal custody and shared physical custody.** Parents share decision-making authority, and the children divide their time fairly equally between their parents.

Chapter 12 contains information on the different forms of custody each state authorizes.

If parents cooperate in drafting and implementing a detailed parenting agreement, the court (if authorized) is likely to issue a shared custody order. On the other hand, if the parents show an inability to reach agreement on important child-rearing issues, the court may issue a sole custody award to one parent, allowing the other "reasonable" visitation. Clearly, a sole custody award heavily favors the "custodial" parent in caring for and making decisions on behalf of the children.

In some states, like New Hampshire and New Mexico, the court must begin with the premise that it will order shared custody unless it would not be in the children's best interests. In many states, a court may order shared custody even when one of the parents disagrees. (See Chapter 12.) So in all of these states, even if you don't successfully negotiate a parenting plan, you may end up with a shared custody order if you are in court.

In Chapter 5, you will select a specific custody arrangement to include in your parenting plan—assuming you and the other parent are ending a legal marriage. Additional information is in Chapter 9, *Understanding Your Children's Needs*, and (if applicable) Chapter 11, *Nontraditional Families*.

MOST OPPOSITE-SEX COUPLES SELECT PRIMARY OR SOLE CUSTODY TO MOTHER

For a variety of reasons, most opposite-sex parenting couples agree that the mother will have primary or sole custody after a separation or divorce and that the father will exercise reasonable visitation. For some, this happens because fathers presume that mothers will be awarded custody. In others, it happens because of the mother's fear that she will be judged poorly if she is not the primary caretaker. In still other situations, the parents agree that the mother has more time, a greater inclination or a better understanding of the children's daily needs.

Preparing to Build Your Parenting Agreement

As any good builder will tell you, you need the right tools and supplies at hand before you start to build, or the building is likely to fall. Your first tasks when preparing to build your parenting agreement are to review all relevant documents and take stock of your relationship with your children. Below are four worksheets to help you with this task.

WHEN TO CONSULT AN ATTORNEY

The ideal situation for taking stock would be one in which you can take the time to evaluate all options before making any decisions. You may not have that luxury right now, however. Consult an attorney as soon as possible if you are in any of the following situations:

- court hearings or deadlines require you to make decisions quickly
- you are involved in court proceedings you don't understand
- you are not sure of what you want or what your rights are
- you feel overwhelmed and unable to adequately represent yourself
- you have been sued for paternity
- a high degree of conflict between you and the other parent absolutely precludes negotiations
- the other parent has hired an attorney
- you are the subject of a "home study" or other custody evaluation, or
- the court is considering terminating your parental rights.

A. Organize and Review All Pertinent Documents

To successfully negotiate with the other parent, or to work well with any professional, you will want to collect and review all relevant documents. These include:

- court documents you have filed or received, such as a "summons," "petition," "complaint," "response," "answer," "declaration" or "affidavit"
- correspondence from an attorney, counselor, mediator or court official regarding a separation, a divorce, paternity, child support, custody or visitation
- court orders regarding a legal separation, divorce, paternity declaration or award of custody

- previously mediated, arbitrated or negotiated agreements between you and the other parent
- documents dissolving your religious marriage, or describing your marital status and your options according to your religious denomination, and
- reports, letters or evaluations from school officials, counselors, therapists or others who have an insight into your children.

Carefully read the documents you gather. If you need help in finding or understanding any of them, an attorney, court clerk, paralegal, marriage counselor, mediator, member of the clergy or other professional might be useful. (Chapter 13 offers tips on finding people and resources to help you.)

You won't necessarily need all of these documents to develop a parenting plan. Nevertheless, having them can help expedite matters, especially if you are going through a legal separation or divorce. For example, if you or the other parent have already initiated a court proceeding, you may have a deadline for submitting your parenting agreement. If you begin negotiations and they seem to be going well, you will probably want to ask the court for an extension of time (called a "continuance") to let your negotiations continue. In short, you need to know where you stand right now so you can take all necessary steps to finalize your agreement, assure your rights and satisfy all legal requirements.

B. Take Stock of Your Relationship With Your Children

Now it's time to take stock of your relationship with your children on the four worksheets set out below. Some of this will be fun, especially when you describe your child. Some of it may be painful. Some of it will be mundane, especially when you gather basic facts and figures. All of this information is important, however, because it will highlight the issues and concerns that your parenting agreement must address. The issues and options you go through in Chapter 5 to build your parenting agreement refer back to answers on these worksheets that might help during your discussions with the other parent.

There are no right or wrong answers for the questions on these worksheets. What is most important is that you try to answer each question thoughtfully and completely. The more information you have at hand when you build your parenting agreement, the better your agreement will meet your needs and your children's needs.

Parenting agreements are meant to focus on children, so you will begin by describing your children. You will need to visualize how the world looks through their eyes. A school counselor or teacher, trusted adult friend, religious leader or other adult who knows your children might be able to add some objective insights.

HOW CHILDREN EXPERIENCE DIVORCE

Drs. Judith Wallerstein and Joan Kelly were the first researchers to investigate and document children's views and reactions to divorce. As a result of their work, therapists, attorneys, parents and courts have a new understanding of the effects of divorce on children. Wallerstein and Kelly found that children experience shock, depression, denial, anger, low self-esteem, shame and guilt (though guilt is primarily experienced by younger children), regardless of their outward behavior.

Behaviorally, different children respond differently to divorce or separation. Some become overly good, some lash out at anyone and everyone nearby, some withdraw into a shell and some regress to a younger behavioral age. These realities can make the task of understanding your children quite difficult. You may have to play detective as well as parent.

To help you clarify your feelings and your goals for your future relationship with your children, complete the four worksheets. You can use them in your own negotiations or to educate any mediator, counselor, lawyer or other person who might help you develop a parenting agreement.

Each parent should complete a separate copy of Worksheets 1, 2 and 3. Working independently lets you each focus on your own feelings and impressions. It also takes some of the pressure off by allowing you to think for yourselves without having to agree about how to answer each question.

Worksheet 4 is meant to be filled out together. You and the other parent use your answers from the first three worksheets to generate a checklist of the core points to include in your parenting agreement. You can start the pro-

cess by reading each other's completed Worksheets 1, 2 and 3. The answers that you record on Worksheet 4 should reflect both parents' views. If you disagree, put down both responses.

For parenting agreements to work, they must be relevant to you, the other parent and your children. If sharing your answers to Worksheets 1, 2 and 3 is difficult or provokes arguments, consult Chapter 4, *How to Negotiate a Parenting Agreement,* or consider bringing in a mediator or counselor. Chapter 7 has information on finding a mediator and making the most of mediation. Chapter 13 has material on finding a counselor.

Below are sample completed worksheets. Blank copies are in the appendix. Before filling out any of the worksheets, make at least the number of photocopies suggested in the instructions. You can make more to allow for mistakes.

The questions on the worksheets are mostly open-ended and are meant to make you think. Fill out the worksheets in order, as each one builds upon the previous.

RESIST THE URGE TO MOVE QUICKLY

Most separating and divorcing parents reach a point when they want to just get it over with and move on with their lives. Those feelings are natural and tempting, but unrealistic. By demonstrating some patience now, you and your children will be far happier as the years go by.

1. Worksheet 1: Describe Your Child

Worksheet 1: Describe Your Child asks you:
- what kind of a person your child is
- what puts your child at his or her best, and
- what makes change easier or harder for your child to accept.

Each parent needs one blank copy of this worksheet for each child. For example, if you have three children, you will need six copies.

If you have more than one child and want to put the same answer for one child as you gave for another, write "same as (child's name)" to indicate which worksheet contains your answer.

FAMILY PROFILE

This family consists of a mother, a father and their only daughter, Susan, who is now 11 years old. Susan's

WORKSHEET 1: DESCRIBE YOUR CHILD

Child's name: _____Susan_____

1. What kind of person is this child?

   Happy, intelligent, but concerned about what is going to happen after our divorce is final.

2. What makes this child special?

   She has a great sense of humor, likes sports, likes to help others, loves animals.

3. How does this child like the current parenting arrangements?

   She is not very happy about having to change homes all of the time, but seems to understand that it's necessary now. She complains about not knowing which house to come home to after school and which room to decorate. She is embarrassed about having to give friends two numbers to call. Although she doesn't like having to spend holidays or her birthday with just one of us at a time, she doesn't seem to mind that she gets to celebrate twice!

4. How has this child's behavior changed since the separation or divorce?

   She has been a lot quieter than usual. She seems to be trying to find ways to get us back together. Her behavior has been pretty good, and I have really appreciated not having to fight with her all the time over the little things like what to wear or who she should play with. She has been helpful around the house and keeps her room clean.

5. Has this child expressed any preferences regarding the future?

   Other than wishing that we would get back together, she hasn't had much to say about the future.

6. How does this child react to change?

   She seems pretty resilient. As long as you tell her what is going to happen and why, she handles it O.K.

7. What makes change easier for this child to accept?

   She needs to be told ahead of time and allowed to ask questions.

8. How does this child let you know that something is wrong?

   She usually says something, but sometimes I have to try and figure it out because her behavior gets worse or she starts fighting with her friends.

9. Who else is important in this child's life?

   Her grandparents on her father's side, her cousins Nick and Tim, my brother and Susan are especially close, and she has lots of friends around where we live.

parents live in the same community, and Susan can easily ride the bus to either parent's home after school. Since her parents' separation, Susan has been living with her mother one week and her father the next week. Susan's mother completed this form.

2. Worksheet 2: Describe Your Relationship With Your Child

Worksheet 2: Describe Your Relationship With Your Child asks you about your relationship with your child, including:

- things that you like to do together
- plans you have for this child's future
- details about your parenting style with this child
- how you would propose to share your parenting responsibilities, and
- whether you are happy with the current parenting relationship.

Each parent needs one blank copy of this worksheet for each child. For example, if you have three children, you will need six copies.

If you have more than one child and want to put the same answer for one child as you gave for another, write "same as (child's name)" to indicate which worksheet contains your answer.

FAMILY PROFILE

This family consists of a mother, a father and two boys: Jimmy, aged six, and Nathan, aged 14 months. The worksheet was completed by the father and describes only his relationship with Jimmy. Jimmy's parents have been divorced for six months; Jimmy's mother has custody and the father has asked that they renegotiate their current arrangements.

WORKSHEET 2: DESCRIBE YOUR RELATIONSHIP WITH YOUR CHILD

Child's name: _____Jimmy_____

1. What do you and this child like to do together?

    We go to the park, the zoo and to his T-Ball games. I try to take him to see my folks at least

    once a month so that he can play with all of the cousins.

2. What are your plans and wishes for this child's future?

    I want him to grow up knowing that both of us love him. He should go to college, but he can be

    whatever he wants.

3. What do you think are the most important things for this child to achieve?

    He should be able to move on with his life and not let our divorce affect him so much. He should

    know that he can come to either of us with his problems. He should be able to grow up in

    exactly the same way as if we had stayed together.

4. How do you and this child handle and resolve conflict?

    For the most part we just talk about it. Sometimes I have to discipline him, but that doesn't

    happen too often.

5. How do you handle discipline with this child?

    Usually he gets sent to his room or loses a privilege, like playing with his friends or riding his bike.

6. How did you share parenting responsibilities and time with this child during the time you were married or living together?

    I did a lot for Jimmy. I always gave him his bath, helped him with his homework and played

    games with him. Sometimes I fixed the meals and I did the housework. I was always involved in

    something to do with raising Jimmy.

7. How do you and the other parent share parenting responsibilities and time with this child now?

    We share the responsibilities just fine. I try to keep up with all of Jimmy's activities. I help out

    with the T-Ball team and go to the open houses at his school. I try to get in at least one

    parent-teacher conference a year. Since Jimmy has so many friends here, I always know how

    things are going with his buddies.

8. Are you happy with the current arrangements? (Please explain)

    Not entirely. I want more time with Jimmy since I am so active in his life. I still feel like I'm being

    treated like the "other parent" and that's not fair. Although we don't fight as much about

    Jimmy, I still feel a lot of tension between us on this subject.

9. Is this child happy with the current arrangements? (Please explain)

   Jimmy says that he misses me a lot and that he wants to spend more time with me. I think

   that would be better because I spend more quality time with him than his mother does.

10. If changes are in order, what would you suggest?

    I think Jimmy should live with me most of the time. The school district for my area is better,

    which means he'll have a better basis for being successful in college. Also, my job is more

    flexible and I have made Jimmy my priority.

3. Worksheet 3: Adding the Details

Worksheet 3: Adding the Details has you identify miscellaneous information needed when drafting a parenting agreement, such as:

- important documents
- work schedules and living arrangements
- your children's activities, needs and interests
- yourself and your children's religious denomination
- counseling histories, and
- histories of domestic violence or substance abuse.

Each parent should start with at least one blank copy.

FAMILY PROFILE

The sample family represented in this form consists of a mother (Marilyn), a father (Sean) and three children: Jennifer (age 12), Brandon (age 10) and Matthew (age four). This form has been completed by Marilyn. Marilyn and Sean were married for 14 years and are about to finalize their divorce. They have been separated for almost a year. Since Sean moved out, the children have been living with Marilyn in the family home. The entire process has been hard for everyone, and the parents have a difficult time talking about anything without arguing.

WORKSHEET 3: ADDING THE DETAILS

1. List of existing court documents, orders or agreements. (Note that the terms listed here might be different in your state. See Chapter 12 for the terms used in your state.)

   Divorce Petition, Response, Separation Agreement

2. Parent's name, occupation and work schedule.

   Marilyn, Accountant, Tuesday - Saturday 8:00 - 3:30

3. Schedule of children's activities (such as school, religious training and after-school activities).

   Jennifer: school, after-school sports, 4-H; Brandon: school, after school sports;

   Matthew: day care

   All three children go to Sunday School and participate in the youth group

4. Children's special needs or interests.

   Brandon needs his ADD medication each day; all three children like to spend as much time as possible riding their bikes and playing with their friends when their homework is finished and they have no other commitments.

5. Religion.

   Parent—Methodist   Children—Methodist

6. Where do you live now?

   123 Main Street, Smithtown

7. Do you have any plans to relocate from the area? (Please explain)

   I might have to move out of the area for work. I won't know that for a year though because our firm hasn't yet decided whether to open a branch office.

8. Do you have any plans for remarriage?

   Not at this time.

9. Are there any adult relatives or friends with whom the children should or should not have close contact?

   The children should continue to see their cousins and grandparents on both sides. They should not be around Aunt Rachel or Uncle George if they have been drinking.

10. Counseling for children.

All three children received counseling from the school counselor and Dr. Jones regarding the divorce and the level of conflict in our home over the last year. I think we should offer them additional counseling, but not force them to go.

11. Counseling for parents.

We received counseling from Dr. Jones regarding the divorce from July-December of last year. I'd be willing to go again if Sean would agree to it.

12. Do you want to address domestic violence issues in your parenting agreement? If yes, why? If no, why not?

Yes. We only seemed to have serious problems at the end, but I'm worried about what might happen now that we're both single parents.

13. Do you want to address the use or abuse of drugs or alcohol in your parenting agreement? If yes, how do you think these issues should be handled in your parenting agreement?

Yes. Sean should start attending Alcoholics Anonymous meetings.

14. Do you have any special concerns about your parenting arrangements?

Yes, I think that all three children need a parent around as much as possible. I don't believe in leaving them alone to take care of themselves like Sean does when he has the children.

15. Do you have any special concerns about your relationship with the other parent?

All three children are doing fairly well, but I think that Sean must be blaming the divorce on me because they seem so angry with me. I wish that Sean would stop bad-mouthing me in front of the children and that we could limit our conversations to the children.

4. Worksheet 4: Checklist of Issues for Your Parenting Agreement

In Worksheet 4: Checklist of Issues for Your Parenting Agreement, you and the other parent work together to identify the issues you want to cover in your parenting agreement. Before you start, you should each read the other's answers recorded on Worksheets 1, 2 and 3. Also skim the table of contents for Chapter 5, which lists 43 issues you can include in your parenting agreement. As you build your parenting agreement in that chapter, you will be reminded to review your answers on these four worksheets.

Make at least two copies of Worksheet 4. Record your answers on one copy unless you disagree. In that case, put one answer on the main copy and the other parent's answer on the second copy, or squeeze both answers onto the main copy. Try to avoid arguments. Your goal in this worksheet is to identify issues, not to start negotiating your agreement.

FAMILY PROFILE

This family consists of a mother (Gloria), a father (Sam) and two boys: David (age nine) and Zachary (age five). Gloria and Sam were married for ten years and have been separated for six months. They are both Catholic and are seeking an annulment of their marriage through the Church. Two years ago, Gloria reached the conclusion that she was a lesbian but did not tell her family until just prior to the separation. She moved out of the family home and lives alone. Sam and Gloria tried counseling off and on for a year prior to their separation. When they separated, they negotiated a temporary parenting agreement and obtained a court order formalizing their agreement. Currently, David and Zachary live with Sam during the week and with Gloria on the weekends. Gloria would like to negotiate a permanent agreement and to expand her time with the children.

WORKSHEET 4: CHECKLIST OF ISSUES FOR YOUR PARENTING AGREEMENT

1. Existing court documents, orders or agreements which must be changed to accommodate your parenting agreement.

   Temporary Order awarding child custody.

2. Existing agreements to consider while negotiating this parenting agreement.

   Temporary parenting agreement reached at the end of marriage counseling.

3. Steps you will have to take to resolve legal or religious issues such as divorce, legal separation, annulment, etc.

   We will have to get a permanent court order and an annulment of the marriage through the Church.

4. Any concerns or recommendations made by a counselor, school teacher, therapist or other interested adult regarding your children's emotional, spiritual or physical well-being.

   The marriage counselor thinks that we need to continue some form of counseling to help the children deal with the divorce and the fact that Gloria has realized that she is a lesbian.

5. Each child's current relationship with each parent.

   David has a good relationship with both of us. As long as we are not fighting, he seems able to get along with each of us. He likes to have Sam help out with his sports and other activities, and wants Gloria to stay active in his school events.

   Zachary seems to be taking the divorce harder than David. He has a good relationship with each of us, but his relationship with Gloria has suffered the most. Zachary is defiant with Gloria most of the time. Sam has an easier time getting Zachary to behave.

6. Each child's feelings, reactions or concerns about separation or divorce.

   Both boys are angry about the divorce but understand why we don't want to live together anymore. They are uncomfortable being around Gloria's new partner, but seem willing to work the situation out as a family. David is closest to Sam. Zachary alternates between being angry with both of us and wishing we could forget about the past and get back together.

7. Changes you think would be good in each child's current relationship with each parent.

    David's relationship with both parents will probably improve on its own over time. Zachary

    needs to get over his anger so that he can regain his positive relationship with Gloria.

8. Changes that may be necessary in each child's current relationship with each parent.

    Gloria and Zachary will have to find some way that they can comfortably spend time together,

    even if Gloria's new partner is around.

9. Current problem areas for children.

    Both boys are having difficulty getting along with their friends right now. David's grades are

    not poor, but they could be much better. Zachary needs to be able to accept discipline from

    Gloria.

10. Current areas of conflict between the parents.

    There is still a lot of conflict over Gloria's new life, although both of us agree that the other is

    a good parent and that we can find some way to both be heavily involved in raising the boys.

11. Changes either parent would like to see in current parenting relationship.

    Gloria doesn't want to have to answer questions from Sam about her partner and her new life.

    Sam would like Gloria to have her partner around less often until the boys are more

    comfortable with the situation.

12. Times when either parent is available to care for children: _____

    Both parents are available on Saturdays and Sundays and most weekday evenings.

13. Times when only _____ Gloria _____ is available to care for children: _____ Tuesday evenings _____

14. Times when only _____ Sam _____ is available to care for children: _____ Wednesday evenings _____

15. Other adults children will be spending time with.

    David and Zachary are very close to both sets of grandparents. Gloria's parents usually take

    the boys on a one-week vacation each summer.

16. Adults or minors the children should not spend time with (or be alone with).

    No one.

17. Any problems with violence, abuse or neglect that would have to be accommodated.

    None.

18. Other comments or issues to be included.

    We should offer the children counseling, but they should not be forced to go if they don't want to.

How to Negotiate a Parenting Agreement

There are two key elements to building a parenting agreement that works: a clear description of how both parents will take care of the children on a daily basis and a process for making larger decisions, resolving conflicts and changing the agreement over time.

This chapter will show you how to negotiate an effective and lasting agreement, how to handle conflict—even intense conflict—and what you should do if the parenting issues become too difficult to handle on your own.

A. Knowing What You Need and Want

Although it sounds simple, many parents find it difficult to describe what they want to get out of their negotiations with the other parent. It is important that you take your time with each step in this process, because it will help you to find workable solutions later. To start this process, you should list:

- **what is or is not working well in the current arrangements,** such as the frequency of visits, frequent conversations about parenting styles or concern about child safety issues.
- **what problems have to be solved,** such as lateness at the exchange, regular arguments over key parenting issues or one parent's concern that a certain activity is completely unsafe for the child; and
- **what you want to get out of the agreement,** such as a clear statement of how exchanges will happen, a better way to solve conflicts or a list of the activities that both parents agree the kids will or won't be allowed to do.

As you make this list, pay attention to what your child and the other parent say about what they think is or is not working well. (The worksheets from Chapter 3 can help you to organize your approach.) Each person's version of "what I need and want" will be somewhat different. Experience shows, however, that the more clearly you can describe your needs and wants, and the more carefully you can listen to the other parent tell you about their needs and wants, the more likely it is you will be able to build an agreement that lasts.

1. Good Negotiations

Good negotiations usually lead to good agreements. But, unless you are a trained negotiator, you might not know how to set your efforts up to succeed, especially when the stakes are high or you have negative feelings about the other parent.

First you should make an effort to communicate your needs and wants clearly. Then listen carefully to what the other parent says they need and want. Once you have each had a chance to outline your needs and wants, you can start to work together to:

- understand what fuels your conflict and what makes it difficult for you to negotiate and reach lasting agreements
- focus on the children and on finding timely ways to solve problems
- develop a realistic parenting plan
- consider more than one approach to solving problems, and
- find ways that each of you will get something you value.

You will know that your negotiations are going well when each of you feels that you:

- are safe in expressing your views (especially if there has been a history of domestic violence or verbal or emotional abuse)
- understand what the other person wants and why (even if you don't agree), and
- know what the other person has to gain from having the agreement succeed.

2. Lasting Agreements

Knowing that you have something to gain from having your parenting agreement work well can make it easier to be flexible as you and the other parent build and carry out the agreement. For example, most parents can handle small changes in the schedule or occasionally late pick-ups and drop-offs for visits if they think that the other parent is considering their needs and the children's needs when making these changes.

There are many ways to measure the things you might gain from a parenting agreement that each of you feels you can live with, including:

- limiting the financial and emotional costs of a court fight
- reducing the tension between you and the other parent
- helping both parents worry less about their children when they are with the other parent
- helping to keep your child out of the middle of his or her parents' arguments by finding new ways to handle your conflicts, and
- showing your children that you and the other parent can agree on some things.

It is possible to create a good parenting agreement when there is little or no trust between the parents. One of the biggest reasons for this unusual statement is that most people consider themselves trustworthy. They know, and will often tell you, that they will stick to an agreement, even if they doubt that the other parent will do the same. When you have two people who feel like this, you are well on your way to building an agreement that lasts. And sometimes negotiations succeed because the parties know that the consequences of failure are often expensive and exhausting legal battles.

Some people think that their negotiations succeed only if they have gotten what they wanted without spending too much time or money on the process of working out the agreement together. These people give little thought to how the other parent feels about the agreement, or whether it makes the most sense for their children. While this strategy might work well for handling some kinds of negotiations (such as buying a used car), it often backfires when people have to cooperate with each other for a long time. Because parenting is a long-term commitment, it pays to lay a strong foundation for the negotiations with the other parent at the beginning.

GAME THEORY OFFERS INSIGHTS FOR IMPROVING YOUR NEGOTIATION STRATEGIES

People who study game theory construct a very simple game to measure which strategies produce the best results for each player. Although life is far more complex than any research game, game theory offers valuable insight into winning strategies that can be applied to real-life situations like your negotiations with the other parent.

By playing a game called "Tit for Tat," invented by Canadian professor Anatol Rapoport, researchers studied the best ways to "win" one-on-one contests. In the short term, playing for one's own advantage produced the best score. Over time, the high score eroded, usually because the other players also played selfishly. In the long run, "niceness" scored better than "selfishness." Most significantly for parents, players who matched a nice move for a nice move and a selfish move for a selfish move tended to score better than when acting only "nicely" or "selfishly" alone.

When players allowed their opponents to get away with one "selfish" move before retaliating with a matching "selfish" move (thus approximating the concept of forgiveness), they scored highest of all. The single most important factor influencing a player's score, other than responding in kind with a small amount of "forgiveness" built in, was having a predictable game strategy.

B. Understanding What Gets in the Way

The single biggest barrier to successful negotiations is conflict. Conflict can range from occasional disagreements or shouting matches to persistent arguing, or go as far as verbal and physical assault, or threats to hurt or kill. A number of studies have confirmed that children witness domestic violence between their parents in 50–75% of divorces, and that nearly half of those children are themselves victims of domestic violence, child abuse or child sexual abuse. Not surprisingly, conflict between parents can feel more like "the clash of the titans" to a child than an example of "Mom and Dad trying to figure out what's best for me."

Some amount of conflict is normal during a divorce or separation. But when arguing, fighting, legal battles and name-calling are a regular part of your co-parenting landscape, you are living in a high conflict situation. Does your situation fit this definition? Ask yourself the following questions:

- Are your court files more than six inches tall when you stack them up on the kitchen table? (Research shows that approximately 5–10% of all divorces are litigated extensively).
- If someone asked both you and the other parent about how things are going right now, one would say, "Great!" and the other say, "Awful"?
- When you or the other parent talks about why the arguing continues, does each of you say that you are right and the other parent is always wrong?

- Arc your extended families and friends lined up on one side or the other ready to do battle?
- Do one or both of you feel that the other parent has nothing good to offer your child?
- Does one parent feel that the other parent has "cut off" the possibility of having a good relationship with your child?
- Have there been threats of violence, physical violence, or verbal or emotional abuse in your relationship (even if it happened only around the time of separation)?

If your answer is "yes" to the last question—or three or more of the other questions—there's a good chance that you fall into the "high conflict" category.

Conflict can be very expensive. The most obvious costs can be measured in the dollars it takes to pay for attorneys, court fees, child custody evaluators, special masters, visitation supervisors, counselors and whatever other professionals you and the other parent must hire to handle your situation.

Less obvious, perhaps, are the enormous costs that each of you will pay emotionally. Your child will pay most of all. Children often feel afraid, sad and confused when their parents start arguing, blaming, threatening each other or letting their anger spiral out of control. A child looks to his or her parents as the people who are most willing and able to provide protection from the scary parts of the world. Children also need their parents to manage the hurt, anger and other calamities that are part of growing up. When it's a child's parents that are arguing or becoming violent, that child loses confidence that their parents will be able to keep them safe and that they will continue to be loved.

In fact, study after study confirms what Carla B. Garrity and Mitchell A. Baris say in their book *Caught in the Middle* (Lexington Books, Copyright 1994):

> *Nothing matters—not custody decisions, visiting arrangements, not whether the child is a boy or a girl—as much as whether parents can minimize fighting. Over time, parental wars take a greater toll on a child's development than any other single factor in divorce.*

WHERE DO WE FIT IN?

Dr. Constance Ahrons, in her book *The Good Divorce* (Harper Collins, 1994), profiles five different types of divorcing couples. Following is a summary (from least to most conflicted) of the five types of co-parenting relationships she describes:

"Perfect Pals": These parents are able to remain good friends, and communicate regularly with very little conflict. These parents may live next door, or down the block. These parents are also more likely to consider "bird nesting" (having the children stay in the family home with the parents switching off living there). When attending the school play or soccer match, they are more likely than not to sit together. These parents are often able to share birthday parties and holiday celebrations, and may keep friendly relationships with their "ex" in-laws.

"Cooperative Colleagues": These parents are generally friendly toward each other, can clearly separate the adult relationship issues from the parenting issues and are more likely than "perfect pals" to have new partners. Although these parents' homes may still be in the same general area, they are less likely to cross paths on a regular basis. Communications are easy, and when conflicts come up, they are usually able to manage them effectively.

"Angry Associates": These parents are frequently angry with each other, have a difficult time separating the adult relationship issues from the parenting issues and while they can often benefit from working with a mediator, counselor or attorney to resolve their disputes, they seldom do. These parents frequently involve their children in their conflict, and the children often dread what will happen each time their parents are in the same place at the same time.

"Fiery Foes": These parents seldom have much to do with each other—but when they do, it often turns into a big battle. These parents go to court regularly, often to resolve even the smallest matters, such as what time the weekend visit must start or finish. Courts will often turn to one or more outside professionals (such as a custody evaluator, attorney for the child, counselor, special master, visitation supervisor, etc.) for help in understanding what court orders might be most effective, and to watch over the parents to make sure that the court orders are followed. These parents are accused of "parental alienation" when children express great fear about being with one parent, or refuse to visit altogether.

"Dissolved Duos": This situation is different from the other four, because it commonly involves one parent who has nearly, or totally, stopped contact with the ex and his or her child. Parents in this group may consider kidnapping or hiding a child after losing custody because they fear that they have no other option for gaining time with their children.

Although it will be difficult, you and the other parent can find effective ways to reduce the levels of conflict that you experience in your co-parenting relationship. Following are some of the strategies that both professionals and parents agree are the most effective.

1. Separate Relationship Issues From Parenting Issues

Most professionals working with divorced or separated families urge the parents to find ways to keep their adult relationship issues separate from the parenting issues. But what does this really mean? In short, it means that you don't mix up the feelings that you have about why you and the other parent didn't stay together with seeing what your child needs, and meeting those needs. It also means that you can see your child's needs as separate from your own, or the other parent's, needs.

2. Deal With Feelings of Revenge

Revenge can be a powerful motivator and a significant roadblock in your negotiations. Although the wish to achieve revenge fuels fewer custody and visitation disputes than you might imagine, it does happen, and it may require attention in your case.

Few parents go through a separation or divorce without at least some fantasies about how good it would be to "pay the other parent back" for some of the feelings of pain, anger, sadness and loss. For some parents, these feelings are more than fleeting. When revenge becomes a central theme for one or both parents, its destructive influence makes finding a settlement outside of court more remote.

Since feelings of revenge are (more or less) a fact of life following separation or divorce, it's time to look for ways to bring the feelings out into the open—and loosen their hold on your negotiations. As with other intense feelings, you may be able to overcome your vengeful feelings by admitting that you have them, and acknowledging how attractive the prospect of acting on them initially appears. Having done this, you might then discard revenge as a productive option and move forward to negotiate an agreement that nurtures your children.

If you or the other parent still can't shake your desire to get revenge, try playing it out in your mind, or in conversation with a trusted advisor. You can start by playing a game of "What if?" Consider that you are not only successful in getting revenge, but that you have exceeded even your wildest dreams! For example, if you want to pay the other parent back for taking a new lover, imagine that you've been able to do that, as well as to guarantee that they will not have another happy moment, or date, for the next ten years. If your goal is to let them know what a comparatively miserable parent they are, imagine that they not only know this, but that a court has sentenced them to walk up and down Main Street with a sandwich board proclaiming their failings and your virtues.

Got the idea? Great! Now imagine the consequences. How well will the other parent be able to function as a caregiver? How will your children react to the other parent's fate? How long will your feelings of triumph last? How long might it take and how much might it cost to actually achieve full victory? How motivated will the other parent be to pitch in on miscellaneous expenses for the children, or to faithfully pay child support?

Revenge may be sweet for the moment, but it is a poor substitute for confidence in yourself, and your value and abilities as a parent, and your own sense of fulfillment.

THE DIFFERENCE BETWEEN CONFLICT AND HOSTILITY

While high conflict relationships are in the minority among all separating and divorcing families, it is common enough to justify a closer look. By looking closely at what you argue about, or why you can't seem to stop arguing, you can learn important things about the ways that either or both of you need to grow in your communication or problem solving skills.

Conflict is a very complex event. For many, conflict starts when they cannot communicate over difficult and emotionally charged issues, and continues because they are not successful in getting over what has made those issues difficult or emotionally charged in the first place. It usually takes several months, or years, for people to deal with all of the feelings that come up when the romantic relationship between the couple is ending. During that time, it can be especially difficult, but critically important, to sort out why the conflict exists, and what it will take to resolve it. Often this means getting help, at least briefly, from a trained professional such as a mediator, counselor, mental health professional or attorney.

Some conflict, however, is so intense that it really should be viewed differently. Hostility occurs when arguing rises above differing opinions about what is right, or what should be done to resolve a problem, and takes on overtones of "making someone pay" for all of the bad things they have done. Hostility is not generally the kind of emotion that can be dealt with simply and logically in a calm negotiation setting between two parents. Hostility is better addressed in counseling or some other controlled setting where a trained professional can help the parents understand what is happening, look for ways to address the underlying issues and provide emotional and physical safety for everyone involved. (You can find more information about the different kinds of mental health professionals that you can turn to for help if you and the other parent are dealing with hostile feelings in Chapter 13.)

3. Don't Undermine Your Child's Relationship With the Other Parent

A number of different mental health professionals have tried to address situations where one or both parents try to undermine a child's relationship with the other parent. Some parents feel that the other parent is trying to "turn" their children away from him or her. In general, professionals suspect that a parent is engaging in alienating behavior when:

- one parent regularly discusses his or her concerns about the other parent's ability to care for the child with the child
- a child has decided to resolve his or her conflicted feelings about wanting to love both parents by choosing only one parent to align with, and seeing the other parent as dangerous, uncaring or incapable
- a child refuses to visit, speak on the telephone or otherwise have any contact with one parent, or
- one parent believes that all would be better off if the other parent were completely absent from the child's life.

Parents give many reasons for trying to undermine the children's relationship with their other parent. Often, this behavior masks a complex range of problems. Sometimes, parents actively try to distance a child from the other parent because there is a history of physical or sexual abuse directed toward the child. In other situations, parents use this as a way of punishing the other parent for leaving the relationship. More often than not, there are many reasons. Untangling these reasons is difficult, but important to do. Generally, parents need a professional's help to address these situations. (See Chapter 5, Issue 34.)

Note: While protecting a child from physical or sexual abuse is critically important, you must be sure to do so in a way that does not also jeopardize your legal situation. For this reason, it is critically important that you meet with an attorney, district attorney, domestic violence counselor, child abuse protection professional or other similarly qualified person who can help you decide the best way to protect your child without getting into a possible legal mess.

4. Stop Arguing!

Constant arguing can become a bad habit. Discovering how you got into the habit in the first place, however, can be difficult. Following are some common reasons that arguing might have become such a large part of your contact with the other parent:

Argument for argument's sake. Sometimes one parent keeps fueling the arguments because he or she likes to argue, or feels like "there's nothing like a good argument to clear the air." Other times, it is because he or she doesn't know any other effective ways to get their points across. If either you or the other parent argues because you "like a good argument," consider that not everyone feels the same —and that after awhile, constant arguing feels like abuse. This chapter can give you ideas about other ways you can make your point, make decisions or feel as if you have been heard.

Yelling to make sure you are heard. Sometimes people feel that arguing and yelling are the only ways to get a point across. If this is true for you, consider trying some of the strategies listed later in this chapter or involving a mediator, counselor or other third party in your discussions with the other parent.

Arguing to stay "connected." Sometimes parents argue as a way to stay "connected." Often, this is because they are unsure about their feelings for the other parent—especially if he or she is not sure about going through with a separation or divorce, or is thinking about getting back together with the other parent. Other times, this type of behavior shows up during a big transition in one parent's life, such as starting a new relationship, having a child with a new partner or making a move out of the area. If you think this might be true in your situation, one or both parents should consider taking this issue into counseling. This way of staying connected can become a destructive influence on all aspects of the co-parenting and parent/child relationships that is hard to correct.

Verbal fighting instead of hitting. Sometimes, people will argue because it feels like a better alternative to pushing, shoving, hitting, throwing things or resorting to some kind of violence or property damage. In this case, arguing seems to offer the only other way to deal with anger that gets out of control. You shouldn't compromise anyone's safety to negotiate your parenting agreement or make important decisions. If arguing is used as an alternative to violence—stop arguing, make sure you are safe and wait to handle your negotiations through a mediator, counselor or attorney. For long-term solutions to dealing with intense anger or physical or emotional abuse, most people find that they need counseling or an anger management group.

5. Shift Your Perspective

Once you have mastered listening to the other parent, try to think about how you will present your ideas to them. One strategy is to think through the issues from the other parent's perspective, and to anticipate his or her concerns. The Native American instruction to "walk a mile in another's moccasins" before deciding that you understand their point of view is a good one. Although you may have known the other parent very well at one time, you may not know how the world looks to him or her now.

To see the issues and potential solutions from the other parent's perspective, you must:

- identify what is important to the other parent (such as making sure the children are supported to do well in school)
- anticipate the other parent's objections (such as worrying that daily tutoring is expensive and gets in the way of a regular Wednesday evening dinner visit)
- develop responses to those objections (for example, you can say that intensive tutoring will pay off in better school performance and self-esteem for the child, or that the program offers discounts for low income parents), and
- suggest alternative solutions that might appeal to the other parent (the other parent can take the child to tutoring and keep the children half an hour later for as long as the tutoring is needed).

6. Take Advantage of Each Parent's Strengths

When emotions are running high—as is often the case in parenting disputes—many people find it difficult to be flexible or to try new problem solving strategies. This is why it is so important for parents to understand what works best for each of them, and to plan for how they will solve problems once they come up.

Each of us has strengths and weaknesses when it comes to how we solve problems. For some, it works best to talk things through from beginning to end before making a decision. For others, it helps to have one person develop a plan that both can consider, instead of having to start from scratch. Also, many parents find that each of them prefers to solve problems in different ways. If each parent comes

to the negotiations prepared to understand—if not accept—the other parent's style, you will have come a long way towards building a parenting agreement that makes sense for both of you and for your children.

C. Using Effective Negotiation and Problem Solving Strategies

Although you may not yet be an experienced negotiator, you can take advantage of the time-tested strategies and techniques that professional negotiators use. What you will notice running through all of these strategies is an emphasis on looking carefully enough at a situation to understand something about why it has been a problem in the past, and to plan for how you might avoid those problems in the future.

1. Establish and Maintain Ground Rules

Establishing and observing a few simple ground rules can help parents keep control of a conversation that might otherwise escalate into a full-blown battle. Ground rules work best when they are simple, easy to remember and few in number. Some of the ground rules to consider include:

- agreeing that neither parent will interrupt the other (sometimes parents keep a pad of paper handy to make notes so that they don't forget a point they want to make)
- agreeing that neither parent will call the other names or make generalized, negative statements about the other (instead of saying, "You never did care much about how the kids were raised," you might say, "I feel as though you left most of the decisions to me while we were married"), and
- focusing on issues and possible solutions, rather than on who is to blame for having created the problem in the first place.

2. Agree on Common Goals

While many parents disagree about decisions affecting their children, they can often identify a list of common goals. For example, you may agree to reduce the conflict between you, find ways that your children can enjoy the best of their relationships with each of you and have your children be confident that they are loved and valued by both parents, regardless of the separation or divorce.

3.   Bring in a Neutral Person

Many parents find it easy to focus on making good parenting decisions rather than blaming each other for their shortcomings if a neutral person, such as a counselor or mediator, moderates the discussion. (See Chapter 7, *Making Mediation and Arbitration Work for You.*)

4.   Recall Times When Negotiations Were Easier

For some parents, the pain, anger and confusion of a separation or divorce is so intense they forget the times when they were able to agree. Remembering what made past discussions more successful is often enough to move parents toward an agreement.

5.   Create a Divorce or Separation Ceremony

Most cultures have complicated rituals associated with marriage to help the partners feel committed to each other, but few societies have separation or divorce rituals. To help themselves untie the ties that have bound them, some parents consider having a divorce or separation ceremony. For some, merely planning the ceremony provides enough closure to the relationship. Others need to read statements to each other, have witnesses present or sign a formal decree.

A SAMPLE SEPARATION CEREMONY

The following ceremony was written by Sharon Wegsheider-Cruse, an author on divorce issues, with some modifications by Virginia Lisenbee Davis. You can consider using it, or modifying it to meet your own particular needs. For example, you may want to add a section on how you plan to treat each other as co-parents, or how you will support your children in having a loving and close relationship with the other parent.

OUR DIVORCE CEREMONY

On this day we come together, with some sadness, to accept that our marriage is dissolved.

On _____ (date) in _____ (city and state), we were married. We thought on that day that we were entering a marriage that would be permanent. We had plans, hopes and fears.

What we didn't know and didn't plan on is the fact that we had each come to the marriage with parts of ourselves unknown. These unknowns prevented us from seeing ourselves clearly and also kept us from getting to know one another. As we have grown and changed, we have not been able to grow together. It has become clear that we cannot go on as a couple any longer.

We have tried to give each other love, comfort and support. We did not set out to hurt one another. Guilt, fear, shame and hurt have become a part of our life. There have been many misunderstandings, and, at times, each of us felt the other was responsible for what was happening. We did not realize that both of us brought pain to the relationship.

Inside each of us were two wounded and frightened children who needed support and healing. Neither of us has been able to give what was needed, and perhaps neither of us was able to receive what was needed. We did our best over the years.

After _____ (# of years) years, we admit defeat. We are not defeated as two individuals; we are simply defeated in making this union work.

We have made a decision to obtain a divorce. Each of us will find our own way to heal. We will cope and lend support to each other as we go our separate ways.

Even though we could not fulfill our plans as a couple, our prayer is that we will fulfill our separate lives in our own way.

We ask forgiveness of each other. We have each forgiven ourselves and ask that our families, our community and our God support our decision.

6.   Remove Labels Such as "Good" and "Bad"

Many parents experience a wide range of conflicting emotions and unusual behavior both during and after the separation or divorce. Many are then tempted to label those emotions or behaviors as being either "good" or "bad." If you can remove these labels, however, and just accept the emotions and behavior as a normal part of the experience, you may have fewer problems overcoming them as you continue your separate parenting relationship.

7.   Choose Your Setting for Negotiations

Choosing when and where you will meet to talk with the other parent is very important. You must find a time and location that is convenient and comfortable and allows you to talk without interruptions. This may mean a pleasant restaurant or coffee shop with tables that offer privacy. But don't choose a restaurant that you used to frequent as a couple, as the associations with past good times might bring up painful emotions best left alone while you are considering the future of your children.

Other options for a meeting location include:

- a meeting or conference room at the public library
- a meeting or conference room at a community center, or
- a picnic table in a park (assuming your children are not present).

8.   Set an Agenda

Your discussions will be more productive if you set out a list of issues that you will cover (called an agenda), and then stick to it. You can use the worksheets in Chapter 2 or the parenting agreement worksheet in Chapter 5 to help you set your agenda, or you can develop your own agenda based on your needs at the time you meet.

Regardless of how you develop your agenda, start each meeting by agreeing on which issues you will discuss at that time. Part of each agenda should be devoted to reviewing your progress so far, and part should be devoted to deciding what should happen next. A sample agenda is below.

SAMPLE AGENDA

1. Review of progress to date.
2. Review each parent's evaluation worksheets.
3. Develop a checklist of parenting issues (Worksheet 4).
4. Discussion of:
    a. medical, dental or vision care
    b. psychiatric care
    c. education
    d. surname
    e. religion
5. Summarize decisions made.
6. Outline issues and set date and time for next meeting.

9.   Give Yourself Enough Time

Negotiations over most parenting issues require that you set aside enough time so you can carefully consider each decision. Don't schedule your meeting for an hour before one of you must leave to catch a plane—give yourself time to be heard and to listen. If any issue on your agenda is likely to involve much discussion, limit the number of issues on your agenda for that sitting.

10. Know What to Cover, and How Much Detail to Provide

It is important to make sure that your parenting agreement covers everything you will need in order to make the arrangements work smoothly. But there is a delicate balance between covering all of the key items, and providing so much detail that you can't handle the real-life changes that are sure to arise.

For some parents, detailed agreements leave little room for misunderstandings or arguments. For others, the details just provide that many more issues to fight about. For parents that do best with lots of detail, the agreement might include a specific list covering each toy and article of clothing, the number of changes of clothes and the number of disposable diapers that need to be packed for each exchange. Other parents might take that level of detail and go wild with arguments over whether the shirts that were packed should have been heavy, medium or lightweight, or whether you can really count a shirt if it is too dirty to be worn. Often, high conflict parents do best when they develop very structured agreements that leave little room for interpretation. You will find more discussion on this topic in section D6 of this chapter.

11. Choose Your Words Carefully

Language is a very powerful tool. It can make communication easier, or it can make communication difficult, adversarial and confusing. By choosing your words carefully, you will be better understood and will be less likely to get into an argument. The following are specific ideas to improve your communication skills.

a.   Be an Active Listener

Listening involves more than hearing the words spoken— you must also understand them. Simple though it may sound, most people need to practice this skill. This is especially difficult when you negotiate with someone you have known—and argued with—for a long time. Try not to fall into the trap of assuming that you know what the other parent will say or what he or she "really" means.

To be sure that you understand the other parent's comments or concerns, ask. Simply say: "It sounds as though you are saying '___;' is that right?" Once you truly hear and understand the other, you can be sure that you are reacting to something real and can make your decisions accordingly. Who knows? You both might be pleasantly surprised to find that some things have changed!

b.   Say "Yes, … If" Instead of "Yes, … But"

Consider the following conversation between two parents:

PARENT A: *"I want the children to live with me during the week, and you can have them on the weekends."*

PARENT B: *"But I want to be able to see them during the week sometimes, too."*

PARENT A: *"There you go again—you always argue. Why can't you just let me have one decision go my way?"*

PARENT B: *"I wasn't arguing! You are as impossible to talk to as always! You can forget it now—the kids will live with me and you can see them when it's convenient."*

When parents are angry or distrustful, it is easy to jump to the conclusion that "yes, … but" really means "no." In fact, the reverse is usually true. When people start sentences with "yes, … but," they are often trying to describe the conditions upon which they might agree—rather than saying "no." You can avoid confusion and the other parent's negative reaction by saying "yes, … if" when you want to condition your approval.

As an alternative, these parents might have approached their discussion like this:

PARENT A: *"I want the children to live with me during the week, and you can have them on the weekends."*

PARENT B: *"That might work, if I can also see them sometimes during the week."*

PARENT A: *"Well maybe, if I know about it in advance."*

PARENT B: *"I could call at the beginning of the week when I know I will have an afternoon free, and the kids could ride the bus home to my house instead."*

In this second conversation, the parents were careful to phrase their responses positively. Their negotiations are almost certainly going to result in an agreement that is clear and acceptable to both.

c.   Use "I" Statements and Give Information

When a parent wants to convey anger, frustration or some other negative emotion, he or she is often tempted to start sentences with "you," as in, "You are so irresponsible!" By turning these into "I" statements, you will find that you are much more effective because the other parent can better understand how you feel and why. Consider how much more effective you can be if you were to say, for example, "I get angry when you are late to pick the children up because I have to deal with their disappointment!" rather than, "You don't even care enough about the children to show up on time!"

d.   Identify Bothersome Behavior and Suggest Solutions

When registering complaints, you will have greater success at finding a solution if you clearly state the problem and suggest solutions.

EXAMPLE: *I get angry when you are late picking up and returning the kids for two reasons. First, it seems to me that you don't think my time is valuable. Second, it doesn't matter to you whether the children get to bed at a reasonable hour on a school night. If you are going to be late, I need you to call at least an hour before, so the children don't sit waiting for you. If you can't get them back again at the agreed-upon time, I need you to agree that they will always be home at least half an hour before their bedtime.*

12. Look to the Future While Learning From the Past

Focusing on the past is valuable, but only if you use it to plan for the future. In fact, getting stuck in the past is a common reason for failing to agree about the future.

When starting in on familiar arguments, many parents say, "Oh no! Not this again!" and stop listening for issues or concerns that can be resolved. Instead of rehashing old issues, shift your focus to making the future work better by asking one or two strategic questions.

EXAMPLE: *I remember that in the past your concerns were "A," "B" and "C." Is this still true? If it is, what should we change so that "A," "B" and "C" are no longer issues?*

A realistic and successful parenting agreement will emphasize the things that work well for your family, and will try to compensate for the things that don't. For this to happen, you and the other parent must work just as hard to identify things that you do well together, as to point out things that are "wrong." When the situation seems especially dismal, remind yourselves of the things you can take credit for, such as:

- how well your children are doing
- how much of the decision-making process you are handling on your own, or
- how much you really agree on about raising your children.

13. Don't Be Thrown Off Course by "Backsliding"

"Backsliding," or changing your mind about things that you've already agreed on, is very common and is not usually a sign of bad faith in negotiations. Rather, backsliding is often a signal that someone is struggling with a very difficult issue. If one of you is retreating from what seemed to be an acceptable resolution of an issue, take the opportunity to:

- reopen the issue
- discuss what doesn't seem right about the resolution
- try to identify the real concerns, and
- ask what alternative solutions might better meet each person's needs and concerns.

14. Conduct an Effective Meeting

The negotiations that you and the other parent conduct on your own must be structured to be productive. The following list of strategies can help your meetings to go smoothly and your negotiations to be more likely to result in lasting agreements:

- Allow each other to speak without interruption.
- Don't criticize each other, even while talking about problems or situations you don't want repeated.
- Describe each problem in terms of your reaction (such as, "When you are late I get angry because the children are disappointed and it seems you don't value my time").
- Use "I" statements (as opposed to "you" accusations).
- Focus on the issues.

15. Expect Success

While some people are naturally optimistic, others tend to see the gloomy side of things. Looking only for problems and threats can be enough to sour almost every negotiation. With practice and conscious effort, however, many people learn to see that challenges and past conflicts offer opportunities to succeed in the future.

People who succeed more often than they fail tend to expect success and to use past mistakes and conflict as opportunities to learn (unpleasant though the experiences may have been). When you expect to succeed, you will work hard to find solutions to your problems. If you expect to fail, you will usually give up looking for solutions, thereby guaranteeing failure.

When you and the other parent are actually making decisions and developing your parenting agreement, you can set your agreement up to succeed if you:

- develop an action plan and assign responsibilities
- find ways to describe what "success" means for your children
- establish how you will know when a problem is really solved, and
- schedule reviews of your parenting plan and make changes when needed.

D. Breaking Through Impasses

Unsolvable disagreements—or impasses—are common during negotiations. In fact, you should probably expect at least one or two serious disagreements during the creation of your parenting agreement. If you hit a dead end, first review the preparation techniques described in Section B, above. If reviewing the preparation suggestions doesn't get you over the hump, consider adopting one of the problem-solving strategies discussed below.

1. Set the Issue Aside for Awhile

One of the easiest ways to deal with an impasse is to set the issue aside for awhile. When setting your agenda, consider resolving the easy issues first—the ones on which you generally agree. This lets you rack up some successes and helps build momentum for resolving the more difficult issues. As you confront increasingly difficult topics, remind yourselves of your successful negotiations to date. Use the decision-making strategies that worked on the easy issues to tackle the hard ones.

2. Reestablish Trust

Trust is an essential element to effective communication and decision making, and yet trust is usually eroded or lost during separation or divorce. This can create enormous problems for parents trying to negotiate and implement a parenting agreement. Fortunately, there are ways for parents to recapture enough trust in each other to be convinced that the other will fulfill the agreement.

a. Understand the Problem

Some parents confuse trustworthiness with acceptable behavior. If the other parent's lifestyle or career changes do not meet your expectations, this does not necessarily mean that the person is not worthy of your trust. If you define trustworthiness with words such as "reliable" and "honest," and by characteristics such as a love for your children, common decency and values you have in common, you may find you are able to trust the other parent again.

b. Measure Trustworthiness

Once you understand the problem, you may be able to resolve your concerns about trustworthiness by describing how you will demonstrate trustworthiness in the parenting relationship.

> **EXAMPLE:** *I am having trouble trusting my children's father because he keeps changing the visiting schedule. To resolve this problem, at a minimum, he would have to call within 72 hours of any change and limit his changes to once a month.*

> **EXAMPLE:** *My trust in our son's mother is gone because she describes her time with him one way and he says something else. These inconsistencies worry me because I don't know whom to believe. She would relieve my anxieties by letting me speak to my son periodically during the course of a visit.*

Forcing yourself to define exactly what the other parent can do to regain your trust will go a long way toward helping you overcome impasses.

c. Agree on Simple Tasks Each Parent Must Carry Out

One way for a parent to believe that the other can be trusted to honor a parenting agreement is to identify simple tasks for each parent to complete in a timely and appropriate manner. One example might be filling out Worksheets 1, 2 and 3 in Chapter 3 in preparation for completing Worksheet 4 together. Other examples include:

- maintaining an on-time visitation schedule for a month
- scheduling and keeping appointments with teachers to learn of your children's progress in school, or
- entering and completing a substance abuse rehabilitation program.

For this strategy to work, the tasks must be clear, achievable and meaningful. State your goals in positive terms by describing the actions that a parent will take, not those the parent will refrain from. For example, you can say that a parent will be on time, rather than a parent will not be late.

3. Find your "BATNA" or "WATNA"

Often, problems that arise in the course of negotiations become easier to solve when the parties consider the alternatives. *Getting To Yes*, by Fisher and Ury (Penguin Books, 1981), of the Harvard Negotiation Project, suggest you consider your "BATNA"—or Best Alternative To a Negotiated Agreement. John Haynes suggests identifying your "WATNA"—or Worst Alternative To a Negotiated Agreement.

An example of a BATNA, or best alternative, might be an evaluation and recommendation by a custody evaluator after observing both parents' homes and relationships with their children. This kind of assessment can be very valuable, assuming it does not polarize you further. One way to avoid increasing the conflict after receiving a professional evaluation is to use it in mediation as a means of breaking the deadlock.

One common WATNA to a negotiated parenting agreement is a full-blown court trial. Considering what a court trial involves often proves to be an effective motivator for parents to negotiate an agreement: seeking a decision by a judge will cost a lot of money, take a lot of time and heighten conflict. There is also the risk that the judge will make a decision that neither parent likes.

4. Play to Your Strengths

List what your current parenting arrangements have going in their favor. Your list might include items such as:

- shared love for your children
- agreement about house rules and expected standards of behavior for your children

- agreement about the community in which you want your children to grow up
- agreement about what school your children will attend, and
- agreement about what religious training your children will receive.

Each area of agreement strengthens your chance of finding further areas of agreement, and reduces the chance of future conflict.

5. Expand Your Options

One effective strategy for overcoming an impasse is to think broadly—most problems have a myriad of possible solutions. If, for example, your homes are not too far apart and your conflict is because one parent feels he or she is not seeing the children enough, consider adding a regular midweek dinner or having the other parent provide after-school care. If your discussions have broken down because one parent wants to move out of the area, consider having both parents move—assuming they can both find jobs.

6. Balance the Power

For any number of reasons, one parent may be at a distinct disadvantage when trying to negotiate with the other. If domestic violence or emotional abuse has been present, then the threat of force or intimidation might be very real. If one parent is articulate and the other is not, the latter parent may have trouble presenting his or her views and interests, or protecting the interests of the children. Also, some parents consider that they have few options because they fulfill a stereotyped role of "Mother" or "Father."

If these or similar situations are present, consider one of the options below.

a. Enlist the Help of a Mediator or Counselor

Counselors and mediators have different strengths when it comes to balancing power between two individuals. Counselors can offer parents a safe setting within which they can vent their feelings and deal with emotional as well as practical parenting issues. Mediators can support one or both parents in their efforts to identify—and communicate more effectively about—practical parenting issues. Because mediators also manage the communication process, they can ensure that each parent is given ample time and opportunity to explain a position.

b. Enlist the Help of Attorneys

An attorney can represent a parent's interests in negotiations. This is especially helpful when one parent feels incapable of representing himself or herself. If one parent is represented by counsel, then both should be represented. Be aware, however, that once attorneys get involved, parents may lose control over the kinds of decisions that are made, the kinds of resolutions they can consider and the costs of reaching an agreement.

While increasing numbers of attorneys support their clients through less adversarial proceedings such as mediation, many still feel more comfortable in a courtroom and may steer their clients that way. Chapter 13 has suggestions on how to find attorneys who are willing to approach separation or divorce cases in the least adversarial way possible.

c. Seek Individual Counseling or Therapy

Some parents have never learned how to stand up for themselves in a discussion or while negotiating an agreement. It may be because these parents cannot deal with the emotional content of the discussions or the stress associated with the separation or divorce. If emotional issues make your negotiations particularly difficult, you may need individual counseling prior to, or as part of, negotiating your parenting agreement.

d. Negotiate Separately

In some situations, especially when domestic violence or emotional abuse has been present, it is best that the parents choose a neutral facilitator and negotiate separately. With this option, each parent meets separately with a mediator or other facilitator to present his or her views, interests and objectives. The mediator or other facilitator helps both parents generate a list of issues and resolutions.

e. Consider a Highly Structured Parenting Plan

Some parents find it nearly impossible to manage their parenting arrangements without having each interaction lead to an argument. Often, the solution is a highly detailed and structured parenting plan that is almost impossible to misunderstand. Almost nothing is left to chance. This also means that there is little, if any, room for making changes, unless the parents sit down (preferably with a mediator's, counselor's or attorney's help) to overhaul the agreement.

A CASE IN POINT

Let's consider a specific example and walk through the process of negotiating an agreement to resolve a particular problem.

Exchanges, or the time your child switches from one home to the other, can be difficult for everyone. The reasons why these times are difficult can be complicated. Let's assume that you and the other parent want to negotiate (or renegotiate) how exchanges happen. In addition to making sure that the exchange is as easy as possible, you might also want to get to the point that your child no longer "falls apart" each time he or she goes back and forth between your two homes.

If you are going to reach agreement about how to manage this issue better, you're going to have to start by figuring out what's right and wrong with the situation now. Each of you can be "experts" on this one. Your first step in the negotiating process, then, is gathering information. You can make a list of what each of you does or doesn't like about the exchange.

For some parents, it might be important to make the time and location of the exchange convenient, or to avoid having an argument during the exchange.

Depending on your child's age, it might also be a good idea to ask about his or her ideas regarding what might make the exchange go more smoothly. Although you don't want to put your child in the position of having to make the final decisions, asking his or her opinion can be a good idea.

Some children need help to talk about what they do and don't like during an exchange. One place to start is to ask your child to tell you what they think about or how they feel just before and just after an exchange. You might also ask what they would change—or what should stay the same.

If you need more information about what makes exchanges difficult, there are a lot of good books, and some videos, about how children deal with divorce and what their parents can do to make things easier. (For some information about good resources, check the Bibliography and Additional Resources sections in Chapter 13). If your child's behavior or "falling apart" seems out of proportion or is alarming, ask a therapist or other counselor about the situation and whether you should consider getting some help.

When you have some idea about the elements of the problem you want to solve, you are ready to think about what kinds of decisions you will need to make. Consider the time of day, where the exchange takes place, who is present, how well the child has been prepared and knows what to expect and how you can handle your information exchange with the least amount of tension.

Some common reasons that a transition might be difficult for a child include:

- regular arguing between the adults
- feeling guilty about leaving one parent alone to be with the other
- wishing that the divorce wasn't real, and
- worrying about what one parent will think if the child shows their affection for the other parent.

Some common strategies to make transitions easier include:

- making the transitions happen at "natural" breaks, such as before or after school, as part of a visit to a grandparent or other relative (if these are stress-free) or before or after an outside activity such as a team sport, youth program or other event
- using notes, emails, faxes or separate phone calls about school, activities, health or special events to avoid an argument or making each other feel guilty
- finding new ways to transfer clothes and toys, such as having parents pick up or drop off suitcases while the child is in school
- addressing each of your own lingering anger, sadness or other unresolved feelings through separate therapy or other counseling services.

Professionals recommend a number of different strategies for helping high conflict families live with a particular parenting plan.

Janet Johnson and Linda Campbell discuss an approach called "parallel parenting" (*Impasses of Divorce*, The Free Press, 1988). With this approach, the child has two clearly defined (and often completely separate) worlds. In this situation, each of the child's worlds is defined by one of the parents. An effort is made to make at least some elements of each world consistent (such as following the same daily routines, using the same child care provider or having at least two or three of the same house rules), no matter where the child is. Parents can use this strategy to lessen the number and intensity of arguments they have by spelling each item out in detail, and then arranging to almost never be in the same place at the same time. The only purpose, then, for the parents to come together would be to renegotiate an element of the agreement, possibly with a mediator, counselor or attorney.

The parallel parenting approach can work well in the short term while the level of conflict is high. For the long term, however, this arrangement can cause new problems. In cases where the differences between the homes are great, and the animosity between the parents remains extremely high (or is regularly boiling just under the surface), children can feel that they lead two lives—one to please one parent, and one to please the other. When these arrangements become a way of life, the child may find it difficult, or impossible, to feel as though his or her needs are seen, respected and met by either parent. Sometimes, children in this situation will go so far as to develop a completely different way of living and relating to others in each home.

Carla Garrity and Mitchell Baris (*Caught in the Middle*, Lexington Books, 1994) discuss a similar approach that they call "demarcated joint custody." With this approach, each parent is given decision-making authority for separate issues. For example, one parent may make all of the medical care and education-related decisions, and the other might make the decisions about religious training and summer activities. The advantage of this approach is that each parent feels as though he or she has a direct and important role to play in their child's upbringing—while minimizing the chances that either will feel as though the other has crossed over onto his or her turf. The downside,

of course, of this type of arrangement is that not all issues are as cleanly divided as they might seem. If you consider the example described above, you can see that these parents will find it difficult to figure out who can decide about summer school if their child has a special educational aptitude or need.

E. Knowing Where to Get Help and Support

Regular and high levels of conflict create significant problems for everyone. While the long-term hope is that you and the other parent will come to understand how to minimize—or prevent—regular conflict, that process can take time. In the meantime, it can help to learn more about conflict, find new problem solving strategies and get hands-on help from trained professionals.

There are a number of professionals to choose from. All are available in the private sector, but an increasing number of courts around the country will order parents to hire the services of one or more of these professionals to help in managing or solving custody and visitation disputes. Although the exact titles these professionals may use will vary somewhat in different parts of the country, a little persistence will generally uncover a few of these professionals in your area.

Attorney (Matrimonial or Family Law Specialist)

A lawyer who specializes in family, matrimonial (marriage) or divorce law.

Attorney for the Child (Minor's Counsel)

A lawyer who specializes in understanding and representing the legal interests of children, especially when the child's parents are involved in high levels of conflict or have been charged with child physical or emotional abuse or neglect.

Child Custody Evaluator (Investigator)

A trained—and usually licensed—mental health professional who specializes in understanding and making recommendations (usually to a court) about what kinds of parenting, visitation or other decisions will be in the best interests of a particular child.

Child Development Specialist

Generally either a medical doctor, nurse, nurse practitioner or mental health professional who has a detailed understanding of:

- how children grow and develop over time
- the effects of a child's physical or mental health on "normal" development, and
- the effects of "environmental factors" such as how the child is parented, their experiences with friends and schoolteachers.

Clinical Social Worker

A licensed mental health professional who is trained in the assessment and treatment of mental health problems and difficulties with relationships.

Court-Appointed Special Advocate (CASA)

A person appointed to accompany and represent the interests of a child through all phases of (generally) juvenile court cases having to do with dependency (a court considering whether to limit or end a parent's rights to raise their child), adoption or other planning for placement in the foster care system.

Divorce Counselor

A mental health professional who specializes in working with adults and/or children experiencing divorce or the end of a similarly committed relationship.

Exchange Supervisor

A person who is appointed by a court to be present when parents exchange their children for visits. Depending on the situation, this can be a friend or relative, a professional or a service offered by a supervised visitation center. The primary purpose is to make sure that no harm comes to anyone at the time of an exchange. Another reason to have an exchange supervisor is to help a child ease the transition from one parent to the other—especially if the child is reluctant to visit.

Guardian Ad Litem

A person, often a lawyer, appointed by a court to make decisions affecting a child's best interests, health, education or welfare.

Marriage Counselor (Marriage Family and Child Counselor)

A mental health professional who specializes in helping couples to address individual and relationship issues in a way that might preserve the marriage or otherwise committed relationship.

Mediator (Child Custody, Divorce)

A trained professional (often either a mental health professional or lawyer) who helps parents or guardians (and sometimes the entire family) address and reach mutually acceptable agreements resolving some or all of the issues surrounding separation, divorce or renegotiating parenting agreements. This may or may not include money and property issues, and filing court papers to get agreements recorded as legally enforceable court orders.

Paralegal

A trained professional who does not give legal advice or represent people in court, but is familiar with routine legal matters such as preparing certain types of forms or researching certain legal issues.

Parent Educator

A trained education or mental health professional who teaches classes or provides individual instruction to parents about child development, parenting, conflict resolution or other matters.

Psychiatrist (Child, Adult)

A licensed medical doctor who is trained in diagnosing and treating mental health disorders and can prescribe medication.

Psychologist (Child, Adult)

A licensed mental health professional who may provide counseling support for individuals, couples, children or families, or conduct assessments of adults or children (including conducting and interpreting psychological tests).

Social Worker

A mental health professional who provides counseling and practical support to individuals, couples or families. This might include referrals to other professionals or community resources, or screening to decide whether someone is eligible to receive certain benefits.

Special Master

A trained professional (usually a lawyer, mental health professional, accountant or other professional) appointed by the court to apply their special expertise to deciding certain types of issues. The special master's decisions are generally binding on the parties as if they were a court order, and can be appealed, but require a court hearing to get them changed.

Visitation Arbitrator

A trained professional (often a court employee, lawyer or mediator) who is either appointed by a court or agreed to by the parties to decide disputes about how visits will happen whenever they come up.

Visitation Supervisor

A person appointed by a court to be present any time a particular parent spends time with his or her child. Generally, this type of appointment is made only when there are concerns about a child's safety when he or she visits with that parent, but these appointments might also be made if a court wants to find out more about how well a parent and child relate together, or a child is not used to being with a parent—especially if the parent has been absent for a long time.

In addition to working with individual professionals, many courts order, or other community organizations, offer helpful resources such as:

Anger Management/Batterer's Treatment Programs

These programs are focused on helping people (generally) convicted of domestic violence who have (almost always) been ordered to attend the program until earning a certificate of completion as part of their probation or other court sentence.

Divorce Support Groups (Parents and/or Children)

These groups may be offered in a variety of ways and can help parents and children deal with issues surrounding separation, divorce or the end of a similarly committed relationship. Some programs have a set curriculum, others allow participants to decide what they will discuss. These types of programs can be open-ended (drop-in, participate until ready to stop, court-ordered for a certain length of time), or operate for set periods of time (such as three, six or 12 months) and lead to a "graduation" certificate.

Legal Information Clinics or Help Centers

A place where people can go for access to get free or low-cost legal advice or information about their legal rights, how to start or handle a court case, the court process, how to fill out and file court forms or other similar issues.

Parent Education

A more extensive program that gives parents detailed information about child development, effective parenting skills, conflict resolution or other subjects.

Parent Orientation

A brief class or session (often less than six hours) that lets parents know about the court, mediation, evaluation, supervised visitation or other process they will be going through as a result of their custody, visitation, dependency or other dispute.

Twelve-Step or Other Substance Abuse Programs

These programs help people with alcohol, drug or other substance abuse issues understand and find new ways to manage these problems in their lives. Attendance might be ordered by the court, drop-in or voluntarily agreed to as part of a marital settlement, mediation or other agreement.

Visitation or Visitation Exchange Supervisors

An organization that provides trained staff members to supervise visits or provide a safe place for parents to exchange a child for a visit. ■

Building Your Parenting Agreement

Raising children to adulthood involves a myriad of parenting issues. Some of these are simple, clear-cut and noncontroversial (at least between the parents). Many others can be hotly contested and lead to expensive, emotionally draining battles. The more parenting issues you can discuss and resolve now, the fewer disagreements you will have later.

This chapter takes you issue by issue through the process of building your own parenting agreement. These issues include who your children's medical providers will be, where they will go to school, where they will live and how they will spend time with both parents. Following each issue are several options for you to consider. As you work through the issues and options, you will find references to questions on the worksheets in Chapter 3 which may help you to address your particular concerns.

In general, parenting agreements have come a long way from the days of "sole custody awarded to mother with reasonable visitation for father." Although some agreements and court orders still use this extremely general approach, more and more agreements are detailed. The reasons for this shift are many, but three stand out:

- "Sole custody with reasonable visitation" lets the sole custodian virtually strip the other parent of a parental role.
- Vague agreements are frequently contested and often lead to arguments over what constitutes "reasonable" visitation.
- Parents denied custody and given only minimum levels of visitation have little incentive to maintain contact with their children or to pay child support.

A. What Works in Building a Parenting Agreement

Two artifacts of a large, steady volume of divorce cases are seeing what works and being reminded frequently of what doesn't. The three key elements that contribute to a successful but separate parenting relationship are outlined below.

1. Cooperate! Cooperate! Cooperate!

It is difficult, but essential, that you and the other parent set aside your differences as you plan for your children's future. Ideally, you will find a way to trust each other. For most parents, this is hardest during the first weeks or months following a separation or divorce. Fortunately, feelings of anger and pain usually diminish over time.

Most parents find that settling into a new life after separation or divorce makes it easier to untangle their "couple" issues from their parenting issues. Regardless of how you feel right now, keep in mind that many parents, feeling just the way you do, have found solutions that benefit everyone—at least in the long run.

2. Get Outside Help

Negotiating parenting agreements can be difficult and complicated. Chapters 8 through 11 cover some of the very complex issues in greater detail. If this is not enough, Chapter 13 provides a list of books, professionals and other information sources.

The parenting agreement in this book does not conform to any specific court's filing requirements. If you are getting a divorce or legal separation, you must check with your local court, the law library, a forms service, a paralegal or an attorney to find out if your agreement must be prepared in any special way.

In addition, because your parenting decisions may have legal consequences, consider having a family law or matrimonial attorney review your agreement. The attorney can help you make sure that the agreement conforms to your state's laws regarding child custody and visitation, says what you want it to say and accomplishes your objectives.

In addition, your agreement, by itself, will not be enforceable the way a business contract is enforceable. However, the attorney can help you turn the agreement into an enforceable court order.

3. Keep Your Agreement Current

You don't need a crystal ball to predict that your children's needs and interests will change over the years. So will yours. For these reasons, few parents negotiate a single agreement that stands, unaltered, until their children reach adulthood. In fact, many parents make at least one major change in their parenting arrangements within the first three years after their separation or divorce. Changes might also be appropriate if a parent intends to move, if work schedules change significantly or if a child wants to live with the other parent.

Section B, below, contains 43 issue/option sets which make up the parenting agreement. Some of these may not be relevant now. As time goes on, however, you, the other parent or your children may discover that previously ignored issues have a new importance. For example, if you have preschool children, you may not care to spend time now deciding about owning and operating a motor vehicle. Similarly, if neither parent is in a new relationship, planning for how to handle new partners may be impossible. Both of these issues, however, may become very important later.

You and the other parent should periodically review your agreement to see if changes are necessary. Issue 41, Making Changes, lets you build a review schedule into your agreement.

Also, keep this book handy for when you want to make changes. Your goal is to create a workable parenting agreement now, and to anticipate the need for changes as time goes on. Agreements that contemplate future changes are better able to respond to your family's changing needs, circumstances or concerns. The earlier you address a request for a change, the greater chance you have of keeping conflict to a minimum. If this edition of the book becomes outdated, you can trade this copy in for the newest edition at a 35% discount. The new material will include legal changes and new issue/option sets contributed by readers and professionals.

B. Complete the Parenting Agreement

You may want to skim the blank parenting agreement in the appendix or the chapter table of contents to see what issues are covered. If issues important to you are not included, use our format to describe the issue and your solution. At a minimum, your agreement should include Issue 11 (Making Decisions), Issue 15 (Where Our Children Will Live) and Issue 39 (Labeling the Custody Arrangement).

As you fill out your parenting agreement, you can select one or more of the options listed or you can include your own solutions. If you have more than one child, you may make different decisions for each. In this case, use the blank lines to record your different decisions or attach additional sheets.

We'd like our database of issue/option sets to keep growing! You can mail in your comments on our pre-addressed reader contribution card, fax your comments to 510-548-5902 or email your suggestions to feedback@nolo.com.

Look over the parenting agreement carefully before you begin. The order that the issues are presented in may seem a little strange, or at least different from what an attorney tells you is important, but there is a reason for it. The vast majority of parents who successfully negotiate parenting agreements handle the less heated issues first—usually issues about decision making. Accordingly, in our agreement, decision-making issues come first and living arrangement issues follow.

You can negotiate your agreement in the order the issues are presented, or you can skip around, tackling the issues that are easiest for you first. Regardless of which approach you take, use the worksheet to record your agreement as it takes shape, not to dictate how you will structure your negotiations.

Here is a suggestion for filling out your worksheet as you go through each issue/option set. Use an uppercase "X" in the space to the left of each item to note which issues you will address. Use a lowercase "x" to identify all options you want to include in that portion of your agreement. When you have finished the entire agreement, go back and number the issues and letter the options you will include. For example, your provision regarding your children's surname might read as follows:

X	Our children's surname is	_Garcia_ .

Any decision to change that surname will be made as follows [choose all that apply]:

_____ Our children will keep this surname until they become legal adults.

_____ Our children may choose their surname.

_X_ Our children may choose their surname after age _16_ .

_X_ We will discuss and agree on any change of surname.

_____ _____ [parent] has the authority to change our children's surname.

_X_ We further agree that [specify]:
Our children must inform us before submitting any documents to obtain a legal name change.

You will work through this section most efficiently if you:

- have Worksheets 1 through 4 from Chapter 3 close at hand (for each issue, refer to the "Worksheet Cross-Reference" chart)
- make at least six copies of the blank parenting agreement
- give the other parent two agreements and keep two for yourself
- complete one copy as you negotiate with the other parent
- write or type your final agreement on one copy, and
- get outside help when you need it.

Issue 1: Medical, Dental and Vision Care

Most parents want their children to receive competent medical care when they need it and at a reasonable cost. Making it happen, however, might not always be easy. Use your parenting agreement to specify the details, including:

- your children's medical providers
- who has authority to make decisions regarding your children's medical care
- how you will exchange medications your children take
- how much medical information you will share (such as every cold and scrape or only major illnesses and accidents), and
- who will take the children for their regular checkups.

ISSUE 1 CROSS-REFERENCES

Worksheet	Questions
Worksheet 3	4
Worksheet 4	4

a. Choose Health Care Providers

When parents live in the same city or within a reasonable distance, they often agree on the primary medical, dental or mental health care provider for their children. If you and the other parent live a considerable distance from each other, however, it makes sense for you each to find providers so that your children can receive consistent care. If you each select medical providers, exchange names, addresses, phone numbers and releases so the providers can exchange records and information. Your doctor should have a release for you to sign.

b. Routine and Special Care

Specify who has the authority to seek routine care for your children, such as immunizations, annual physical exams and blood tests. Many parents agree to let either parent handle routine care for the children without first discussing it with the other. Some circumstances, however, such as immunizations, require coordination to avoid duplication.

You also need to specify how your children's special medical, dental or vision care needs, such as hospitalization, surgery, medication or experimental treatment, will be met. Most parents who share legal custody (or joint custody in states that do not differentiate between legal and physical custody) require discussion and agreement before allowing this level of treatment. (See Chapter 2, Section D, for definitions of joint, legal and physical custody.)

c. Emergency Care

Clearly state how much authority each parent has to seek treatment in a medical emergency. If the children spend a fair amount of time with both of you, you will probably want to allow either parent to obtain emergency treatment without first consulting the other. If you choose to restrict a parent's authority to seek emergency treatment, the parent who must make, or be consulted about, emergency decisions must include a medical release during visits with the other parent, or be available at a moment's notice.

d. Ongoing Medical, Dental or Vision Care

Some children have medical or physical conditions (such as diabetes, a physical disability, poor vision or periodontal disease) which requires attention for months, years or even the rest of their lives. In such situations, you must decide whether medications, physical supports or enhancements (such as crutches or prosthetics) will be kept in each home or will travel with the children.

The American Academy of Children and Adolescent Psychologists cautions that "the child with a serious medical illness is at risk for developing associated psychological problem." For this and other reasons, you should give serious consideration to addressing this possibility in Issue 2, below.

Issue 2:   Psychiatric and Other Mental Health Care

Although many parents are willing to consider providing some mental health or emotional support for their children, few know what signs to look for in the child's behavior. Perhaps the most obvious indicator of emotional or other mental health care needs is a dramatic change in your child's behavior which persists over some period of time. Some of the warning signs include:

- unusual stress, clinging and/or nervous tics
- regression to previous behavioral stages (for example, bedwetting or thumb-sucking)
- loss of motivation for school, making friends or having fun
- sleeping too much or too little
- becoming unusually rebellious or argumentative, and
- becoming unusually cooperative and compliant.

Psychiatric or other mental health care can be a source of serious disagreement. If you and the other parent discuss this issue, keep in mind that you need to decide the following:

- whether you will permit or require psychiatric or other counseling for your children
- whether you will permit or require psychiatric or other counseling for either parent
- who may provide the care, and
- how you will determine when the need for counseling has ended.

If mental illness is already part of your family's situation, you should pay close attention to your children's needs in this area. Although hereditary links to mental illness are not always clearly defined, professionals note that when parents suffer from manic-depression (bipolar disease), schizophrenia, alcoholism or other drug abuse, their children are particularly prone to become mentally ill.

Counseling for parents is included here because a parent's state of mind and mental health can have a significant impact on children. Whether the parents attend counseling together, or set out goals to strive for in separate counseling sessions, time spent in counseling will usually result in better parenting plans.

Specific provisions in your parenting plan might:

- identify the issues to be addressed (such as anger, frustration, jealousy or violence)
- allow the counselor and patient to agree when these issues are resolved, and
- provide for a letter from the counselor to the other parent stating that the counselor and the patient agree that the counseling has accomplished its objectives.

ISSUE 2 CROSS-REFERENCES

Worksheet	Questions
Worksheet 1	4
Worksheet 2	9
Worksheet 3	4, 10, 11
Worksheet 4	4, 6, 9

Issue 3: Education

School often becomes a dominating influence in children's lives after the age of five. Whether your children attend a public school, private school or home school, parental involvement in children's education is critical. Making decisions about your children's education is more complicated than simply deciding on the type of school they will attend. In addition, you must consider:

- how you will make decisions about changing your children's school
- how you will address your children's special needs or talents

- who will participate in, and remain informed about, your children's school activities and performance
- whom the school should contact in the event of an emergency
- how you will define and encourage your children's good school performance
- the kind of education you will consider after high school, and
- how you will pay for post-high school education.

ISSUE 3 CROSS-REFERENCES

Worksheet	Questions
Worksheet 1	2, 9
Worksheet 2	2, 3, 10
Worksheet 3	3, 4
Worksheet 4	10, 18

a. Public, Private or Home Schooling

Although most children attend the local public school, many do not. If you are not content with the local public school, investigate before assuming you have no other options.

Some public school districts are large enough to allow for specialized schools (such as schools that emphasize art, science or math). Other school districts allow parents and students to choose from more than one school.

Private schools come in all sizes and configurations. You can choose from parochial, secular, same-sex or coed schools. The school may let students live at home, or require them to live in residence on the campus.

Home schooling is an option when a parent is willing and able to commit to full-time teaching. Home schooling requires an enormous commitment by one or both parents, and the curriculum must adhere to state educational standards.

You must consider your children's educational needs, academic needs and preferences before settling on a solution. If your option costs money, you must make sure that you put aside adequate funds. Specify your arrangement in your parenting agreement and your child support agreement, and be sure to include the same decision in both places.

If either parent or the children want to change schools, you can plan now for how that decision will be made. You can establish criteria (such as the child attaining certain skills or staying within a budget), or specify who will be authorized to make the change.

b. Supporting Special Needs or Talents

Some children need help with keeping up with certain skills or subjects. Others have special talents which can be cultivated through extra classes or activities. Parents need to be sensitive to these possibilities, as well as to the children's changing needs.

If your children have special needs or talents, consider:
- requesting support from their current school
- supplementing the school resources with private tutors, counselors or after-school activities, or
- switching schools.

c. Participating in School Activities

You and the other parent must agree on who will:
- participate in any parent-teacher associations
- help in the children's classroom
- attend parent-chaperoned functions, or
- attend other similar activities.

d. Attending Parent-Teacher Conferences

You and the other parent must also decide who will attend parent-teacher conferences. Some parents attend together, some designate one to attend and inform the other parent of the matters discussed and some opt for separate conferences.

e. Listing Parents' Names on School Emergency Contact Forms

You and the other parent must determine who will be listed on the school's emergency contact forms and in what order these persons will be listed. The school will also need to know who has authority to make medical decisions in the event of an emergency. (See Issue 1.)

f. Encouraging Good Performance in School

Parents often disagree about how to encourage good school performance or what the consequences will be for poor performance. For example, some parents give their children money or other rewards for earning good grades. Some parents withhold allowances or other privileges if their children get poor grades. If you and the other parent decide to reward or punish good or poor school performance, you will want to define the terms and specify the rewards or punishments you will use.

g. Sex Education

If you or the other parent want to prevent your children from participating in sex education classes, specify it here. In addition, you must find out whether you will be asked to give permission for your children to take the class or your children will take the class unless you deny permission.

h. Post-Secondary Education

Although most children and parents think about post-high school education for their children, such as college or technical training, many families fail to plan until their children reach high school. In fact, there are many planning options available, some of which require more preparation and thought than others.

Consider setting up a special account which you will use to pay for your children's education. If you do this, you will want to indicate how money will be deposited into that account. You can also investigate different loans, grants or scholarships. If the type of training your children receive is important to you, you can specify what programs you are willing, or refuse, to pay for, such as:
- pay-to-learn apprenticeships
- trade schools, or
- two-year or four-year institutions.

Issue 4: Surname

Many parents never question what last name their children will use after divorce or separation; however, the issue does come up. In general, courts require that a child's surname be chosen with the child's best interests at heart.

In some families, everyone has the same last name. In other families, they are all different. Some of the options you can consider after separation or divorce include:
- give the children one parent's surname
- create a new name from both parents' surnames (such as a hyphenated name), or
- have the children use one parent's last name from a new relationship or marriage.

After separation or divorce—especially if one or both parents changed names when the couple married or began living together—either or both parents might choose to return to a previous name. Additionally, a parent who begins a new relationship after divorce or separation might change his or her last name to match the new mate's surname.

Your children will need to know what their last name is and who has the authority to change that name. Some parents let their children choose their name; others allow the children that choice only after they reach a certain age.

Some parents change their children's last name without the other parent's consent. Later, they register the children in school, with the doctor or elsewhere under the new name. Asking children to assume a new last name without the other parent's consent can be confusing for the children and often provokes an argument with the other parent. It also means that your children's school, medical and other records might be difficult to piece together.

In most states, when you change a minor's last name, you must obtain court approval.

ISSUE 4 CROSS-REFERENCE

Worksheet	Question
Worksheet 3	8

Issue 5: Religious Training

After separation or divorce, parents may need to plan for their children's religious training. For some parents, this is easy; for others, it presents difficult choices. In many families, parents have different religions. Whether you will expose your children to one religion, agree to disagree, teach two religions, give your children no formal religious training or let your children choose for themselves, religion can be an important aspect of a child's development. It can also have a big influence on how you decide other elements of the agreement such as medical care (Issue 1), mental health care (Issue 2), school (Issue 3), child care (Issue 20) and outside activities (new Issue 26), among others. (Additional information on multicultural families is in Chapter 10.)

ISSUE 5 CROSS-REFERENCES

Worksheet	Questions
Worksheet 1	9
Worksheet 2	1, 2, 3
Worksheet 3	3, 5
Worksheet 4	3, 4, 18

a. Teach One Religion

This is quite probably the approach you will take if the parents have the same religion. But even if your religions differ, you may choose, for the sake of simplicity or because one parent has stronger religious ties, to raise your children with only one religion. This is especially common when children have two Christian parents who belong to different denominations, or have one parent who strongly identifies with being Jewish while the other parent has nominal ties with a Christian denomination.

b. Teach Both Religions

Some parents agree that while neither plans to convert to the other's faith, they want their children to grow up understanding both parents' religious beliefs. If this is your choice, consider whether either parent will be allowed to confirm, convert or otherwise formally indoctrinate the children in a particular faith.

c. Agree on Basic Tenets and Allow Children to Choose Denomination

Some parents have no strong preferences about which denomination their children must be raised in, as long as the principal values follow a general religious belief, such as Christian, Moslem, Jewish, Hindu or Buddhist. In this situation, consider who will expose the children to the faith and take them to services. Also consider what you will do if your children express an interest in a particular denomination.

d. Let Children Choose Religious Participation

Some parents do not subscribe to any particular faith, are not active in any congregation or have no interest in providing religious training for their children. In this situation, decide how you will respond if your children some day express an interest in religion. You might decide to take them to religious services of their choice, expose them to several different religions or refuse to let them participate. Also, if you and the other parent *do* participate religiously but you want to let your children choose for themselves, consider what you will do if your children select no religious training.

Issue 6: International Travel and Passports

Some families want or need to travel out of the U.S. with their children. Almost all foreign travel requires a passport—even for children. International travel becomes a concern if you fear that a trip abroad might become an attempt to change custody or to take the children away from you altogether. If your children have dual citizenship, you may have a hard time enforcing your court orders outside of the U.S., as there might be a question about which country has legal authority to make decisions.

Some U.S. courts are beginning to order economic sanctions against a parent who tries to change a custody agreement while outside the United States. Some courts have cut off child support if a parent has tried to live permanently and have jurisdiction transferred to a foreign country. Some judges have also required a parent to post a bond before taking a child out of the country.

ISSUE 6 CROSS-REFERENCES

Worksheet	Questions
Worksheet 2	2
Worksheet 3	6, 7, 14
Worksheet 4	10, 18

⚠ WE ASSUME GOOD INTENTIONS

This books assumes that neither parent intends to take the children out of the country to steal them from the other parent. If this is an immediate concern, see a lawyer for help in securing a court order that will minimize this possibility.

a. Issue Passport but Set Limited Travel Time or Destination

With this option, parents might permit travel out of the U.S. but incorporate restrictions specifying permitted countries or amounts of time their children can be abroad, or both.

b. Issue Passport but Require Supervised Travel

Your parenting agreement might require that an adult accompany your children and the other parent for international travel. If this is your inclination, you might seriously rethink whether issuing a passport is advisable at all, given

that it might not be possible for a travel "supervisor" to prevent child-snatching under all circumstances.

c. Require Both Parents' Permission to Obtain a Passport

In the event that one parent seriously fears flight or abduction of a child, then that parent should seriously consider requiring that both parents give permission before passports are obtained for their children. International agreements provide some relief if this happens, but are not as effective as withholding the passport in the first place.

d. Instruct the State Department to Withhold a Child's Passport Unless Requested by the Custodial Parent

If one parent has sole custody, he or she can inform the State Department not to issue a passport for the children unless it is the custodial parent who applies for it.

Issue 7:   Driving and Owning a Car, Motorcycle or Off-Road Vehicle

Parents often disagree about when their children will be allowed to drive or own a car, motorcycle or off-road vehicle. While most parents let their teens take driver's training with their peers, the rules regarding when, how far and under what circumstances they may drive without an adult vary. Parents also often disagree on the following:

- whether or not their teens may own a car, motorcycle or off-road vehicle
- under what circumstances the teens may own a vehicle (for example, only if it is brand new, if it is formerly the "family car" or if a teen pays for it), or
- who will pay the insurance, tickets, repairs and other costs—the parents or the teens.

Because driving and owning a vehicle can be very important for your children in their teen years, this decision is especially worth thinking through in advance.

ISSUE 7 CROSS-REFERENCES

Worksheet	Questions
Worksheet 1	4
Worksheet 2	5
Worksheet 4	4, 9, 18

Issue 8: Military Service

Minor children need a parent's permission to enter the military. Some options you can consider would allow your minor children to enlist as follows:

- without restriction
- in the event of war
- after a certain age
- with the approval of one or both parents, or
- never.

Issue 9: Allowing Underage Marriage

You may wonder why underage marriage has been included as an issue you should consider when negotiating your parenting agreement. The reason is simple. Underage marriages are increasing, and you are now more likely than ever to have a child who considers this option. In 1960, there were approximately 8.5 underage marriages per 1,000 women between the ages of 15 and 18. After hitting a high of 10.6 marriages per 1,000 in 1980, that number has stabilized as of 1988 to just under 10 marriages per 1,000 women between the ages of 15 and 18.

The divorce rate for these underage marriages is also staggering. The U.S. Department of Commerce, Bureau of the Census, reports that the number of underage marriages which end in divorce has doubled during the period between 1950 and 1992. In that time, underage marriages ending in divorce have jumped from 10.3 per 1,000 women ages 15 to 18 to 21.2 per 1,000. For purposes of comparison, the divorce rate among 15- to 18-year-olds is more than three times greater than the rate for adults. Although underage marriages tend to last for an average of 7.1 years (slightly longer than the 6.8-year average for adult marriages), these marriages are just as likely to include children, and generally include more than one child.

You have at least five options when considering whether you will let your minor children get married, including:

- allow it at the child's discretion
- allow it in the event of a pregnancy
- allow it after a certain age
- allow it with consent of one or both parents, or
- not allow an underage marriage.

Because teenage pregnancy and underage marriage are such emotionally charged issues, you might make a tentative decision now and reevaluate that decision if the issue actually arises.

ISSUE 9 CROSS-REFERENCES

Worksheet	Questions
Worksheet 1	9
Worksheet 2	2, 3

Issue 10: Insurance

Insurance coverage can help with both the predictable and unpredictable expenses of child-rearing. Parents can provide insurance for medical, dental, vision and psychiatric care, and for prescription drugs. Parents can insure their own lives for the benefit of their children, and can get life insurance policies for their children which they can later convert to cash to pay for college.

Insurance coverage might be available through a parent's employment, secured as a stand-alone individual policy or converted from employee coverage to an individual policy if a parent changes jobs. Some parents agree that both will obtain whatever insurance coverage they can as long as it is available at low or no cost through their employer. If you both have insurance, you will have to agree on submitting claims, seeking treatment on the child's behalf and paying deductibles and other uncovered expenses.

⚠ **INSURANCE AND CHILD SUPPORT**
Most states require one or both parents to provide health insurance for their children as an obligation of child support. If you are also making a child support agreement, make sure your decisions in this section are consistent with what is in your child support agreement.

A list of resources that answer insurance questions is in Chapter 13.

ISSUE 10 CROSS-REFERENCE

Worksheet	Question
Worksheet 3	4

Issue 11: Making Decisions

When parents are married or living together, they work out their own system for making decisions. Only rarely does a court or other outsider, such as a therapist or physician, get involved in either the process or the actual decision.

When parents separate or divorce, however, they have to figure out how the big and little decisions affecting their children will be made, and who will make them. The question of who makes decisions is especially relevant if either or both parents have new partners. The parents also have to accept that only the larger decisions can be made in advance. Most decisions will be made as the issues arise.

Good decisions take your values and needs, and your children's values and needs, into consideration. Good decisions also stand the test of time because everyone involved gains something important. Whenever possible, the advantages of a decision should outweigh the disadvantages for everyone concerned.

You can take some of the guesswork out of the decision-making process by building a sound decision-making framework. To build this kind of framework, ask and answer the following questions for each decision which must be made:

- What must this decision accomplish?
- Who will gain by the decision?
- Who might lose by this decision?
- Whose needs must be met by this decision?
- How will I know that this decision has accomplished my objectives?

Take, for example, the need to choose between two schools for your children. Your answers to the above questions might go something like this:

- What must this decision accomplish? ("The school must provide a good college preparatory education.")
- Who will gain by the decision? ("Our children will gain a good education.")
- Who might lose by this decision? ("We will lose money if we choose an expensive private school. If we select a public school where only one of us lives, the parent who doesn't reside in that district may lose weekday contact with the children.")
- Whose needs must be met by this decision? ("Our children's needs must come first but we must be able to afford any private school and have money left over to continue most other important activities.")
- How will I know that this decision has accomplished my objectives? ("We will see the children's grades and test scores improve, and the school counselor will be confident that the children will have a good chance of getting into a good college.")

There are basically four models for making decisions, each with its own advantages and disadvantages:

- the parents reach an agreement
- one parent decides and later informs the other
- one parent decides but need not tell the other, or
- another responsible adult (such as a grandparent, aunt or close family friend) has the authority to make decisions.

ISSUE 11 CROSS-REFERENCES

Worksheet	Questions
Worksheet 1	5
Worksheet 2	6, 7, 8, 9, 10
Worksheet 3	12, 14, 15
Worksheet 4	1, 2, 3, 4, 10, 17

a.   The Parents Reach an Agreement

Provisions which require the parents to agree work well when both parents are active in their children's lives, can set aside their conflicts and have the same child-rearing values regarding raising their children. This does not mean you must see things identically, but that you are generally able to reach agreements on your own.

The best way for your parenting agreement to succeed is for you and the other parent to work together to find solutions that are in your children's best interests. Additionally, you both must remain informed about health care, school and outside activities so you can make decisions with an understanding of how they are likely to play out over time.

You can structure this option in any way that feels comfortable—just be specific. If, for example, you want to let a parent make everyday decisions when the children are with that parent, but will require discussion and agreement for significant decisions, you must describe what you mean by "everyday" and "significant" decisions.

Parents usually agree that, in an emergency, the parent caring for the children at the time will handle the situation and inform the other parent as soon as possible thereafter. Conversely, parents usually require consultation and agreement on major decisions, such as a change in residence, surgery, remedial tutoring, support for special talent or participation in a hazardous activity.

Parents can choose to meet in person, talk by telephone or start out their discussions by letter. Writing letters is good if you and the other parent are currently arguing. If you must communicate in writing because of constant arguing, however, reevaluate whether you and the other parent can actually make this decision-making model work.

b.   Parent With Primary Care of Children Decides and Informs the Other Parent

This option allows parents who argue frequently over child-rearing to make sure that decisions get made, while both parents remain aware of what is going on in their children's lives. It keeps both parents in the loop and eliminates opportunities for perpetuating the conflict. The parent who makes the decisions may have to provide the other parent with a medical release when the children are in the other parent's care. Otherwise, you can handle emergencies as described in Section a, above.

c.   Parent With Primary Care Makes All Decisions

This option may be necessary with parents who have a history of harassment, abuse or violence between them, or when a parent has had little involvement in raising the children. It allows decisions to be made for the children without fear of fighting or interference.

When the parent who does not have the authority to make decisions on the children's behalf spends time with them, that parent may need a medical release from the other parent to cover emergencies. This decision-making model is consistent with agreements that include supervised, or otherwise very limited, visitation.

d.   Parents Choose Another Responsible Adult to Make Decisions

In some families, the parents are either unwilling or unable to make decisions on their children's behalf. Sometimes this is the case with very young parents who need to grow up themselves. Other parents are incapable of making responsible decisions because of illness, abuse, substance abuse or neglect. In this situation, a court often determines who will take over the parenting role.

If you are unwilling to make decisions about your child's welfare, you may consider appointing a legal guardian for your children who would have complete decision-making authority. Or you could consider giving a guardian more limited powers—to make medical or financial decisions, for example—by signing a document called a "power

of attorney." Either way, these steps may affect the legal custody label in your parenting plan. (See Issue 39.)

Issue 12:   Resolving Disputes When Making Decisions Together

Even the most experienced negotiators may find themselves unable to resolve a particular issue. This is called an impasse. You and the other parent must plan for how you will resolve an impasse, that is, how necessary decisions will be made even when you cannot reach agreement on these issues on your own.

Part of the problem when trying to resolve a difficult issue is understanding the nature of the conflict. In addition to differing views, values and cultures, we are all driven—at least in some part—by jealousy, anger, bitterness or revenge. Often we may insist that our views are in the best interests of our children when, in fact, they are not. Many disagreements between parents are motivated by a desire to improve their adult lives rather than to meet the needs of their children. One effective strategy you can use to resolve conflict is to examine your motives for taking a particular position.

You have several options for resolving disagreements. As you consider these options, make sure that the option you choose allows for decisions to be made in a timely fashion. Your options include:

- giving the primary caretaker authority to decide
- resolving the underlying problems before making decisions
- developing temporary agreements
- using a counselor, therapist or attorney
- role-playing to see what is best for the children
- mediation, or
- arbitration

For more information on this subject—especially for dealing with high conflict situations—see Chapter 4.

ISSUE 12 CROSS-REFERENCES

Worksheet	Questions
Worksheet 2	6, 7, 10
Worksheet 3	7, 12, 15
Worksheet 4	3, 10, 17

A COURT'S ROLE IN MAKING DECISIONS

When parents cannot resolve their parenting issues, they can consider taking the issue to a court. Courts will not decide what clothes your children may wear to school, friends they may spend time with or sports they can play. A court, however, will decide who has authority to make decisions affecting your children, where your children will live and how they will spend time with both parents.

Most parents and professionals use the court as a last resort for resolving disputes. Going to court can be quite expensive and take a lot of time. More importantly, the judge making the decision will not know either you or your children, and will have little time in which to hear the matter and make a decision. As a result, you risk getting a decision that is less sensitive to your particular needs than might be the case if you and the other parent reached an agreement on your own. Furthermore, if you already have a court order, a court will not modify it unless you show that there has been a substantial change in circumstances.

Many states provide their judges with some guidance in making custody and visitation decisions. Some judges are urged to avoid contested proceedings whenever possible. These judges usually rely on the recommendations of a custody evaluator when making their decisions. Also, most judges give significant weight to a teen's preference about custody and visitation.

a.   The Primary Caretaker Has Authority

If your children will spend significantly more time with one parent than the other, consider giving that parent final authority to make decisions when you otherwise can't agree. Alternatively, you could give one parent final authority on certain issues when you disagree and give the other parent similar authority for different issues.

To put some limits on the parent with decision-making authority, you could require that before making a final decision the parent consult with someone whose opinions both parents value, such as a counselor, religious leader or family member. Even when parents cannot agree about something, they can often agree on whose advice they will trust and follow.

b.   Resolve Hidden Conflicts, Then Resolve the Dispute

One option is to try to "get underneath" the problem by trying to understand why it is a problem in the first place. Mental health professionals are especially skilled at this, and can often help parents who are regularly battling over certain things to untangle the issues and develop a plan for solving them over the longer term. Regular conflicts over exact pick-up and drop-off times, or whether visits over school holidays should start at the end of school on Friday or some other time may have more to do with worries over larger issues. For example, some parents want to make sure that visitation schedules do not vary more than a few hours or so one way or the other so that the child support amounts won't change. Other times, parents will refuse to allow a later or earlier pick-up time because they want to "teach" the other parent to be on time (in a way that they perhaps were not during the marriage, for example).

c.   Use a Counselor, Therapist or Attorney

One option is to ask for an evaluation of your situation from a trained professional, such as a psychiatrist, marriage and family counselor or other mental health professional. You can accept any recommendation that the evaluator makes, use the recommendation to try and reach an agreement on your own or bring the recommendation into mediation.

Another option is to each consult with an attorney—or meet with one attorney together—to get information about the law. (Be aware that many lawyers refuse to meet with both parties in a divorce dispute.) Many parents insist on knowing "what the law says" before making a decision. For example, if your state requires that a noncustodial parent be given a certain minimum amount of visitation, consulting an attorney might help you by guiding your decision about where the children will live (Issue 15), holidays (Issue 23) and vacations (Issue 24).

d.   Develop Temporary Agreements

Mistrust thwarts most parenting agreements. Therefore, it helps sometimes to take baby steps before trying big ones. So parents fighting over big decisions might try sharing decisions on simple issues for a short time. Hopefully this will improve their ability to communicate, resolve conflicts and make decisions together on more controversial questions.

For example, you might agree to make decisions about outside activities together for three months before trying to tackle larger decisions. Then you might be ready to tackle larger decisions, like who will provide after-school care, and then even larger decisions, like which schools your children will attend.

e.   Parent A/Parent B Plan

This tool for resolving impasses involves assigning parental roles involved in a particular issue to two hypothetical parents—Parent A and Parent B. Once these roles are assigned, you can then start deciding, based on the situation, which real parent is best suited to be Parent A and which Parent B. For instance, if you decide that the child should spend Christmas with Parent A and three weeks in the summer with Parent B, you would then decide which role is most appropriate for you and the other parent—that is, who would be the best Parent A and who the best Parent B.

The Parent A/Parent B approach is in fact most often employed when deciding where the children will live a majority of the time (Issue 15). Especially if you have trouble making that decision when you get to it, you may wish to return here and review this decision-making option.

f.   Mediate Disagreements

Many parents select mediation as a method to resolving disagreements. When the mediator has no authority to make an independent recommendation to the court, the process allows parents to control their own decisions. As a result, the parents are able to focus on their children and on persuading each other of what choices should be made.

Mediation is covered in Chapter 7.

> ### EXAMPLE OF HOW TO USE PARENT A/PARENT B PLAN
>
> Sometimes, parents cannot agree on where their children will live, not because they differ, but because they want the same thing. For example, you and the other parent might decide that "Parent A" will be the primary caretaker for the school year and "Parent B" the primary caretaker for the summer. You agree on how the children will visit each parent when they are with the other, and how they will spend holidays, weekends, special occasions and vacations. The only question remaining is who gets the nine-month chunk of time with the children, and who gets only three.
>
> In deciding who will be Parent A and who will be Parent B, you might consider the following:
> * who provided most of the daily child care when you were a couple
> * who lives near the better public schools
> * whose home is more conducive to studying
> * who lives closer to community recreation programs and sports facilities in which your children participate, and
> * who lives closer to the children's friends or in a neighborhood with similar-aged children.

g.   Arbitrate Disagreements

A few states allow parents to submit parenting decisions to an arbitrator when they cannot reach agreement on their own. Unlike mediators, arbitrators are decision makers. In arbitration, each parent presents his or her views to the arbitrator, who resolves the issues in dispute.

WHEN CONSULTING OUTSIDERS

If you turn to an outsider for help in resolving disputes, be sure you maintain control over the process. No matter what type of outsider you use—mediator, counselor, therapist, attorney or arbitrator—you must decide the following in advance:

- how the outsider will be chosen—will you require any minimum qualifications?
- how the outsider will be paid
- exactly which issues the outsider will be helping you resolve, and
- the scope of the process—will you limit the number of mediation or counseling sessions? Will certain legal rules apply in arbitration? Will attorneys be present in arbitration?

See Chapter 7 for more information on mediation and arbitration, and Chapter 13 for information on working with therapists and counselors.

Issue 13: If Extended Family Members or Close Friends Are Fueling the Dispute

Sometimes, the greatest stumbling block parents face as they separate or divorce is dealing with "over-involved" grandparents, other family members or close friends. This can be an extremely difficult and emotionally charged issue, because while you will want to encourage your children to maintain their relationships with other significant adults (see Issue 27: Grandparents, Relatives and Important Friends), you do not want to allow those very relationships to undermine your ability as parents to make decisions.

When parents ask for help in coping with a troubled marriage, separation or divorce, that "help" can sometimes become a hindrance. Occasionally, grandparents, other relatives or close friends decide that they have a "stake" in the decisions that you and the other parent make as part of your separation or divorce (or even that they would be the better custodian for your children). When this happens, their influence on your negotiations can be overwhelming—thereby making an already difficult situation even worse.

Grandparents or others may become overly involved—first with trying to save the marriage, and then in blaming

one or the other parent when the marriage fails. Alternatively, the grandparent, other relative or close friend may feel that the marriage, or otherwise committed relationship, is destructive, and that one partner is incapable of ending it on their own. This is often the case when domestic violence, child abuse or child neglect has been involved.

In extreme cases, grandparents or other close relatives fear that the natural or adoptive parents are incapable of providing the consistent, and appropriate, care children need. The result can be a custody battle in which parents, grandparents or others try to prove their fitness, the unfitness of the others or that they have a significant relationship to the children. In the event someone other than the parents is trying to gain custody of the children, it often helps to get an opinion on the matter from a trained mental health professional.

As well-meaning as this outside intervention may be, it can sometimes take on a life of its own, which then obscures the parents' efforts to reduce conflict and negotiate child-focused agreements. While it can be very difficult to ask an over-involved grandparent or other relative or close friend of the couple to stay out of the middle of the conflict, it may be the only way parents have to discover their own priorities and negotiate their own agreements.

Some of the ways that you can tell if grandparents, other relatives or friends are becoming over-involved include:

- receiving regular calls from the same person who is "just asking how everything is going" (translate—wants an update about the latest "horror story")
- receiving regular calls to report about the other parent's activities (especially activities that don't have much to do with parenting, like who the other parent went out with on Saturday night)
- hearing how many people are lining up "for" or "against" one or the other parent
- being told that others are willing to back you "if you want to get serious about it and sue," or
- being told that an outside party might sue for temporary custody if both parents can't make progress in their custody battle soon.

When trying to sort out the positive contributions by grandparents, other relatives or close friends from the negative, consider who is:

- raising the key issues in dispute
- fueling the conflict surrounding those issues, or

• recommending against agreements that you and the other parent have been ready to reach on your own.

ISSUE 13 CROSS-REFERENCES

Worksheet	Questions
Worksheet 1	9
Worksheet 3	9, 14, 15
Worksheet 4	4, 10, 11, 18

a.   Limit the Information You Share

One of the easiest ways to prevent others from fueling your conflict is to limit the amount of information you share. This may be difficult if they are your primary source of emotional support, but it is often necessary. Consider holding back details of your parenting agreement negotiations. Think about what you would tell a casual acquaintance in the grocery store and limit your comments to that. Detailed descriptions of difficult negotiations may lead those who care about you to want to intervene, rescue your children or even try to solve the problem themselves. If, for example, you are used to turning to your mother for a sympathetic ear, this may be a good time to find a friend or counselor who can listen compassionately without offering lots of advice, or choosing to get involved on your behalf.

b.   Schedule a "Family" Meeting

Often, the simplest way to diffuse a difficult situation is to tackle it head-on. If you and the other parent believe that a significant source of your troubles lies with over-involved grandparents, other relatives or close friends, consider convening a meeting among the three or four (or more) of you during which you say politely, but firmly, "thanks, but no thanks."

As part of this meeting, you will need to name the problem and then describe the impact the problem has in your and your children's lives. Depending on the details of your situation, this may have to be stated more or less bluntly—but under any circumstance, you will need to be understood. In order for that to happen, you and the other parent will need to agree about a number of things, including:

• how much outside input you are willing to accept as you negotiate your agreement

• whether you are willing to share information about your agreement with this grandparent, other relative or close friend once it has been completed, and

• how you will ensure that unwanted intervention will be handled.

Introducing this subject at a "family" meeting feels scary, but it needn't be harsh. For example, you might say something like, "Over the past year each of us has turned to you for help while we tried to save our marriage, and we both appreciate the fair hearing, moral support and great ideas you offered. While we know that the road ahead is going to be difficult, we also know that it will be harder if we have to find an agreement which satisfies everyone in the family. Recently, it has become almost impossible to resolve our conflict now that others in the family are so heavily involved. Our priorities are on figuring out what we need to do in order to meet the children's needs, while satisfying our own. We know that more than almost anything else, our children need to know that they can rely upon their parents to make necessary decisions on their behalf— whether or not we are together as a couple. While we are not experts at this, we are both sure about what we are doing and why, and we feel that it is our responsibility to make the decisions which will make this divorce final. We will probably make some mistakes along the way, but we feel confident that we each have the children's best interests at heart, that we are willing to get help from experts as needed and that we will be able to make whatever changes may be necessary as time goes on."

c.   Ask Your Attorney, Mediator or Counselor to Help Communicate the Message

For some, confronting others directly is either too difficult or has already proven to be unsuccessful. For others, direct confrontation is virtually pointless because they know they will not be taken seriously. If either of these scenarios describes your situation, you might consider bringing in another person who will be viewed as an "authority" because of their standing as a professional or expert. Attorneys, the mediator, a clergy person or a counselor to any of the parties may be just the authority to accomplish this task. If this is an option you are considering, talk it over first to determine:

• whose opinions or expertise would be best

- what the grandparents', other relative's or close friend's reaction to this kind of contact is likely to be
- how the information should be delivered (that is, in person, in writing or by telephone), and
- when the contact should be made in order to have the desired effect (that is, immediately, only after the parents have made an effort to resolve the problem, etc.).

d. Discuss the Matter in Mediation or Counseling

Sometimes it is difficult for an over-involved grandparent, other relative or close friend to understand where their natural concerns for you, the other parent or the children may have departed from the norm and become intrusive. When this is the case, it may help to discuss the problem, its impact and possible resolution with the assistance of a mediator, counselor or other trusted third party.

e. Adapt the Traditional Native American Talking Circle to Meet Your Needs

Another interesting option for dealing with this issue can be drawn from the Native American "talking circle." The talking circle is used in many Native American tribes, and offers a unique setting for discussing important issues and finding solutions. While some aspects of the circle are ceremonial and religious, this process might be adapted to meet your needs.

Your talking circle should include all of those who are directly affected by the dispute or issue under discussion (trying to balance the number of people from each "side" as much as possible). Sit in a circle, so that everyone can see each other. Next, identify some object that can be used as your "talking stick." The person who convened the circle starts the process by explaining why the gathering is taking place, and reminds the participants to observe common courtesies when addressing each other and expressing their views. In general, the first clockwise pass of the talking stick allows each participant an opportunity to explain why they are there (for example, as a relative, friend, support person, silent witness, etc.). On subsequent passes around the circle, each speaker may express their thoughts about the effects of what has happened within the family and may later propose and discuss solutions. The stick continues to be passed around the circle until all who choose to do so have aired their views and a consensus has been reached. Throughout this process, the circle maintains equality among the par-

ticipants, and encourages "deep listening and full speaking" (Diane Le Resche). Because no speaker is hurried, it takes time and patience to allow the results of the talking circle to unfold.

In a variation of the talking circle, the primary parties to a dispute, such as the parents, sit with a facilitator in a small circle at the center of the larger circle which includes all significantly interested extended family members or friends (but probably not the children). In this way, those sitting in the center circle carry on the bulk of the conversation, and the outer circle is used as a resource for finding solutions or gaining perspective. Participants in the outer circle are empowered to speak only after being recognized by the facilitator in the center circle. This model of the talking circle offers an advantage to participants by placing the decision-making focus on the parents, while allowing other interested and involved family members or friends to be witnesses to the discussion and supportive only as needed.

f. Get Protective Orders

In rare instances, over-involvement on the part of a grandparent, other relative or close friend becomes so severe that it is destructive. This may be especially true if this individual is trying to fight for custody of the children. Some extended family members may even threaten to kidnap the children "for their own good." Any of these scenarios can have a potentially damaging impact on the children, and may therefore require court orders to protect the children, you or the other parent until the matter can be sorted out and resolved. To get more information about these orders, contact an attorney or your local District Attorney's office, battered women's shelter, police department or Children's Protective Services department.

Issue 14: Exchanging Information

Both parents will need and want at least some information about their children's health care, school, outside activities, interests, abilities and special needs.

Talking with the other parent can be difficult. When parents are angry or hurt over the separation or divorce, or still hope for a reconciliation, they may use information exchanges about the children as an excuse to rehash the adult issues. While discussing the adult issues is fine under many circumstances, you might easily get sidetracked and forget to discuss your children and their needs. Also, some parents use information exchanges about the children as a chance to criticize or pry into the other's new life, partner or activities. When this happens, the children's interests suffer or are forgotten altogether.

Parents often need to find new ways to communicate effectively. Below are a few options to consider putting into your parenting agreement. Consider choosing more than one so you can use one when things are going well and another when communication is difficult.

For additional help, consider the following:
- review Chapter 4 on negotiations
- evaluate your agreement to see if it addresses everyone's needs
- get help from a mediator or counselor, or
- consult with any other third party whose opinions you respect.

The more ideas you can generate to solve problems, the better.

ISSUE 14 CROSS-REFERENCES

Worksheet	Questions
Worksheet 1	8
Worksheet 2	6, 7, 10
Worksheet 3	12, 14, 15
Worksheet 4	4, 9, 10, 17

a. Don't Put Your Children in the Middle

One of the worst mistakes you can make—and lots of parents make it—is to put your children in the middle by having them carry messages. You and the other parent must find a way to keep each other informed without passing messages through your children.

Children are apt to forget, distort or misunderstand your message. Children also soon resent the role and cringe when they deliver a message that the other parent doesn't want to hear. Some children may temporarily like the power of being the "information highway," but that soon fades. If you need to change plans, collect child support, find out about the other parent's activities or understand what discipline is being used in the other parent's home, talk to the other parent directly.

b. Establish a Businesslike Relationship

Many therapists, mediators, counselors and attorneys know that to let hostilities cool, the relationship between the parents has to change from intimate partners to business partners. Parents who have been through this can tell you how difficult that change can be. Nevertheless, the strategies for bringing this new relationship about are fairly simple.

You and the other parent must learn to make your conversations brief, focused only on the children and courteous. You must make an effort to inform each other about the little things, such as what your children have been doing for fun or have accomplished recently, as well as the significant information about illnesses, behavior, special events and report cards.

If things don't go well when you talk in person, consider scheduling telephone calls. If that doesn't work, exchange notes through the mail, via email, at a convenient drop-off location or, as a last resort (and only if your children can't read yet), in your children's suitcase.

c. Establish Separate Relationships With Activities and Care Providers

For some parents, exchanging information about health care, school, counseling or outside activities doesn't work. These parents must establish separate contacts with the children's health care providers, school officials and event and activity coordinators.

Be sure that if one of your plans is to have each parent get information separately from schools, doctors or others that they are legally entitled to this information. Often, this means that you will have to have a joint legal custody agreement. If you are not sure whether you are entitled to this information, or you do not have a joint legal custody agreement, you will need to check with an attorney to find out what the law allows in your state.

Many schools, doctors, counselors, club leaders or coaches do not usually communicate with parents separately. You may need to be persistent. Keep in mind, however, that scout leaders, coaches, doctors and others dread getting between parents battling over control of their children. You will have an easier time dealing with these people if you make your contacts brief, friendly and to the point. Don't rely on these people to give you information about the other parent or to relay messages. If children resent being made into message carriers, outsiders resent it even more.

Issue 15: Where Our Children Will Live

Perhaps the most hotly contested provision in a parenting plan establishes living arrangements. If you and the other parent agree to a sole custody (or sole legal and physical custody) arrangement, then this issue will be obvious. With any other custody arrangement, however, be prepared for some intense, but critical, negotiations.

Your goal, in most cases, should be to have your children spend as much time as possible with each parent, without ignoring their needs for stability, routine and emotional and physical safety. This can be challenging if domestic violence, emotional abuse or child abuse have been issues in the past. (See Issue 16 for situations involving abuse.) It can also be difficult if the parent and child have little or no relationship or if the children are old enough to have their own desires and schedules to consider.

In evaluating the options below, consider:
- the ages, needs, wishes and temperaments of your children
- the distance between your homes
- available transportation
- what you can afford, and
- how well you and the other parent work together.

With a little creativity, you should be able to come up with several possible solutions, each presenting advantages and disadvantages.

In Issue 12, option e, we discuss the Parent A/Parent B method for resolving impasses around custody issues. If you find that you reach an impasse on where the children will live, go back and review that discussion. Essentially, the Parent A/Parent B method asks you to first assign parental roles to hypothetical parents and then examine the circumstances to determine which of you would best fit each role.

ISSUE 15 CROSS-REFERENCES

Worksheet	Questions
Worksheet 1	3, 5
Worksheet 2	1, 3, 4, 7, 8, 9, 10
Worksheet 3	2, 3, 4, 6, 7, 14
Worksheet 4	1, 2, 4, 5, 6, 7, 8, 12 ,13, 14, 15, 17, 18

AVOID CREATING A "VISITING" PARENT

Sometimes, changing the way you view the parenting agreement and living arrangement is as simple as changing the words you use. In *Mom's House, Dad's House*, by Dr. Isolina Ricci (Macmillan Publishing 1998), the author recommends that parents and children describe the time spent with each parent as "living" with that parent. Further, she points out that when parents and children describe their arrangements to others, they should acknowledge that they have two families, one with each parent. If at all possible, avoid the notion that children live with one parent and just visit the other. By making one parent the everyday parent and one parent the visiting parent, you run the risk that you and your children will either resent or exploit the lopsided roles and relationships that follow.

"Everyday" parents are sometimes viewed (and often view themselves) as the only ones responsible for the day-to-day realities of child-rearing. As a result, it is easy to assume that the everyday parent is the only real parent. Some everyday parents prefer to control all substantive aspects of their child's life. Others feel overwhelmed and that they are being taken advantage of by missing out on relaxation times, especially if the children live with their other parent on weekends and holidays.

"Visiting" parents are sometimes accused of becoming the fun or party parent. The reasons some visiting parents adopt this role are as varied as the people who live with these arrangements. Some visiting parents are so starved for time with their children that they try to cram every conceivable activity into short periods of time. Some parents miss the giving that is part of daily caretaking, and compensate with gifts that are more frequent, more expensive and sometimes problematic.

Although no one can fault parents who seldom see their children for wanting to make every minute count, their relationships with their children will be far more balanced and fulfilling if they can intersperse fun activities with the routines of everyday life. Familiar, daily routines often provide an opening for conversations about thoughts and feelings. If all visits are filled with activities, the parent and children will have few opportunities to "talk," and are apt to drift apart. As a result, visiting parents often become "special," but less significant, influences in their children's lives.

a. One Primary Residence

For many children, designating one home as the primary place that children live makes the most sense. Joan B. Kelly, Ph.D., of the Northern California Mediation Center, has developed a comprehensive array of visitation plans for both school-age children and infants and toddlers. Following are several sample plans for your review. Each plan relates only to the routine schedule each week, without regard to holidays or other vacation periods. The discussion includes a description of the amount of time spent with the noncustodial parent (NCP), and the comments parents have made regarding these plans.

- **Alternating weekends (Friday 6 p.m. to Sunday 6 p.m.).** This arrangement allows four overnights in 28 days; the 12 days between contacts with the NCP can be too long for many children; the NCP-child relationship diminishes in importance to the child; the NCP is not involved in school or academic/achievement activities; in addition, the custodial parent has little time "off duty."
- **Alternating weekends (Friday 6 p.m. to Monday a.m.).** This option allows six overnights in 28 days. It allows the NCP to have a larger weekend block of time with the child, allows the NCP to take the child to school on Monday, necessitates fewer transitions for the child and provides less opportunity for conflict between parents.
- **Alternating weekends (Friday 6 p.m. to Sunday 6 p.m.), weekly midweek visit (Wednesday 5 p.m. to 8 p.m.).** This arrangement allows four overnights in 28 days but provides NCP-child contact at least every seven days. The three-hour visit on Wednesdays can be "rushed," not allowing enough time for homework; and the transition back into the custodial parent's home each Wednesday can be difficult.
- **Alternating weekends (Friday 6 p.m. to Sunday 6 p.m.), weekly midweek overnight (Wednesday 5 p.m. to Thursday, start of school).** This arrangement allows eight overnights in 28 days, provides no more than six days between visits with the NCP and allows the NCP to maintain involvement with homework assignments and school activities. The transitions at school times help avoid conflict. The NCP has an opportunity for bedtime and morning rituals on school days, and the custodial parent has midweek evenings off duty.

- **Alternating weekends (Friday 6 p.m. to Monday at school), weekly midweek overnight (Wednesday 5 p.m. to Thursday 7 a.m.).** This arrangement allows ten overnights in 28 days, provides no more than six days between visits with the NCP and allows longer weekends for the NCP.

For infants and toddlers, where the child has a minimum relationship with the noncustodial parent, the arrangements may be quite different. For example, you might consider:

- **Two to three weekly contacts for two to three hours each; Saturday or Sunday visits gradually expanded to six hours each as the child gains security; overnight visits added approximately six to 12 months after visitation starts as child is secure.**

Other single primary residence options are as follows:

- **Live in home "A" except for alternating weekends, alternating holidays and a portion of the summer.** This option allows some geographic distance, and accommodates parents who don't get along too well or children who don't want or need more frequent contact.
- **Live in home "A" except for midweek overnights, most weekends, alternating holidays and a portion of the summer.** This allows for some geographic distance between the homes, but may require both parents to live in the same school district.

- **Live in home "A" and visit other parent for short or daytime visits only.** This accommodates extreme geographic distance or situations where violence, abuse or neglect require limited and/or supervised visitation.

b.   Dual Residences

Some families prefer to have their children live with each parent for extended periods of time, or to divide their time almost equally between the two homes. Again, there are many possible variations. These living arrangements require extensive coordination between the parents and a willingness to encounter each other and any new partners. Dr. Kelly's examples of this type of arrangement follow, together with other variations on this theme.

- **Monday afternoon to Wednesday a.m. with Parent A, Wednesday p.m. to Friday a.m. with Parent B, alternating weekends, Friday to Monday a.m. with each parent.** This arrangement allows 14 overnights per 28 days with each parent; all transitions can be managed through school or day care; the routine for weekday overnights remains fixed.-
- **Monday a.m. to Wednesday a.m. with Parent A, Wednesday a.m. to Friday a.m. with Parent B, each weekend is split (Friday p.m. to Saturday p.m. with one parent, Saturday p.m. to Monday a.m. with other parent).** This arrangement allows 14 overnights per 28 days; the time apart from either parent never exceeds three days; transitions are more frequent.

For infants or toddlers who are attached to both parents:

- **Tuesday and Thursday 4 p.m. to 7 p.m. and Saturday 10 a.m. to Sunday 10 a.m. / or Tuesday 4 p.m. to Wednesday 9 a.m., Thursday 4 p.m. to 7 p.m. and Saturday 5 p.m. to Sunday 5 p.m.** This arrangement allows frequent contact throughout the week; overnights become a regular activity.

Other dual-residence arrangements are as follows:

- **Children alternate living in home "A" and "B" at approximately equal intervals such as every week, two weeks, month or six months.** This requires homes in close proximity, especially if children are school-age.
- **Children live in home "A" during the week and in home "B" on the weekends.** This option allows somewhat more geographic distance.

- **During the school term, the children live in home "A" during the week and in home "B" on the weekends. In the summer, the children live in home "B" during the week and in home "A" on weekends**. This option will work only if there is a moderate geographic distance between the parents' homes, and won't work if the children attend school year-round.

c.   Children Live With Someone Other Than a Parent

For some families, it makes sense for the children to live with an adult other than a parent. This third adult may also have custody of the children or may be appointed their guardian.

   If this option appeals to you, make sure your parenting agreement specifies the arrangements. The more specific you are, the more everyone will understand their responsibilities to the children and to each other. For example, if one or both parents are struggling to finance separate apartments, get jobs and recover from a drug addiction, having the children live with a grandparent could be a good idea—as long as you specify how each parent will maintain a relationship with the children.

d.   Bird Nesting

Bird nesting means that the children remain in one home and the parents alternate moving in and out. The parents might have separate homes, sleep at a friend's house or stay with a relative.

   Bird nesting is chosen infrequently, but can be especially good for infants or very young children. It requires an unusual degree of coordination and cooperation between the parents. And you must be clear about who will make decisions regarding the layout, furnishing and routines of the household.

THE FATHER-CHILD RELATIONSHIP IS IMPORTANT

The fathers' rights movement has gained considerable steam over the last few years. For any number of reasons, a large number of fathers are either minimally involved or absent from their children's lives. Some of the more common reasons given to explain this phenomenon include:

- The bias in the legal system traditionally favors giving the mother custody.
- Fathers feel powerless to control how their children are raised when living with the mother.
- Fathers resent being treated as a "cash cow" ("mother stays, father pays").
- Vague court orders for "reasonable" visitation allow custodial mothers considerable latitude to limit the amount of time fathers can spend with their children, therefore eroding the parent-child relationship as contact becomes increasingly limited and sporadic.
- Men can often earn more in the workplace, making them less available for full-time parenting arrangements.

Researchers have tried to assess the impact on children when one parent, generally the father, leaves the home and does not maintain significant ongoing relationships. Their findings range from intensified separation anxiety, poor grades or substantially below-ability performance, aggression toward parents and diminished self-concepts, to long-term anger, depression and a sense of profound loss.

   Most researchers agree that when children have little or no access to their fathers, they have a better than even chance of:

- committing suicide
- running away from home
- exhibiting behavior disorders
- committing rape
- being involved with the juvenile justice system, or
- serving time in prison as an adult.

While it is probably not accurate to say that all of these problems would go away if fathers were awarded custody instead of mothers, fathers' rights advocates, as well as joint custody advocates, insist that many problems would be resolved by allowing both parents to have substantial roles to play in their children's lives—especially after a separation or divorce.

Issue 16: Domestic Violence, Child Abuse and Child Neglect

Domestic violence, child abuse and child neglect are serious issues that affect all members of a family. Reports of violence, abuse and neglect are on the rise nationwide. Domestic violence, child abuse and child neglect happen in all kinds of families, from all parts of the country and at all income levels. Domestic violence can be directed at women, men and children. It may or may not be associated with drug or alcohol abuse. Some estimates show that approximately one in five marriages will experience at least five violent episodes each year. Other statistics estimate that in approximately 50% of the families in which a mate is abused, so are the children.

Get professional help if there is abuse in your home. Do not assume that violence directed at an adult does not affect the children. Children are very aware of their surroundings. Furthermore, violence, abuse and neglect come in many forms. Hitting, molestation, name-calling, intimidation, abandonment, kidnapping and neglect of basic needs for food, shelter, care and protection all harm children—whether or not they are the intended targets.

KIDNAPPING IS A FORM OF CHILD ABUSE

Some 360,000 children are abducted each year in the United States. Significantly, only one in 750 of these is a stranger-abduction. A substantial number of children abducted by a parent are under the age of six (implying that children are easier to hide prior to their entering school). In an effort to understand the meaning these statistics might have for parents negotiating a parenting agreement, it may be helpful to learn some of the most common reasons why parents abduct their children. These are:

- to exert control, power or revenge in the parenting relationship
- to protect a child from physical abuse or sexual assault
- the abducting parent suffers from Narcissistic Personality Disorder, or
- the abducting parent cannot accept responsibility for his or her own contributions to the marriage and divorce troubles.

Kidnapping, or child abduction, is a form of child abuse. While it may happen in response to physical abuse or as a result of mental health problems, it is just as likely to happen when one parent feels powerless to influence his or her children's upbringing in the separate parenting arrangement. Quite simply, this means that parents who feel that they have nothing to gain by accepting little or no contact with their children are more likely to abduct those children.

Jill Krementz' book profiling children's experience with separation and divorce is instructive (*How It Feels When Parents Divorce*, Alfred A. Knopf, 1988). Jimmy, a ten-year-old, was the object of repeated kidnappings by both his parents. As his parents fought over who should be his primary caretaker, he was taken from one home to the other—always in secret. Court battles and orders followed each abduction—and placed his father deeply in debt.

Jimmy relates how this nightmare began when he was seven: "… the court decided that I should live permanently with my Dad, but keep seeing my mother on weekends. Well, that made my mother so mad that she decided to steal me. One weekend while I was visiting her, she and Don packed up their car with a lot of stuff and we all piled in … I remember asking her, 'What about Daddy?' And she just said, 'Don't worry about it.' " After having been "stolen" at least three times, Jimmy was finally settled in his father's home. He lost a year of school and all contact with his mother.

Families with a history of violence, abuse or neglect often use mediation, counscling or attorneys to make their parenting decisions. Mediation can be a problem, however. A battering victim may be intimidated when making decisions with the batterer in the room. If your state requires mediation in custody and visitation disputes (see Chapter 12), ask for separate meetings with the mediator so you can speak without fear or feeling intimidated.

In some states, judges appoint a social worker to evaluate both parents' homes and make a custody or visitation recommendation to the judge. In that situation, be honest about what has gone on and your concerns for the future. If you would feel more comfortable with a support person with you during an evaluation, ask the judge or social worker if it's possible. It's unlikely you'll be told no.

If your children are a target for either parent's uncontrolled anger, sexual advances or violence, consider bringing in someone trained in assessing domestic abuse to help you decide whether or not your children will be safe in that parent's care. (We explain how to find domestic abuse experts in Chapter 13.) If violence or abuse against any family member was or is a fairly common event, the expert can recommend a treatment plan so that children are not placed into the same situations within that parent's new home or family setting.

If you were the target of violence or abuse in this family relationship, get help from a counselor or therapist to make sure that the decisions you are making on behalf of your children are not based on fear or intimidation. You should also find out about what protective court orders might help out during the time when these decisions are being made, and afterwards.

ISSUE 16 CROSS-REFERENCES

Worksheet	Questions
Worksheet 1	4
Worksheet 2	5, 10
Worksheet 3	4, 9, 12, 15
Worksheet 4	1, 3, 4, 5, 7, 8, 9, 10, 11, 16, 17

a. Make Protective Orders Work

If you are concerned about violence or abuse, you can get a protective order from a court that tells an abuser to stay away. While a piece of paper is not a guarantee that the abuse will stop, most abusers adhere to the terms of an order.

Whether you are trying to negotiate or implement decisions regarding your children, protective orders can help in the following ways:

- provide time and space to let a situation cool down
- keep specific people away from each other
- require supervised visits with the abuser, and
- limit telephone calls between the abuser and victims.

Be aware, however, that the time you decide to get a restraining order can be the most dangerous of all. This is often because the target of the order may want to scare you or hurt you to prevent you from getting help. This is why it is important to talk with a professional to evaluate how dangerous your situation is, and to plan for your family's safety.

A court may issue a temporary protective order, which can be modified, extended or made permanent, as needed. Some people want to change, or even drop, their protective orders after they have them if they impose restrictions that no longer seem necessary. This might be the case, for example, if the violence only happened once at the time of separation and was not too severe.

If you are thinking about dropping the protective order before it runs out, consult with an attorney, counselor or other domestic violence expert first. They may advise you to modify the order, rather than drop it altogether. This would keep the power of the court behind you, but make it a little easier to handle visits or exchanging information about the children. Remember that your existing court orders stand until they are formally changed by a judge's decision. That means that the restrained parent can be arrested or found in contempt of court if they do anything that is not allowed by the existing court order.

b. Require Counseling or Emotional Support

One of the best steps you can take in stopping violence, abuse or neglect is to deal with the issue openly and honestly. Many parents agree to undergo counseling to learn how to change their behavior. (See Chapter 13 for more information.) A parent who doesn't volunteer may be ordered to go by a court.

The abusive or neglectful parent may not be the only one who needs counseling. No doubt, so will the victims. If the abuse or neglect has ended, the parents may need joint counseling to learn how to work together.

c.   Find a Safe Way to Care for the Children

You must find a way that your children can be cared for without losing safe contact with both parents. Often this translates into supervised visits between the abuser and the children. If you decide to have your children's visits with one parent supervised, be sure that you spell out exactly what this means. Any court order you get should include:

- who will supervise the visits, and what kind of training this person will need (some states and courts insist on the use of trained volunteers or professional visitation supervisors)
- how long the visits will last
- whether the visits can take place at the parent's home or at another location, like a playground or visitation center
- whether there will be limits on the types of activities the children can do with this parent
- how you will know whether the supervised visits are succeeding, for example, are the children are becoming more comfortable around a previously absent parent, or is an angry parent demonstrating more self-control?
- how often the need for supervised visits will be reviewed, and
- when the supervised visits can end.

You should also identify an adult whom your children can call if they ever fear for their safety while in a parent's care. Be sure your children know that they will never be punished for calling this adult, even if their fears were unfounded.

d.   Looking for and Responding to Signs of Child Abuse

Many parents wonder what signs to look for in a child who has been a victim of abuse. This question is a difficult one, and not just because abuse is such an emotionally charged issue. One of the most difficult aspects of assessing whether abuse has actually occurred, unless of course you witness that abuse, is that the signs or cues you must look for can also indicate other problems—some psychiatric and others developmental.

Professionals in the American Association of Child and Adolescent Psychiatry (AACAP) caution that even severe abuse may not surface in the child's awareness until adolescence, or even later, but they proceed to list some the most common behaviors children exhibit if they have been victims of abuse. As you look over this list, be careful not to jump to any conclusions. This list should provide a starting point from which you will develop a greater sensitivity to the fact that the child is experiencing some kind of problem, and that abuse may be one of the causes. The AACAP notes that, regardless of whether the child reports abuse, he or she may exhibit one or more of the following behaviors:

- a poor self-image
- an inability to depend on, trust or love others
- aggressive, disruptive and sometimes illegal behavior
- passive or withdrawn behavior
- fear of entering into new activities or relationships
- school failure, or
- serious drug or alcohol abuse.

Most parents, or other adults, have little idea about what they should do if they suspect that a child has been abused, or if a child tells them they have been physically or sexually abused. Commonly, the adult who encounters this kind of information feels shocked, angry, confused, skeptical or even afraid. How you handle this situation, however, is critically important. Regardless of whether you believe that either the suspected or reported abuse has occurred, professionals recommend you communicate your support for the child first, and then try to understand the reality of the situation.

The first step in supporting the child who reports abuse is to allow him or her to convey as much information to you as they are able, with as little pressure from you as possible. Next, you must enlist the help of one or more trained professionals, such as a doctor, nurse or other medical professional, police officer, domestic violence counselor, mental health professional or other trusted advisor to help unravel the child's experiences and feelings and understand what further responses are appropriate to the situation. Specifically, the AACAP recommends adults respond to the child who reports abuse as follows:

- encourage the child to talk freely
- don't make comments that appear to judge the child or the situation
- show that you understand and take the child's comments seriously
- assure the child that they did the right thing by telling you about the situation

- tell the child that they are not to blame for the abuse
- offer the child protection, and
- promise to take prompt steps to end the abuse—and then do just that.

How can you know if claims of child sex abuse are true? Much has been made recently of false claims of child sexual abuse. As a result, many question whether children, or adults, can be trusted when they report child abuse—especially if these reports surface for the first time as part of divorce proceedings or modifications of existing custody and visitation orders. While some assert that claims made during divorce or custody battles are manufactured in order to ensure a "win," others worry that legitimate claims are dismissed because they cannot be proved not to have been manufactured. Unfortunately, there will probably never be any clear-cut formula for guaranteeing the legitimacy of each and every claim.

Most professionals underscore the fact that any allegations of child sex abuse are serious and should be treated as such. Regardless of the validity of the particular claims, however, the child who is at the center of this whirlwind will be affected and will need help to deal both with his or her own feelings and with the investigations and battles that are sure to follow.

e. Get an Independent Evaluation

A trained professional can provide parents with an objective opinion about how to deal with violence, abuse or neglect. Depending on the issues involved, parents can learn new strategies for dealing with stress, disciplining their children and understanding their children's behavior. Unless you are low income and qualify for financial help, you will probably have to pay for this kind of evaluation.

f. Require Supervised Visitation

Supervised visitation means that when your children spend time with an abusive parent or a parent who presents a serious threat of kidnapping, another adult is with them. Your court may recommend specific people who have been trained to perform this function. If not, you and the other parent must find your own supervisor. This might be a relative or friend, or a social worker or battered women's shelter employee whom you may need to pay. Some courts will require the supervisor to file a report with the court, describing the visit and the children's reactions to being with the parent.

g. Take a Break

If the violence you're experiencing is the result of the stress of separation or divorce, take a break. After the parents have established new homes, get some counseling and then slowly resume visits between the children and the abusive parent.

Issue 17: Alcohol or Drug Abuse

Many parents have alcohol or drug problems. For some, it is an ongoing problem. Others use alcohol or drugs to escape the pain of the separation or divorce. You and the other parent will be more successful in dealing with these issues if you allow the addicted parent to help define and control his or her own recovery.

ISSUE 17 CROSS-REFERENCES

Worksheet	Questions
Worksheet 1	4
Worksheet 2	5, 8, 10
Worksheet 3	9, 13, 14
Worksheet 4	4, 10, 16, 18

a. Attend a 12-Step or Similar Recovery Program

Throughout the country, a myriad of 12-step recovery programs, such as Alcoholics Anonymous, meet daily. (Chapter 13 provides information on how to locate these types of programs.) Some programs will provide a written record of a person's attendance to whoever needs to verify it. In some instances this will be the court, while in others it might be the other parent.

b. Require Counseling or Emotional Support

Consider requiring a parent to get counseling. Some courts require the completion of a particular course of counseling or group therapy. If you agree to counseling without court intervention, check with a mental health agency, doctor, hospital, police department, community organization or church to find a qualified counselor.

Your agreement will be more likely to succeed if it:
- describes what specific behavior must stop
- describes what issues must be covered (such as ending the substance abuse and dealing with feelings of anger, jealousy and abandonment), and

- gives the addicted parent and the counselor a method of defining when the problem is under control.

c.   Structure or Limit Access to the Children

Getting a handle on a substance abuse problem can take a long time, and you may want to establish certain conditions before allowing the parent with the problem to care for the children. Here are some suggestions:

- The parent with the alcohol or drug problem will not operate a vehicle containing the children within 12 hours of consuming any alcohol or nonprescription drugs.
- The parent with the alcohol or drug problem will not consume alcohol or nonprescription drugs within 12 hours prior to, or during, any visit with the children.
- The parent with the alcohol or drug problem will submit to alcohol or drug testing if the other parent so requests. If that parent passes, the other parent will pay for the test. If that parent fails, he or she will pay for the test and forfeit scheduled visits until he or she can pass a test. (Alcohol or drug testing might be available through your police department, hospital or public health facility. You will have to investigate what services are available in your area as there is no universal way these services are made available to the public.)
- You can limit visits, or require them to be supervised (see Issue 16, option f), until the parent with the alcohol or drug problem successfully completes a rehabilitation program.
- Identify an adult whom your children can call if they ever fear for their safety while in a parent's care. Be sure to let your children know that they will never be punished for calling this adult, even if their fears were unfounded.
- The parent with the alcohol or drug problem will not allow any person to consume alcohol to excess or nonprescription drugs in the children's presence.

Issue 18: Maintaining Contact When the Children Are With the Other Parent

Neither children nor adults can be two places at once. Keeping up with your children, their interests and activities is important. By planning now for how to stay in touch, you ensure that you will maintain, and even deepen, your relationships with your children.

Maintaining contact with your children demonstrates your love and support, keeps communication channels open and offers new ways to have fun together—especially if you are creative. Your contact with your children can be both scheduled and spontaneous. Ideally, you will find a mix of both that works best for everyone.

Scheduled contact should occur at regular times and be convenient for everyone involved. Spontaneous contact is, by definition, unscheduled, but it should not be disruptive. Following are a number of options parents consider to create a happy medium of both scheduled and spur-of-the-moment contact that can make for rich, well-balanced relationships, regardless of the distance between you and your children.

ISSUE 18 CROSS-REFERENCES

Worksheet	Questions
Worksheet 1	3, 4, 5, 8
Worksheet 2	1, 2, 7, 8, 9, 10
Worksheet 3	3, 4, 7, 8, 14
Worksheet 4	4, 5, 6, 7, 8, 9, 18

a.   Set Up a Contact Schedule

Many parents agree to a minimum number of calls between the children and the other parent. For example, you might agree that the parent with whom the children aren't living would initiate at least one call per week to the children. Many parents allow their children to initiate additional calls whenever they like.

In some families, the problem isn't too little communication, but too much. Calling a child too frequently may cause problems. If you call as often as once or twice a day, you may be communicating that you fear for your children's safety while in the other parent's care, or that you are desperately lonely. By pacing your calls, you can stay in touch without introducing unnecessary worry or anxiety. If, in fact, you are extremely lonely or anxious, discuss the situation with a trusted advisor or mental health professional.

b.   Set a Regular Contact Time

Some parents forget that calling their children when they are eating dinner, doing homework, doing chores or getting ready for school can be disruptive. To avoid this, many parents schedule regular times each week when they can be reasonably sure that their children will be free to talk. Telephone time is set up to be as convenient as possible for both parents and their children. It may take some planning to find this time, but it usually pays off in enjoyable conversations and a minimum amount of disruption in daily routines.

c. Give Children Their Own Telephone Line

It is common for many parents to have less than friendly feelings for the other parent after separation or divorce. Therefore, receiving calls from the other parent, even for the brief moment of calling your children to the telephone, can be distasteful. To avoid this, consider getting your children a separate telephone line, or a line with a different ring, so that when it rings only the children answer.

If you choose this option, be prepared to establish ground rules on acceptable telephone use. Your telephone company may have ideas for regulating telephone use and blocking certain types of calls (such as 900 numbers).

d. Schedule a Midweek Dinner

When the parents' homes are in the same general area, scheduling a regular midweek dinner might be a great way to shorten the time between visits and create a special occasion for everyone. If you set up regular midweek dinners, you must specify who will transport your children, as well as the pick-up and drop-off times. (See Issue 28.)

e. Plan for Contact During Trips

Parents need to plan for how they can stay in touch with their children when they are away on a trip with the other parent. The simplest solution is to leave an itinerary and include telephone numbers for where and when the children can be reached.

f. Be Spontaneous—and Creative!

Letters, care packages and the like are all inexpensive, non-intrusive ways to stay in touch with your children. Care packages can include books, toys, interesting shells, dried flowers, games, cookies or almost anything else you and your child might enjoy. Pictures can be mounted on construction paper and assembled into quick "memory" books and sent along to fill your child in on your activities, share your vacation vicariously or learn about places or things that interest you. Computers and fax machines expand the possibilities even further. Consider faxing cartoons, interesting or funny stories or your favorite jokes. Email offers instant communication, and the Internet offers the possibility for private "chats" in real time, or even a treasure hunt throughout the World Wide Web.

g. Find Ways to Extend a "Personal Touch" Into Your Child's Daily Life

Another way for parents to stay in touch is to buy or make small, personalized things that your child can wear, use or see on a daily basis. While these things need not be expensive or fancy, they can provide a regular reminder that you care. For example, consider personalized pencils, barrettes, a sticker for the bathroom mirror, notepaper, a box for small treasures or a bookmark.

Issue 19: Reinvolving a Previously Absent Parent

Parents drop out of their children's lives for a variety of reasons. Some parents are better able to cope with the separation or divorce if they have little or no contact with their family. Others leave or are kept away because of substance abuse, violence, child abuse or incarceration. Regardless of the reason, reinvolving a parent is often a difficult task.

While children are remarkably adaptable, flexible and loving, they typically experience a mixture of hurt, anger, happiness, confusion, hope, jealousy, anxiety and anticipation as a result of a parent's absence and return. So does the parent who remained. Both parents will need a lot of time to get used to the one parent's return. Consider incorporating many of the options below into your parenting agreement.

a. Deal With Your Feelings

Everyone—the children, the parent who remained and the returning parent—can benefit from counseling. The children and the parent who remained may need to talk about their fears and hopes. The returning parent may need help in understanding both his or her own feelings, and the feelings of the children and the other parent.

b. Develop a Businesslike Relationship With the Other Parent

When a parent returns, tension with the other parent is both natural and common. Parents need time to develop trust, resolve the issues that existed before the parent left, and come to terms with the changes that are inevitable when only one parent remains to care for children.

Often, returning parents want to pick up where they left off. A parent who remained often resents the underlying assumption that the returning parent can just "waltz back in, become an instant parent and be a hero!"

To help ease this transition, you and the other parent can behave like business partners. Maintain your separate adult lives, but work together to raise your children. As with all good business relationships, the partnership works best when the parents can exchange information, respect each other's privacy and relationship with the children and keep a cool head when conflicts arise.

c. Go Slowly and Respect the Children's Feelings

Children often act out to avoid being hurt again. Young children may feel that they can't get enough of the returning parent, and not let that parent out of their sight. Older children, on the other hand, may test the parent's commitment through weeks, or even months, of short tense visits before resuming a normal relationship. The returning parent may develop a deep and satisfying new relationship with the children if he or she respects the children's feelings. You might ask your children how much contact they can handle.

If you are the parent who has been absent, be prepared to talk honestly about what happened and to answer your children's questions—even if it takes awhile for the questions to surface.

d. Keep an Open Mind

If you are the parent who remained, you probably have mixed feelings about the other parent's return, although anger may be high on the list. Depending on the length of the absence, your life and your children's lives may have changed considerably.

You need to maintain an open mind about the possible ways in which the other parent might reenter the children's lives. At the same time, be realistic and keep your support systems in place. The other parent may find the transition back too hard and may leave again or assume a very limited parenting role. If, however, the other parent wants to take an active role in your children's lives, consider ways to accommodate this request, as long as it is not harmful to the children.

e. Negotiate Short-Term Agreements

When a parent reenters his or her children's lives, it is a good idea to negotiate simple, short-term agreements. These agreements allow both parents and children to test the waters and to learn what works best.

Trust, a critical element of any parenting relationship, is built over time. By adhering to these short-term agreements, returning parents demonstrate trustworthiness—and make more reliable negotiators for long-term agreements.

f. Consider Reevaluating Your Sole-Custody Arrangement

Parents who remain behind have de facto sole custody of their children, whether or not a court makes such an order. If the returning parent appears to be reestablishing a long-term parenting role, you might consider modifying the custody arrangement.

Knowing whether a parent is back for good can be difficult. One way to test it is to negotiate and adhere to several temporary agreements, as described in option e, above. After everyone is satisfied that the returning parent is reliable, it may make sense to give that parent a larger parenting role.

The parent who remained behind may balk. But researchers repeatedly find that parents actively involved in their children's lives maintain regular visitation schedules, pay a higher percentage of court-ordered support and have more satisfactory relationships with their children than do parents less involved in their children's lives.

Issue 20: Child Care

Child care is an important issue for many parents as they go their separate ways. Assessing the need for adult-supervised child care can be difficult, and there are no magic ages by which all children are ready to care for themselves while home alone. While many teens can care for themselves for limited periods of time, those same teens may not be able to resist inviting friends over, spending unlimited amounts of time on the telephone or accessing "adult" materials on cable TV or the Internet. Younger children may be very compliant about following your rules, but may not be as well equipped to handle a medical or other emergency, know how to respond to strangers who call or come to the door or observe basic safety precautions when preparing or heating up food for themselves. Similarly, children who are skilled baby-sitters for others may not be as responsible, or may have more difficulty getting cooperation, when caring for siblings.

Although parents may feel that they have few childcare options, there are actually quite a few different possibilities. You must consider your child's age, where you live, how well you know your neighbors, how far away you will be, how long you will be gone and whether you can easily be reached in an emergency. Some different ways to handle this include:

- children care for themselves
- older children care for younger children
- family member or friend cares for children
- parents participate in a "baby-sitting co-op" (parents trade caring for each other's children)
- occasional babysitters from neighborhood
- after-school care
- community recreation programs/child care centers
- licensed daycare
- agency-provided sitters (usually licensed or bonded).

As you consider whether your children need some form of adult-supervised child care, you should create guidelines for their time alone, and then assess whether each of your children can realistically fulfill your expectations. For example, do you trust the children to:

- follow basic safety rules regarding strangers who call or come to the door
- respond in an appropriate manner to medical or other emergencies
- provide responsible care for siblings
- follow your rules for when friends may visit, and
- follow your rules for using the telephone, watching television, using the Internet, etc.?

If you do decide that at least some adult-supervised child care will be necessary, you should deal with this issue in your parenting agreement, although you may have difficulty finding such care. In some families, a grandparent, other relative or friend has been a frequent care provider, and will continue to be available after the separation or divorce. In other families, finding child care providers that are acceptable to both parents is more difficult.

Below are some options that parents commonly consider. For ideas and information on finding child care providers and what qualifications you might want in a child care provider, see *Nolo's Law Form Kit: Hiring Child Care & Household Help*, by Attorney Stephen Elias (Nolo).

ISSUE 20 CROSS-REFERENCES

Worksheet	Questions
Worksheet 1	3
Worksheet 2	6, 7, 9
Worksheet 3	2, 3, 7, 8, 9, 12, 13, 14
Worksheet 4	1, 4, 9, 12, 15 ,16, 17

a. Agree on Care Provider's Minimum Qualifications

Parents may not have a clear idea of who will provide child care, but may be able to agree on certain minimum qualifications. Parents often consider the care provider's age, physical location and licensure. Depending upon the distance between your homes, you can use the same provider (offering more continuity in your children's care) or each find a provider with the minimum qualifications you agree upon.

b. Agree on Ineligible Care Providers

You may be more anxious about preventing certain people from caring for your children than defining who can provide care. If this is the case, name these individuals in your parenting agreement or describe the characteristics you find unacceptable, such as being under the age of 17, using drugs or alcohol or operating a child care facility more than 10 miles from your home.

c. Address the Role of a Parent's New Partner

Sometimes, the care provider that a parent wants to exclude is the other parent's new partner. This can fuel a fairly intense battle, so approach the situation with caution.

First, ask yourself your motive for not wanting the new partner to care for your children. If your concerns are motivated by jealousy, rivalry or a fear of being "replaced" as a parent, consider more direct and productive ways to express and resolve your fears than to exclude that person as a care provider. Feeling jealous of the other parent's new partner is common, even if you don't want to have the other parent back as a partner. Similarly, a fear of being displaced is natural, and can be handled by:

- agreeing that your children will never be told that you are anything other than their parent
- finding special names for the new partner other than "Mom" or "Dad," and
- talking directly to your children about your fears.

Additional decisions about new partners are in Issue 38. If you find yourself unable to manage your feelings about the other parent's new partner, a counselor might be able to help.

d. Agree to Call the Other First for Child Care

When parents' homes are close by, they can consider providing child care for each other. For some parents, this means that one parent provides all after-school care until the other returns from work. For others, it means that one parent "covers" for the other for business or vacation trips.

This option offers several advantages:

- It allows parents to extend the time they spend with their children.
- It provides for greater continuity in care, which is especially important for young children.
- It keeps child care costs down.
- It shows children that their parents can still cooperate—at least about them.

There are at least two disadvantages. First, some parents use the chance to be called whenever child care is needed as "proof" that the other parent leaves the children too often. Second, you may find it difficult to maintain a separate life

if the other parent is constantly around and able to keep track of your activities.

Note: This kind of child care arrangement could affect child support payments if one parent increases the amount of time that they care for the children over a long period of time.

e. Find an Adult Neighbor Who Can Check on Your Child

Some children are old enough to stay home by themselves for short periods. Others can take care of themselves with a neighbor's help. If your children need only minimal supervision, consider asking an adult in the neighborhood to call or stop by to see how things are going, or to be available by telephone in the event of an emergency.

⚠ DON'T PUT YOUR CHILDREN AT RISK

Do not leave your children home without adult supervision unless they are fully capable of caring for themselves and know who to call in the event of an emergency. Although you may have difficulty finding child care, unless your children can care for themselves, or your oldest child is truly capable of caring for younger siblings, you could be taking a dangerous risk by leaving them unattended. (Chapter 13 contains referrals to books which can help you to assess your children's readiness to stay home alone.)

Issue 21: Moving

Some parents want to move away after a separation or divorce. A career change, job change, enrollment in school, new partner's job change, desire to be near a parent who can provide child care, inability to afford to live in the community or desire to just start over are common reasons for wanting to move.

Moving, however, almost always becomes an emotionally charged issue for both parents and children. When children move, they may experience any number of stress-producing events, including:

- interrupting existing friendships
- forming new friendships, often after other age-mates have established social circles
- adjusting to different school curricula and teacher styles
- coping with either or both parents' stress or arguments over the move, and

- having considerably less contact with one parent.

Children who are allowed to remain in their neighborhoods because of a custody modification may be spared a change of schools, friends and contact with extended family members, but they will certainly miss the level of contact they had with their previous custodial parent if that parent moves away.

Regardless of what happens with legal custody (decision making on behalf of your children), the further apart parents live, the more difficult it is for the children to spend significant amounts of time with both parents. Any parent who wants to move should, therefore, examine his or her motives and options carefully.

In general, any proposal by a primary custodial parent to move away will trigger a dispute with the other parent if the move will either reduce the amount of time the other parent spends with the children, or increase the difficulty, time or expense of maintaining the current level of visitation.

If you are thinking about moving, you should be aware that child support might change significantly if the move will change the amount of time your children will spend with each parent. This is because many child support formulas are based not only on what each parent earns, but also the percent of time the children spend with each parent. More often than not, this means that the parent who earns more income or spends less time with the children will end up paying a higher amount of child support.

In the typical dispute, custodial parents want to know whether they are permitted to move under the terms of the existing custody order, and noncustodial parents want to know whether they can either prevent the move or acquire primary physical custody of the children. Unfortunately, a definitive answer is hard to come by, even for experienced attorneys and judges, although the trend is to permit a custodial parent to relocate without changing custody if that parent:

- has provided significantly more care for the children than the other parent
- is making a sincere effort to accommodate visitation by the remaining parent, and
- there are no obvious reasons to conclude that the move will harm the children.

Move-aways have recently become a hotly contested issue in a number of states. The reasons for this are many, of course, but often boil down to the fact that:

- we live in a highly mobile society

- local economies often require parents to move in order to find work or advance in their careers
- requiring parents to surrender custody as a condition of moving away may violate their constitutional right to travel, and
- it is usually difficult to assess whether a child's interests will be either better served or compromised as the result of a parent's move.

The decision as to whether a custodial parent should be able to both relocate and retain custody involves addressing such questions as:

- Will the move adversely affect the relationship between the children and the noncustodial parent?
- Will the move adversely affect the relationship between the children and extended family members and friends?
- Will the move adversely affect the children's education?
- What impact would restricting the custodial parent's right to move have on his or her ability to lead an independent life?

Coming to a decision in the face of these and related issues involves a very delicate balancing act, which is performed in countless courtrooms, mediation sessions, attorney offices and counseling sessions, and few parents ever emerge from the process without feeling completely frustrated both with the process and its results. Some legal trends, however, seem to be emerging as these difficult and controversial decisions take shape.

Certain factors tend to make it easier for a court to approve the move, and others make it easier to prevent the move. When courts approve a move, it is often because the moving parent:

- has been the primary caretaker
- previously discussed his or her intent to move with the other parent
- has never hidden the child or prevented or frustrated the child's visitation schedule with the other parent (except for instances of child abuse or other violence)
- is willing to share in transportation costs so that the child can spend as much time as possible with the other parent
- is willing to allow visitation with the other parent at every reasonable opportunity
- supports the child in maintaining an ongoing relationship with grandparents, other relatives and close friends, and

- has not tried to coach the child to convince the judge, mediator, custody evaluator or other professional to approve the move.

When courts prevent a proposed move-away, it is often because the moving parent has engaged in one or more of these behavior patterns:

- has already tried to restrict or eliminate visits with the other parent by hiding the children or fabricating excuses about why visits cannot take place
- has tried to coach the children into convincing the judge, mediator, custody evaluator or other professional that they do not want to remain behind
- is unwilling to find ways to accommodate the other parent's visits with the children in view of the increased distance between the parents' homes
- ignores the wishes of teens who wish to switch custody arrangements in order to remain in familiar surroundings, or
- wants to move solely for the purpose of getting a fresh start.

Clearly, a move can be one of the most volatile issues parents face as they live with the demands of parenting separately. Accordingly, prevention is the best way to keep this issue from getting out of hand, and saves you the time, expense and emotional cost of financing the next supreme court decision in your state. This holds true whether or not either of you intends to relocate in the future. By taking the time to plan for how you will resolve this issue in the future, how much notice the moving parent must give the other to allow for review or renegotiation of the existing parenting agreement and how you will resolve any disputes that arise, you will do yourself, your children and the other parent a huge favor.

Each of the resolution options described below will highlight a different approach to this complex problem. Among the key elements of this decision you will need to consider when the subject of a proposed move comes up are:

- your children's ages and attachments to their school, community, extended family and friends
- the frequency of your children's visits with their other parent, and the depth of those relationships
- the urgency of your need to leave, or need to prevent the other parent from leaving
- your reasons for leaving, or preventing the other parent from leaving, and

- whether any other of the related issues (such as child support, which court will have jurisdiction over the issues and enforcement of your orders) may be compromised.

In the event you and the other parent feel that you simply cannot resolve these matters on your own, you should refer back to Issue 12, Resolving Disputes When Making Decisions Together. If a proposed move will mean that your children must spend less time with one parent, refer to Issue 22, If Our Homes Are Far Apart.

The information provided here is intended to help you and the other spouse come to terms with the possibility of one of you moving and to help you negotiate a reasonable agreement covering that issue. If you need to know how a judge would rule in your state, you will have to research this question on your own. (See Chapter 12, Section A.)

ISSUE 21 CROSS-REFERENCES

Worksheet	Questions
Worksheet 1	3, 4, 5, 6, 7, 8, 9
Worksheet 2	1, 2, 6, 7, 8, 9, 10
Worksheet 3	1, 3, 4, 6, 7, 8, 9, 10, 12, 14, 15
Worksheet 4	1, 2, 4, 5, 6, 7, 8, 9, 11, 12, 13, 14, 15, 17, 18

a.   Both Parents Relocate

In some parts of the country, the economy is so depressed that both parents may have to leave following a separation or divorce. Or, if both parents are originally from the same area, both may want to move back to that area after the divorce or separation to take advantage of the support that may be forthcoming from family members or old friends who have remained there.

You and the other parent can consider several options, including relocating together to a city or other area large enough to support you both and let you pursue your own lives. Many parents consider this alternative when they agree that their children need to have frequent contact with both parents, and feel that they might each benefit by making a move.

b. One Parent Relocates, Physical Custody Changes to Remaining Parent

For some parents, relocation is a necessity if they are to earn a living, gain an education or meet other pressing needs. Children don't always make the move with their parents, however, even when it is the primary custodial parent who needs to relocate. Some families prefer to raise their children in a particular community, and will alter the physical custody arrangements to ensure that the children can stay in that community as long as one of the parents is able to remain.

c. Allow a Move as Long as Children Are of a Certain Age

Mental health professionals note that both kindergartners or first graders and teens are particularly vulnerable during a move. This is because the five- to seven-year-old is learning to separate from their parents' authority and to accept direction from other adults, and teens are increasingly dependent on their peer groups, and may resent losing this support and social resource. Accordingly, some parents choose to either delay or time a move so that they can avoid moving their children during these critical age ranges.

d. Time a Move With a Change in Schools

Some parents choose to delay a move until children are either ready to start school, or will otherwise be changing schools (for example, moving between elementary and middle school, or between middle school and high school).

e. Allow Children to Choose Whether They Will Move

Some parents agree that they will allow their children to decide whether they will move with a parent after they have reached a certain age. Many parents decide to allow their children to choose whether they will move with a parent when the child is between the ages of 12 and 15, because that is when their children are either approaching high school, or entering their sophomore year (the one that really starts to count for college applications).

f. One Parent Relocates

With this option, the parents agree that there is no compelling reason for both parents to either remain in the same area or move to the same new area. You must choose a living arrangement that accommodates the distance between your homes. Issues 15 and 18 suggest options.

g. Parents Remain and Find New Ways to Meet Their Goals

You may decide that, although you or the other parent might prefer to relocate, the children's interests would be better served if both parents remain in the area. You'll need to adopt some creative solutions to address the concerns of the parent who considered moving. Here are a few suggestions:

- The parent who wanted to move could return to school to gain new job skills to find employment in the area.
- The parents could alter the living arrangements to allow the parent who wanted to move to "commute" between two cities to work.
- The parents could alter the living arrangements (and child support payments) so that the parent who wanted to move becomes the primary caretaker for the children.

Issue 22: If Our Homes Are Far Apart

If a parent moves a significant distance from the other, the parents face the challenge of helping the children maintain a close relationship with both. Transporting the children is covered in Issue 28, below.

ISSUE 22 CROSS-REFERENCES

Worksheet	Questions
Worksheet 1	3, 4, 5, 7, 8, 9
Worksheet 2	1, 2, 3, 7, 8, 9, 10
Worksheet 3	1, 3, 4, 6, 7, 8, 9, 14
Worksheet 4	1, 2, 3, 4, 5, 6, 7, 8, 9, 15, 18

a. School Year With One Parent, Summer With the Other

The most common solution parents choose when they live apart is for the children to spend the school year with one parent and the summer with the other. If your children's school district is on a year-round calendar, however, this option isn't very feasible.

b. Change Primary Residence With Change in Schools

Some parents consider alternating each school term—for example, third grade with one parent and fourth grade with the other. Few professionals would recommend it, however, because it provides little continuity in the children's education and social life. Here is a compromise: The children live with one parent during elementary school, the other parent during middle (or junior high) school and then choose where they live during high school. These transitions often involve minimal disruption because so many children change school districts at these times.

c. Children Attend Private Residential School

A few families send their children to a private residential school. The children alternate vacations with their parents according to a predetermined schedule. See Issue 23, Holidays, just below, for suggestions on alternating times with parents.

Issue 23: Holidays

Deciding who your children will spend holidays with can be difficult unless you can think beyond one year. Remember that every holiday comes around every year.

First, make a list of all holidays and other occasions important to your family, including extended school breaks and holidays you celebrate because of your faith, cultural heritage or family traditions. Then consider the following possible schedules:

- alternate on an odd-year and even-year basis
- split extended holidays in half
- celebrate certain holidays twice
- assign the same holidays to the same parent every year, or
- decide how your children will spend the holidays as each holiday approaches.

ISSUE 23 CROSS-REFERENCES

Worksheet	Questions
Worksheet 1	3, 5, 8, 9
Worksheet 2	1, 7, 8, 9, 10
Worksheet 3	1, 2, 3, 4, 5, 7, 9, 12, 13, 14
Worksheet 4	1, 2, 3, 5, 8, 9, 11, 13, 14, 15, 16, 17, 18

a. Alternate on an Odd-Year/Even-Year Basis

This option assigns certain holidays to each parent in odd years, and then reverses the schedule in even years. For example, your children might spend Thanksgiving with you in 2000, and with their other parent in 2001. This plan is comforting because parents know they will never miss spending a holiday with their children more than one year in a row. By contrast, this schedule can be frustrating if a particular holiday is meaningful for only one parent.

b. Divide Holiday Celebrations in Half

Some parents divide the actual holiday celebration (and associated vacation days) in half so that their children can spend part of the time with each parent. This option allows everyone to see each other on the "big day," but requires advance planning so that your children do not miss the main part of the celebration because of travel. Often parents use the odd-year/even-year plan to alternate who spends the first and second halves of the holiday with their children.

c.   Celebrate Important Holidays Twice

Some families celebrate their holidays twice. For example, one parent might celebrate Christmas with the children a week before the actual date, and the other celebrates it with the children on December 25th. This is certainly easier when one parent's family already celebrates a holiday one week before or one week after the actual date so that they can also fit in a "family reunion." Fortunately, few children complain about getting to celebrate twice!

d.   Develop a Fixed Holiday Schedule

If you and the other parent differ on which holidays are special, you can assign holiday time so that each of you celebrates the same holidays every year with your children. This option is ideal when, for example, one parent participates in religious celebrations and the other parent chooses nonreligious holiday times for vacations, trips or other activities.

e.   Make Decisions as Each Holiday Approaches

Some parents prefer not to be tied down to a holiday schedule. As long as you are communicating effectively and your ideas about a holiday schedule are similar, this plan works well. It means, however, that you must spend considerable amounts of time arranging every holiday. If you choose this option, decide how far in advance of each holiday you will make your plans.

Issue 24: Vacations

Vacationing can raise a multitude of questions. Among other things, you and the other parent should discuss:

- travel out of the area, out of the state or out of the country
- whether each parent must provide the other with an itinerary and contact information
- whether certain activities (such as hang gliding) will be permitted
- how long the children can be away, and
- whether you will schedule "make up" visits.

Informing the other parent well in advance of your intentions allows everyone to deal with schedule changes more easily. If you know how much vacation time you will have in a given year and how you'd like to spend it, you and the other parent can start early to figure out how the children will fit in.

ISSUE 24 CROSS-REFERENCES

Worksheet	Questions
Worksheet 1	3, 5, 9
Worksheet 2	1, 6, 7, 8, 9, 10
Worksheet 3	1, 3, 4, 7, 8, 9, 12, 13, 14
Worksheet 4	1, 4, 5, 7, 8, 11, 12, 13, 14, 15, 16, 17

Issue 25: Special Occasions and Family Events

Although you and the other parent have gone your separate ways, your children may want either or both of you to attend special events or ceremonies. By planning ahead, these decisions are considerably easier to make. With very little imagination you can expect this issue to come up over back-to-school night, a football game, a family picnic for your children's scout troop, graduation or a school play.

Although these events are meant to be fun and special for the participating families, they can also become frustrating and confusing. You, your children and the other parent need to develop a strategy for dealing with these invitations so that the events remain fun and are as simple to plan as possible.

Some parents alternate who attends each event ("You go to back-to-school night and I'll go to the open house"), others attend together and still others attend the events that have the most meaning in their relationship with their child ("I'll do scouts if you do baseball").

ISSUE 25 CROSS-REFERENCES

Worksheet	Questions
Worksheet 1	5, 9
Worksheet 2	1, 6, 7, 8, 9, 10
Worksheet 3	1, 3, 4, 5, 7, 8, 9, 12, 13, 14
Worksheet 4	1, 2, 3, 4, 7, 8, 9, 10, 15, 16, 17

Issue 26: Outside Activities

Scheduling a child's outside activities can become more complicated during a separation or divorce. Participating in team sports may conflict with visitation schedules or other scheduled family time. It is also possible that one parent might not approve of a child's interests—like possibly dangerous contact sports—or insist on certain activities such as bible study, bar mitzvah preparation or extra academic classes. For these reasons, it may make sense to decide in advance what types of activities you will encourage, discourage, insist on or prohibit altogether.

ISSUE 26 CROSS-REFERENCES

Worksheet	Questions
Worksheet 1	1, 2, 5, 9
Worksheet 2	1, 2, 3, 6, 7, 9
Worksheet 3	2, 3, 4
Worksheet 4	4, 7, 12, 13, 14, 18

Issue 27: Grandparents, Relatives and Important Friends

After your separation or divorce, it is important to your children that you find ways for them to maintain relationships with other adults who are important to them—namely, grandparents, aunts, uncles, neighbors and family friends. Children need the security of familiar friends and relationships. These familiar people can help ease the transition for children when their parents no longer live together.

You should consider the following options in your parenting agreement:

- Each parent ensures that the children maintain relationships with the parent's own extended family.
- The parents agree on specific holidays or times when the children will be with particular extended family members.
- One parent arranges for all visits with extended family members. (This option is especially appropriate if one parent has moved out of state while all of the extended family lives near the parent who remains).

Once you have agreed on these issues, be sure to explain them to the relatives and friends involved.

ISSUE 27 CROSS-REFERENCES

Worksheet	Questions
Worksheet 1	5, 9
Worksheet 2	6, 7, 10
Worksheet 3	7, 8, 9, 12, 13, 14
Worksheet 4	1, 4, 9, 11, 15, 16, 17

Issue 28: Transporting the Children

Transporting children for their time with each parent can be simple if you live near each other. Some children walk, ride their bicycles or take the city bus back and forth. For most parents, however, this subject is more troublesome. One way to ease your frustration is to agree on as many details as possible—how you will make exchanges, the time for pick-ups and drop-offs, how each parent will notify the other of last-minute changes and who will pay for transportation costs.

Your options will depend on several factors, including how far apart you live, how often your children will see each parent, who has access to a car and the costs of transportation. If there has been violence between the parents, you may want to choose a busy public location for your exchanges. If weather is an issue in your area, you will want to choose a location that allows you, the other parent and your children to wait indoors—such as a shopping mall or museum—in the event of bad weather. If you or the other parent must use public transportation to make the exchanges, you will need to know the schedules and plan accordingly.

ISSUE 28 CROSS-REFERENCES

Worksheet	Questions
Worksheet 2	8, 9, 10
Worksheet 3	2, 3, 4, 6, 7, 9, 12
Worksheet 4	1, 9, 10, 11, 16, 17

a. Meet at a Midpoint

This option lets the parents share the travel time by choosing a neutral location for making exchanges. It requires that each parent has access to a vehicle and arrives at the exchange point at approximately the same time.

b. Alternate Travel Responsibilities

In an effort to share the responsibility fairly equally, some parents alternate transporting the children over the entire distance. This option requires that each parent can obtain reliable transportation when it is his or her turn to drive, but allows more flexibility in setting a time for the exchange.

c. One Parent Transports

This option is ideal for parents who cannot absorb equally the time and vehicle maintenance necessary for transporting children. If one parent is without a vehicle, or cannot take the time to provide transportation, perhaps that parent can compensate by reimbursing the cost of gas or other expenses.

d. Parent Travels to Children

Some parents travel to the children and either rent an apartment or motel room, stay with a friend nearby or live with the children for the visit. This option allows parents to visit without otherwise disrupting their children's normal activities.

Parents often consider this option when the distant parent has more travel time available than do the children. Usually this happens during the school year when the recess is too short to allow the children to visit at their other parent's home. If you choose this arrangement, you will need to decide where the parent will stay, how travel expenses will be allocated and which parent will participate in the children's activities.

e. Parent Brings Children to Other Parent and Leaves

With this option, one parent takes the children to the other parent's home, and then vacations or visits friends before picking the children up at the end of the visit. This option probably won't work for other than occasional visits, but it can add variety or help one parent out if he or she has vehicle problems.

f. Children Travel by Themselves

Some parents let their children travel alone between homes —by train, bus or airplane—once they reach a certain age. Of course, the parents must still get the children to and from the stations, but this option can save a lot in time, money and aggravation.

Issue 29: Improving Transition Times

Many parents have difficulty handling the inevitable ups and downs that come when children travel between homes. This is especially true just after the separation or for a parent who hasn't seen the children in quite some time. Many parents have high expectations when their children are about to arrive, and get depressed when their children leave.

For children, the ups and downs are worse. Young children, especially, gear up when anticipating a visit with one parent and simultaneously crash because of the separation from the other. A child may be afraid of forgetting the schedule, particularly if it is new or irregular. Some children worry a good deal about going to the right home after school or getting in trouble for making a mistake.

Difficult transitions should not persist, however. If they continue for more than a couple of months after you set your parenting agreement in motion, you should look for a deeper cause. Often, persistently difficult transitions indicate that there are larger, more troubling issues that deserve some time and attention. Allowing the difficulties to go on for long periods of time will only make things worse—possibly damaging your children's relationships with one or both parents for a long time to come.

ISSUE 29 CROSS-REFERENCES

Worksheet	Questions
Worksheet 1	1, 3, 4, 6, 7
Worksheet 2	7, 9, 10
Worksheet 3	2, 3, 4, 7, 8, 12, 14, 15
Worksheet 4	4, 5, 8, 9, 11, 18

a. Time the Exchange With Other Regular Transitions

By timing your exchange with a drop-off or pick-up at school, after a sporting event or before or after some other regular activity, the exchange won't feel artificial or forced.

b.   Make Exchanges Simple and Quick

Children generally have an easier time of saying good-bye to one parent and taking up with the other if the actual exchange is quick and casual. One strategy is to carry out the exchange at a busy public place, such as a park, restaurant or shopping mall.

Another way to expedite the exchange is for parents to minimize their communication. Speak the day or evening before to discuss necessary information about the children's health, school and activities. Not only does this allow the exchange of the children to be brief, but it also helps parents exchange vital information without making the children sit around and wait. It is especially useful when tension is high.

c.   Give Children Your Undivided Attention at the Start of the Visit

The start of any time with your children can be easier and more relaxing if you delay other activities, at least briefly, to give your children some time during which they have your undivided attention. This may be as simple as giving them uninterrupted time to tell you about their activities while with the other parent. If you have more than one child, taking them to a park or the zoo gives each child a chance to talk while the others play. This might be especially helpful if your children have half-siblings or stepsiblings from your new relationship.

d.   Give Your Children Some "Breathing Room"

Some children need quiet time at the start of a visit to get reacquainted with you and your household. For these children, jumping right into a frenzy of activity will often backfire. You might give this child some pictures to look through, a book to read or some paper to color on, take this child on a short walk or find some other low-key activity to do together.

e.   Be Patient When Your Children Ask Questions

Children have many questions after their parents go separate ways. Depending on their age and temperament, they may ask why you are no longer together, how decisions are being made, how they will be cared for, whether they will be able to form lasting intimate relationships as an adult or any number of other questions. You can best help your children by hearing and answering their questions

patiently. Eventually, your children's questions will decrease and their comfort with the situation will increase.

Most mental health professionals agree that children don't really need, or necessarily want, to know the intimate details of your relationship. Be careful that in answering your children's questions you don't burden them with your frustration, anger or disappointment over your partner's sexual performance or compatibility. If they ask, don't ignore them, but redirect the conversation to a more appropriate topic.

f.   Establish New Rituals

Children thrive on routines and love rituals. It's important to make sure children have some personal belongings—such as a favorite toy, outfit or book—with each exchange. You can also set aside a small amount of time at the beginning and end of each visit for a special activity or small ritual and keep the exchanges predictable, setting them for approximately the same time of day, and at fairly regular intervals. Some children do better making exchanges in the morning or afternoon. Other children handle exchanges better if they are dropped off at the other parent's home. These are some ways to ease the awkwardness of coming together and the discomfort of separation for both you and your children.

Issue 30: Treating Each Child as an Individual

Many parents assume that visits should always be the same for each child, and that children should always visit their parents together. Parents, however, can often do their children a great service by tailoring some visits to meet the needs, personalities and interests of only one child at a time.

In the book *Divorce and Your Child* (Yale University Press, 1984), authors Sonja Goldstein and Albert Solnit observed that:

> *While it is generally preferable for brothers and sisters not to be separated by their parent's divorce, it does not follow that in a smoothly working joint custody situation … all the children must spend the same day or parts of days with the same parent in the same manner. This is not the way it is for children whose parents live together; older and younger brothers and sisters do not have the same activities, and it would place an unwarranted burden on children of divorced parents if joint custody were to hamper them.*

This is not to say that all visits should be separate, but only to suggest that parents consider occasional arrangements to allow each child time alone with each parent.

ISSUE 30 CROSS-REFERENCES

Worksheet	Questions
Worksheet 1	1, 2, 3, 4, 5, 7, 8, 9
Worksheet 2	1, 3, 4, 5, 7, 8, 9, 10
Worksheet 3	3, 4, 14
Worksheet 4	4, 5, 6, 7, 8, 9, 18

a. Schedule Short, Separate Visits With Each Child

Scheduling a separate visit with each child allows you and each child to plan a special activity for just the two of you. It is a good strategy for smoothing over rough spots in the relationship, as well as providing a fun time that only the two of you have shared. To make the most of this kind of visit, have your child help plan the activities, and take pictures or collect mementos of your "adventure" for your child to keep.

b. Children Take Turns Being the Center of Your Attention

You may not have the option of scheduling separate visits for each child. In this case, you can still carve out special time for each child by:
- setting aside a small amount of time for each child during each visit
- having the children take turns deciding which activities everyone will engage in during your visits, or
- staggering the arrival or departure times for each child (school or other activity schedules may facilitate this) to allow special time for each child.

Issue 31: When Parenting Styles and Values Are Very Different

Parents frequently differ in beliefs, values and expectations for themselves and their children. Children whose parents have substantially conflicting child-rearing rules and disciplinary styles sometimes feel as though they are two different people—one to please each parent. You can guard against this by not criticizing the other parent's style and, if possible, finding some common ground.

Differences are not necessarily bad—in fact, they are what make the world go 'round. While some children tolerate the variety, others find it overwhelming. You need to tailor your agreement on this issue to fit what best suits your children.

If the differences between you and the other parent come from differences in cultural backgrounds or religious beliefs, see Chapter 10 for more information. If your differences are because one of you recently came out as a lesbian or gay man, or have chosen a less than traditional way of living, read Chapter 11.

ISSUE 31 CROSS-REFERENCES

Worksheet	Questions
Worksheet 1	3, 4, 5, 8
Worksheet 2	3, 4, 5, 7, 9, 10
Worksheet 3	4, 5, 8, 9, 12, 13, 14
Worksheet 4	2, 3, 4, 5, 6, 8, 9, 10, 11, 17, 18

a. Focus on Your Child

Some parents can agree only that they both love their children. If this is true for you, use it as a starting point for a new partnership with the other parent. The key to making this option work is recognizing your children's skills, interests and personalities and finding ways to complement them.

Children's needs and interests depend a lot on their ages. Young children often find security in being with or near a close extended family. By contrast, teens often like to "hang" with their friends and need a parent who can supervise from a distance. (For more information on how differences in parenting styles affect children of various ages, see Chapter 9.)

Sometimes, parents are able to resolve these issues on their own. But often they need help refocusing their energy from trying to change everything about their former partner to finding ways to work together. First, each parent must decide and then articulate what they think isn't working well. Then each parent must find a way to make the situation better, or just less bad. For a step-by-step approach, parents with different parenting styles or values should try to:

- define the problem
- propose solutions
- identify areas of agreement
- evaluate any disagreements
- decide if more help (or help from a different professional) is needed
- decide how they will know if the situation has improved
- make the agreed-upon changes
- measure their progress in accomplishing their goals, and decide if any further changes are needed.

If you and the other parent come from different cultural or religious backgrounds, teaching your children about who they are can give parents a way to focus on their children. In particular, consider having your children:

- hear stories from grandparents or other elders
- attend special religious or cultural functions
- learn skills unique to a particular culture, or
- attend special camps.

b. Structure the Living Arrangements or Transition Times to Reduce Conflict

If the lives your children lead are radically different in each parent's home, then you may find transition periods particularly difficult for your children. Several researchers have found that children adjust better to two homes with very different rules and standards than to open conflict between the parents.

Nevertheless, it may be very difficult for your children. To ease the contradictions, you have two options. One is to modify the living arrangements (Issue 15) so that your children go back and forth infrequently. For example, one parent can have the children during the school year and the other in the summer, again, with frequent communication but no physical exchanges.

Your other option is to improve transition times. (For suggestions, see Issue 29.)

c. Agree to Disagree

For some parents, the differences are so great that they do not try to bridge the gap. If you are in this situation, do your best to have some consistent standards for your children's conduct and to respect your children's right and desire to know, understand and love the other parent. Beyond that, each parent must be willing to let the other parent enforce his or her rules in his or her own home.

d. Take These Issues to Counseling

Communication is often the first casualty in a failing relationship. But it is communication that will save the children (and each other) from emotional pain and suffering. If each parent can spend a little time trying to see the world through their former partner's eyes, they may gain insight into why they do the things that they do. Each parent may also be more able to modify his or her behavior to suit the other parent's needs if they understand why the other parent desires the change. But this type of role-playing can be difficult alone. For all these reasons, counseling can sometimes take the edge off of a certain set of conflicts—or even help parents to find new strategies that help the sources of conflict go away. For example, parents might agree to disagree on bedtimes and eating times, as long as each is satisfied that the children won't go hungry, will eat nutritious foods and will still be in bed at a reasonable time.

Issue 32: Consistency in Raising Children

Children need their parents to be as consistent as possible in approving or disapproving their conduct—whether the parents live together or apart. When parents separate or divorce, this is hard to achieve. As a start, you and the other parent might agree on certain daily routines, such as meal times, bedtimes and finishing homework before playing.

Children, as a rule, are remarkably flexible. They know that their parents are different people, and they can usually handle the variations in each home. Some of the differences between your two homes can be passed off rather simply by saying, "Yes, at the other house you are allowed to do that, but I do things differently." Others cannot be dismissed so easily and require that the parents try to reach a common ground. If your parenting styles are vastly different, consider the additional options in Issue 31, above.

ISSUE 32 CROSS-REFERENCES

Worksheet	Questions
Worksheet 1	3, 4, 7, 8
Worksheet 2	3, 4, 5, 7, 9, 10
Worksheet 3	4, 5, 12, 13, 14
Worksheet 4	1, 4, 5, 7, 9, 16, 17, 18

a.   Establish a Few Common Rules for Both Homes

Even when parents approach raising children differently, they can maintain a minimum level of consistency by agreeing on a few rules that will be enforced in both homes. Be creative—find issues that matter to you both and that you agree on. No two people disagree on absolutely everything. For example, you might agree on allowed snack foods, television shows (or the number of hours each day the children can watch television) or requiring the children to show respect for both parents.

b.   Exchange Information About Behavior and Discipline

Parents can avoid problems by talking to each other about behavior and disciplinary issues. If you don't, your children will find the chinks in the unified front you may try to maintain, and will play one of you off the other.

With this option, each parent lets the other know about any behavior or discipline problems, and what actions the parent took to deal with the situation. In this way, you and the other parent can support each other, even if you might have handled the situation differently.

c.   Acknowledge Your Differences

Along the lines of "variety is the spice of life," you can accept that you have different child-rearing styles. You must acknowledge, however, that this can be difficult for your children. Encourage them to describe exactly what bothers them and to talk to the other parent directly to work out a resolution. If you agree to this arrangement, you must also agree to let go—that is, to not try to tell the other how to handle situations in his or her own home.

Issue 33: Disparaging Remarks

You won't score any points with your children if you criticize the other parent, or his or her new partner or lifestyle. However critical children may be of their parents, most children love and revere them and don't want to hear the negative remarks.

A parent who makes disparaging remarks about the other in the children's hearing creates two serious problems. First, the critical parent weakens the children's relationship with their other parent. This can make it difficult for the children to live with and rely upon the other parent for care and companionship. Second, the critical parent conveys,

quite clearly, that their children cannot express love or admiration for the other parent in that home. Children often grow to resent and distrust the critical parent for interfering in the children's other important relationships.

You can read Chapter 4 for more information on handling high conflict situations, and understanding the negative and alienating effects that these types of behaviors can have on parent/child relationships.

ISSUE 33 CROSS-REFERENCES

Worksheet	Questions
Worksheet 1	3, 4, 5, 9
Worksheet 2	5, 7, 8, 9
Worksheet 3	4, 9, 10, 11, 12, 13, 14, 15
Worksheet 4	4, 5, 6, 9, 10, 16, 18

Issue 34: Undermining the Parent/Child Relationship

Many parents are uncomfortable with their children's relationship with the other parent. Children seldom miss the message. When parents cry out in frustration, "You are just like your (mother/father) when you do that," their children hear this as a warning that they possess a bad character trait or personality flaw that they will have to work to avoid.

Some parents are quite direct in trying to undermine their children's relationship with the other parent. Most commonly, a parent will force the children to sit through lectures on all of the other parent's faults. Less commonly, a parent will punish a child for talking about the other parent or asking to see that parent, or will bar the children from talking to, spending time with or accepting gifts from the other parent.

In some instances, a parent might physically inspect the children upon each return, looking for evidence of mistreatment. Unless you have real reasons for suspecting child abuse, do not examine your children in this way. You are likely to instill real, yet unwarranted, fear in your children that they must worry about their safety when they are with the other parent.

Whether your undermining efforts are indirect or direct, the effect on your children is the same. They will be torn between a desire to love both parents, and the need to earn approval by saying they love one parent and hate the other.

ISSUE 34 CROSS-REFERENCES

Worksheet	Questions
Worksheet 1	3, 4, 5, 8
Worksheet 2	4, 7, 8, 10
Worksheet 3	10, 11, 12, 13, 15
Worksheet 4	4, 5, 10, 11, 18

Issue 35: Denying Access to the Children

Some parents limit the relationship that their children have, or might have, with the other parent. It may be because of lingering anger or pain from the separation or divorce. More commonly, when communication breaks down and conflict heats up, a parent stops adhering to the schedule governing when each parent is to spend time with the children. Difficult as it may be, your first responsibility when drafting and carrying out your parenting agreement is to look at the world through your children's eyes.

If you feel that your only recourse in a particularly troubling situation is to deny the other parent access to the children, you must obtain outside help. If you've already decided Issue 12—Resolving Disputes When Making Decisions Together—follow your agreement. If you haven't, consult Chapter 4 for information on negotiating, Chapter 7 for information on mediation and arbitration and Chapter 13 for ideas on finding appropriate resources.

ISSUE 35 CROSS-REFERENCES

Worksheet	Questions
Worksheet 1	3, 4
Worksheet 2	5, 6, 7, 10
Worksheet 3	4, 9, 10, 11, 12, 13, 14, 15
Worksheet 4	4, 5, 6, 7, 8, 9, 10, 11, 16, 17

Issue 36: When a Parent Needs to Develop Parenting Skills

Many parents need help with their role as a parent. For parents who were previously uninvolved in the day-to-day care and discipline of the children, having full responsibility for their children, even for relatively short periods of time, can be overwhelming. A parent who has abused or neglected his or her children in the past needs special help so that discipline and other child-rearing situations do not further harm the children. Fortunately, many agencies and other resources offer help in honing or developing parenting skills. (See Chapter 13.)

ISSUE 36 CROSS-REFERENCES

Worksheet	Questions
Worksheet 1	4, 5, 7, 8
Worksheet 2	3, 4, 5, 7, 10
Worksheet 3	4, 10, 11, 12, 13, 14
Worksheet 4	1, 3, 4, 5, 6, 7, 8, 9, 10, 17, 18

Issue 37: When Nonrelatives Live in the Home

Housing is expensive, especially on only one income. After a divorce or separation, you (or your ex) may need to share your home, especially if it means you can afford to live somewhere large enough to accommodate your children overnight.

You or the other parent may imagine the worst when you hear that one of you has roommates. Any concerns about roommates should be included in your parenting agreement. For example, you can:

- require the children to have separate sleeping quarters
- bar the roommates from having or using drugs in the home
- prohibit the roommates from disciplining the children, or
- restrict the number of outside visitors.

ISSUE 37 CROSS-REFERENCES

Worksheet	Questions
Worksheet 1	3, 4, 5, 9
Worksheet 2	4, 5, 7, 8, 9, 10
Worksheet 3	6, 7, 8, 9, 12, 13, 14
Worksheet 4	1, 2, 4, 5, 7, 8, 9, 10, 11, 12, 13, 14, 15, 16

Issue 38: When Parents Have New Partners

When a separated or divorced parent develops a new intimate relationship, both parents and the children are likely to have fairly intense feelings about the situation. The other parent may be jealous, even if he or she has no desire to get back together. That parent may also be afraid that the children will get attached to the new partner and lose their bond with their parent.

These feelings can be very powerful and can seriously disrupt your parenting relationship. Although you both know that you cannot tell the other whom to choose as a partner, you still must address certain issues, such as:

- how the children will relate to the new partner—in particular, whether that person will supersede the children's relationship with the other parent
- what the children will call the new partner
- ensuring that the children have their own sleeping quarters, and
- whether the new partner will make parenting decisions.

One of the most challenging problems is figuring out the new partner's role in discipline. Many parents want new partners to have nothing to do with discipline at all. But children can become confused and difficult to handle if there is an adult in their lives who does not set any limits or who fails to support the rules or disciplinary practices of the household. For these reasons, it makes sense to carefully discuss what issues the new partner should deal with and which should be left to the parents alone. Depending on the situation, this conversation can be handled best if all of the adults can talk these issues out together. Often this kind of conversation is most successful if you involve a mediator or counselor.

If the new partner has children the situation is more complicated. Blended families are common, and children whose parents have parted ways are likely to live in one at some point in their lives. In their article entitled "Stepfamilies as Settings for Child Development," E. Mavis Hetherington and Kathleen M. Jodl summarize the reseach findings about how common stepfamiles are this way:

Life in a single-parent family is often only temporary, given that estimates of rates of remarriage are 66% to 75% for women and 80% for men. Before the youngest child reaches the age of 18, 40% of family members currently in a first marriage will eventually become members of a stepfamily, with 86% of these stepfamilies composed of a biological mother and stepfather. (From *Stepfamilies: Who benefits? Who does not?*, edited by Alan Booth and Judy Dunn, Lawrence Erlbaum Associates 1994.)

With these new families, a second set of issues becomes important to consider and accommodate. These new issues include things like:

- scheduling each child's visits with his or her various parents
- resolving conflicts among the three or four adults
- handling discipline, especially if the parents in the stepfamily handle discipline differently
- balancing the sibling and stepsibling relationships, especially if the parent and their new partner have a child together
- deciding whether the stepparent can or should handle exchanges.

Although each family's situation is somewhat different, here are some strategies for dealing with the realities of blended families.

a. Describing the New Partner's Role

This issue can lead to some pretty heated arguments. But it is often easier to tackle them directly than to let negative feelings about a new partner infect all aspects of a parenting plan. Issues should include what the children will call the new partner and how the new partner will be involved in daily decision making and discipline, as well as in the larger decisions such as where the children will live or where they will go to school.

b. New Partners, Decision Making and Conflicts

Parents must consider how the new partner will (or will not) be involved in altering or updating the parenting agreement or what types of issues the other parent can legitimately raise about the new partner's relationship with the children (read: "Knowing when the other parent's partner is or isn't any of your business").

c. Talk Before Problems Come Up

If it looks like a new partner will be around for a while—either through marriage or just a committed relationship—it helps if there is good communication with the other parent. Since the new partner and the other parent will likely be working together, it helps if they get to know each other before any problems crop up. Then, when conflicts do come up, there is at least some framework for working together to find a solution.

Even if neither of you has a new partner, you can include this provision in your parenting agreement in anticipation of that time. Or, you can skip this issue now and modify your agreement when necessary.

(Additional information on new partners is in Chapter 9, Section A4, and Chapter 11.)

ISSUE 38 CROSS-REFERENCES

Worksheet	Questions
Worksheet 1	3, 4, 8, 9
Worksheet 2	2, 5, 7, 9, 10
Worksheet 3	1, 4, 5, 7, 8, 9, 12, 13, 14, 15
Worksheet 4	1, 3, 4, 5, 6, 7, 8, 9, 10, 11, 12, 15, 16, 17

Issue 39: Labeling the Custody Arrangement

Living arrangements and custody labels are two different issues. You described your children's actual living arrangement in Issue 15. Here you decide what these arrangements mean in terms of custody—the term used by the court in a divorce or legal separation.

Three custody labels are the most common:
- sole custody, which gives one parent authority for all decisions
- joint custody, which generally means that parents share child-rearing, and
- split custody, which divides the children between parents.

In some states, custody is further defined as "legal" and "physical." Legal custody refers to making decisions regarding health, education and the child's best interests. Physical custody describes providing the majority of physical care for the children. A common arrangement in these states is for one parent to have sole physical custody, while the parents have joint legal custody. (Chapter 12 indicates which states differentiate between legal and physical custody.)

No matter what custody label(s) you use, you have tremendous latitude to spell out with whom your children will spend their time. For example, even with a sole custody arrangement, your children may live with the non-custodial parent every other weekend. Similarly, you can

agree to joint custody, but have your children spend little time with one parent.

COURTS AND CUSTODY

In general, a judge will guarantee a parent's right to spend time with his or her children and a parent's obligation to care for and support his or her children. Furthermore, in most states, custody laws are gender-neutral. This means that neither parent is presumed to be more fit simply because that parent is a mother or a father. A few states retain one exception to this, called the "tender years" doctrine. In these states, a court may assume that very young children should live with their mothers whenever possible.

A parent could be denied contact with his or her children if the judge rules that:
- a parent is legally incompetent (even then, the court may permit supervised visitation)
- a parent is not related to the children by blood or legal adoption—such as a stepparent or same-sex co-parent (you can give that person the status of parent in your agreement, however), or
- the contact would be harmful to the children.

In extreme cases, a court can terminate a person's parental rights—usually after finding that the parent has abandoned the children or engages in behavior highly damaging to the children. If you are named in a hearing to terminate your parental rights, you will have the right to defend yourself—in many states, you will have the right to an appointed attorney if you cannot afford one yourself.

ISSUE 39 CROSS-REFERENCES

Worksheet	Questions
Worksheet 1	3
Worksheet 2	1, 2, 6, 7, 10
Worksheet 3	1, 7, 12, 14, 15
Worksheet 4	1, 2, 7, 8, 10, 11, 12, 13, 14, 17, 18

a. Sole Custody

Parents frequently choose sole custody when distance, acrimony or other factors make it impossible for parents to collaborate on the decisions that affect their children. If your decision in Issue 11 (Making Decisions) is to have only one parent make decisions, you'll probably want to select sole custody.

A parent with sole custody cannot prevent the other parent from visiting the children. The sole custodian does have considerable discretion in scheduling visitation, however. The more specific you can be about your visitation schedule, the easier your plan will be to live with. The decisions you make here should also be consistent with the decisions you made in Issue 18.

> **⚠ SOLE CUSTODY AND CHILD SUPPORT**
> A sole custody arrangement does not exempt the noncustodial parent from paying child support.

b. Joint Custody

Most parents who choose to make decisions together (Issue 11) choose joint custody or joint legal custody if their state differentiates between legal and physical custody. Joint legal custody can mean anything from consulting each other on every decision larger than the clothes to be worn to school, to consulting only on major issues, such as whether to allow underage children to marry, and everything in between.

Joint physical custody agreements may also vary widely. The most common joint physical custody awards specify that the children:

- spend equal time with each parent
- spend the school year with one parent and the summer with the other, or
- live primarily with one parent and spend weekly midweek visits or overnights, weekends and half of the holidays and summer vacation with the other parent.

For joint custody to succeed, you and the other parent must be willing to work together to make decisions, without using your children as either a weapon or an excuse. You can help your joint custody arrangements to succeed by being specific in your parenting agreement about how you will make decisions and how your children will share time with each of you.

All states allow parents to choose joint custody arrangements. A small number of states permit courts to order joint custody, even over the objections of a parent. (Your state's rules on joint custody are spelled out in Chapter 12.)

c. Split Custody

Splitting custody of the children between the parents is not recommended except under special circumstances. Such circumstances include:

- a history of irreconcilable conflict between a parent and one or more of the children
- incest or violence between the children, or
- children with different fathers or mothers.

Unfortunately, some parents split custody because it makes each of them feel as though they have "won." If this is your reason for considering it, be careful. Often, the bond between siblings is the only reliable support system children have after their parents split up. Eliminating it can have very serious consequences, even if the children have only one parent in common.

Consult a mental health professional before splitting custody of your children. If you still decide to opt for it, schedule a lot of time that your children can be together.

d. Third-Party Custody

Some parents are unwilling or unable to care for their children. The parents may be children themselves, or may be undergoing psychiatric, substance abuse or physical rehabilitation. No matter what the reason, if you are in this situation you will have to choose a third person, such as a grandparent or other relative, to care for your children. You must also specify how you and the other parent will spend time with your children and how you will regain custody of your children.

You should know that you might find it difficult to re-establish your parenting role with your children if you have created a voluntary guardianship. This is because, in some situations, it can be hard to prove that there is a good reason to change guardianship back, especially if the guardianship has been in place for some time. For this reason, it is very important that you get legal advice before deciding to give up the guardianship of your children to someone else.

Issue 40: Separating the Adult Relationship Issues From Parenting Issues

As you have undoubtedly noticed, this book rarely misses an opportunity to emphasize how important it is for you and the other parent to keep your children out of the middle by separating your adult relationship issues from the parenting decisions you must make. This issue/option set is meant to help you to avoid two common problems that parents face while parenting separately. The first pitfall is getting so wrapped up in the adult relationship issues that you either forget to discuss the children or get so angry that further discussion and agreement become impossible. The second problem is that when adult relationship issues are continually entangled with parenting issues, it becomes increasingly difficult to focus on your children's best interests.

While most parents see the value in separating their adult relationship issues from the parenting issues, many wonder just how they will be able to do it. Following are some concrete ideas you can incorporate into your agreement to help you to keep the two issues as separate from each other as possible.

a. Agree to Resolve All Parenting Decisions First

Perhaps the simplest way to ensure that your parenting decisions are made without being clouded by the adult relationship issues is to agree that you will always resolve the "kid issues" before discussing whatever adult issues you or the other parent wishes to raise.

b. Schedule Separate Telephone Calls

Some parents have a difficult time following the ground rule described in section a, above—that is, agreeing to resolve all parenting decisions first. For them, it often helps if they can at least agree to set up a separate telephone call or meeting time when they will discuss whatever adult relationship issues need to be resolved. This often works best when parents have already agreed to have regular telephone calls to discuss the children. If either parent wishes to raise extraneous issues for discussion, they can let the other know during the regularly scheduled "kid update" call, and set another time for that conversation to take place.

c. Arrange to Discuss Adult Relationship Issues When Away From Your Children

Some parents are able to get the parenting issues resolved first, but unfortunately proceed to take up adult issues within their children's earshot. For these parents, incorporating a provision of this kind helps to remind each of them that they must handle their adult business elsewhere.

d. Discuss Adult Relationship Issues During Joint Counseling Sessions

Many parents still have substantial and reoccurring adult issues to resolve long after the divorce is final. If this is true for you and the other parent, it may be more productive—and better for your children—if you save your conversations for a joint mediation or counseling session when someone can facilitate your discussions and help you to look for ways to resolve those issues on a more permanent basis.

ISSUE 40 CROSS-REFERENCES

Worksheet	Questions
Worksheet 1	4, 8
Worksheet 2	6, 7, 8, 10
Worksheet 3	7, 8, 9, 11, 14, 15
Worksheet 4	7, 8, 10, 11, 17, 18

Issue 41: Making Changes

Although many parents wish to negotiate a single parenting plan that will remain viable throughout the course of their separate parenting relationship, the reality is that changes are almost always unavoidable. Anecdotal evidence gathered from experienced mediators indicates that parents will generally need to renegotiate substantial portions of their parenting agreement approximately every two-and-a-half to three years.

Any number of things might require changes in your parenting plan, not the least of which are your children's changing needs, interests and activities as they get older. Some of the other events that commonly trigger the need for a modification of your existing arrangements include:

- one or both parents "settle down" with a new partner or spouse

- one parent plans to move a substantial distance away from the other parent
- your preteen or teen wants to change their primary residence, or develop a primary residence, rather than spitting the time equally between both homes
- one or more children develop a serious discipline problem in one home
- the schools in one parent's area no longer meet the children's needs
- the primary caretaking parent needs to devote more time to school or a career, or
- the primary caretaking parent is making it difficult for the children to spend time with their other parent, in violation of existing court orders.

All parents need to respond to the inevitable changes in their children's, or their own, lives. By anticipating the need to modify your agreement in the future, you can minimize much of the conflict parents normally experience when troublesome issues arise, or if your children ask for modifications. (For more information on this particular issue, see Chapter 8, *Dealing With Changes in Your Existing Agreements.*)

ISSUE 41 CROSS-REFERENCES

Worksheet	Questions
Worksheet 1	5, 8
Worksheet 2	2, 3, 8, 9, 10
Worksheet 3	4, 7, 8, 14, 15
Worksheet 4	4, 6, 7, 8, 9, 11, 18

a. Set Up Regular Reviews

Consider reviewing your parenting agreement:

- once a year
- when your children change schools, or
- as your children reach certain ages.

In the first few years after you separate or divorce, you might consider more frequent reviews (such as every six months) until you are sure you have settled upon a final agreement.

Give yourselves enough time to negotiate whatever changes are necessary. Scheduling the review approximately one month before the school year begins or about one month before the start of the summer break should give you plenty of time.

When you review your agreement, you may discover that you have already informally negotiated changes, or that certain aspects of the agreement no longer work. If you negotiate changes to the agreement, modify it in writing to reflect the changes.

b. Allow Your Children to Share in Decisions

You may want to give your children a role in deciding where they will live and how they will spend time with both parents. Some parents solicit their children's opinions no matter what their ages; others wait until the children are teenagers.

While it is often a good idea to ask your children for their thoughts on what they would like the most—or what kinds of arrangement they think would work best—you and the other parent need to be careful that you are not putting too much pressure on your children. It is a very difficult, but critically important, balancing act. The balancing act can become even more challenging if a child wants to be involved. Often, this will happen with later elementary school-aged children or adolescents. The key is to hear what they have to say, ask questions to see if you can understand why they want what they are asking for and then tell the child that their views will be taken into account as you and the other parent go through your decision-making process. Some of the ways that parents put too much pressure on their children when they involve them in the discussion about making changes to the parenting agreement are by:

- making the child feel that he or she has to "choose" between one parent or the other
- making the child demonstrate which parent he or she loves more by making the choices that parent wants, or show who he or she wants to be with more by choosing to be with that parent more of the time
- treating them as if they have the same authority as an adult to decide what is in their best interests (almost setting them up as a co-parent, or allowing them to make the decisions as if they were the parent).

c. Consider Mediation

You may be willing to evaluate or renegotiate your parenting agreement only if a third party is present. In this situation, include an automatic mediation schedule for reviewing your agreement, or allow either parent to schedule mediation as necessary. (More information on mediation is in Chapter 7.)

d.   Get an Expert Opinion

You will find a long list of services and professionals that can support separating or divorcing parents in handling almost any problem they might encounter in their separate parenting relationship.

Issue 42: Making Substantive Changes to This Agreement

If you make substantive changes to your parenting agreement, such as living arrangements, decision-making authority or making a move, you will want to modify any existing and relevant court orders so that your agreement is enforceable. This may seem unnecessary if your relationship with the other parent is working well; if it deteriorates, however, you may not be able to enforce your agreement.

ISSUE 42 CROSS-REFERENCES

Worksheet	Questions
Worksheet 1	5
Worksheet 2	2, 3, 10
Worksheet 3	1, 7, 8, 14, 15
Worksheet 4	1, 2, 3, 8, 11, 18

Issue 43: Explaining the Agreement to Your Children

You and the other parent must consider how you will tell your children about your parenting agreement. If possible, tell them together. If that won't work, decide who will tell them and what that person will say. You must also decide how your children's questions will be answered. You can agree that either parent will answer any question that the children have. Alternatively, you can select one parent to field most, if not all, questions.

Some children, especially younger children, have difficulty understanding that they will continue to be loved even though their parents no longer love each other. Many children fear that they were the cause of the separation or divorce, especially if you and the other parent argued frequently about child-rearing issues. To help your children,

stress that the decision to separate or divorce was made because of the relationship between the parents, not because of anything that the children did or did not do. No matter what you say, find a way to ensure that your children know they are loved.

Preschoolers, especially, have little use for calendars, but do understand the sequence of familiar events. Try explaining when they will see you or the other parent again in relation to other events that they enjoy. For example, if your children attend preschool, a play group or swimming lessons on Tuesdays and Thursdays, explain that you will see them after two more swimming lessons.

Some other ways parents have found to help explain the parenting plan to their children include talking briefly (about five minutes) and often about how the new arrangements will work and giving children age-appropriate books, videos or workbooks that explain what it's like to live in two homes, or to live primarily with one parent and visit with the other parent on weekends or holidays. Ideally, children should be told about the parenting plan and how it will work *before* any changes are made. While some children can handle this kind of information fairly well on their own, other children need help, such as from a counselor, to deal with all of the feelings that come up when they see how their lives will change. Some of the ways that parents chose to tell their children about the parenting plan for the first time include:

- telling the children together
- having only one parent tell the children
- one or both parents explaining the plan during a counseling session (especially if they are already seeing a counselor), or
- inviting the children to attend the last part of a mediation session to learn about the new agreement.

Regardless of which option you choose, your children should *not* find out about the parenting plan by reading any of the court documents, especially if they include evaluations or declarations about a parent's weaknesses or why they should or should not have primary custody of the children.

ISSUE 43 CROSS-REFERENCES

Worksheet	Questions
Worksheet 1	6, 7
Worksheet 2	4, 6

Parenting Agreements and Money

This book is primarily about how to fashion an effective parenting agreement. However, if you are separating or getting a divorce, child custody is but one of the issues that you may be facing. Other issues typically include child support, alimony (also commonly called "spousal support") and the division of jointly owned property. While it is certainly possible to keep all these issues separate, many parents find that all of these issues are connected. For instance, the decision regarding who gets the family home may be made after determining which parent can best afford its upkeep and debt load. Alternatively, if a paramount goal is for the children to continue living in the family home, then the parent who becomes the children's primary caretaker is likely to be the parent who remains in the family home.

Child support and alimony can also obviously effect custody arrangements in that a parent who receives substantial child support and alimony may have an easier time caring for young children than if all family income must come from employment. Property division other than the house may affect a parent's ability to raise the necessary money to purchase a home or move to a neighborhood which is more attractive, offers a better public school system, offers more social and cultural amenities or allows that parent to be closer to extended family members or to pursue education or employment opportunities.

Fortunately, if you truly focus on the best interests of your children issue by issue and option by option, you will find that most decisions about how the children are to be raised can be made prior to, and independently of, the money issues. By basing your custody decisions squarely upon what is best for the children, you may even find that you will also be able to resolve such fundamental and potentially divisive issues as who keeps the house and how much alimony or child support, if any, should be paid. For example, some parents are tempted to argue for custody in order to receive or avoid paying child support. For most parents, however, this line of reasoning fails because the actual costs associated with being a custodial parent are almost always higher than any child support payment a court is likely to order.

The balance of this chapter will provide you with some basic information about divorce-related money issues that may help you as you negotiate a mutually acceptable parenting agreement. As you review this information, you should understand that each of these issues is likely to involve legal or other issues, including some with tax consequences. For this reason, you should consider consulting an attorney, accountant or other advisor prior to finalizing any particular agreement.

A. Understanding Child Support

What follows is a brief introduction to the subject of child support. If you want more detailed information, refer to Chapter 13, *Help Beyond the Book*, for a bibliography of more detailed information and resources.

Every parent is legally responsible for supporting his or her children until:

- the children reach the age of majority (and sometimes longer, particularly if a child is disabled or still in school)
- the children go on active military duty
- the children are declared emancipated by a court, or
- the parents' rights and responsibilities are terminated (such as when a child is adopted).

Separated or divorced parents must satisfy this legal obligation in one of two ways. Either:

- the parent who has the children most of the time satisfies his or her obligation by becoming the primary caretaker, or
- the parent who has the children the least amount of time satisfies his or her obligation through monthly child support payments.

When the time that the children spend with each parent is more or less equal, the parent with the larger income will be expected to pay at least some support to the parent with the smaller income.

1. How Child Support Payments Are Calculated

Each state has its own method for calculating the amount of child support that will flow from one parent to the other after separation or divorce. An increasing number of states use a standard formula to compute the basic support payment that a judge will impose if the issue is presented to the court for resolution. The factors that are used in these formulas are usually:

- the relative amount of time each parent cares for the children
- each parent's net income and necessary expenses
- each parent's earning potential
- each parent's eligibility for public benefits, and
- the number and ages of the children.

Most states allow the parents to negotiate a support payment that is higher or lower than the statutory amount, but also allow the family court judge to reject the parents' agreement if it appears that the children will not be adequately supported by the provisions in that agreement. (A few states require that at least a minimum obligation be imposed on the parent paying the child support.)

In addition to the guidelines imposed on them by most states' laws, judges are supposed to strive for fairness in establishing the dollar amount of child support obligations. They are thus given at least some discretion to apportion child support responsibility between parents according to their relative financial circumstances. Some states' laws specify additional factors which must be considered in determining who pays child support, and how much child support they will pay. These factors include the needs of the child—including health insurance, educational needs, day care and special needs of the child—the needs of the custodial parent, the payer's ability to pay and the children's standard of living before the divorce.

a. Relative Financial Circumstances

When determining child support orders, a court normally considers the relative income and assets of both spouses. If the custodial parent earns more than the noncustodial parent, child support may be a nominal amount. Accordingly, when courts consider the relative assets and income of the parties, they usually end up awarding at least some child support to the custodial parent. In general, the statistics show that mothers are most often the custodial parent and that fathers generally pay child support. As a result of a number of factors, custodial mothers generally have considerably less household income than do noncustodial fathers.

b. Ability to Pay

Courts always consider a person's ability to pay when establishing his or her child support obligations. To do this, a court totals the payer's gross income from all sources (such as wages, public benefits, interest and dividends on investments, rents from real property and profits from patents), and then reduces that total by the amount of any mandatory deductions (such as income taxes, Social Security, health care and mandatory union dues) to arrive at a figure which represents the payer's net income.

In most states, deductions for credit union payments, wage attachments and the like are not subtracted when calculating net income. By example, consider that John makes $2,000 per month, and his income tax, Social Security, unemployment insurance benefits and other government deductions reduce his income by $500 per month. John's net income for purposes of calculating child support is now $1,500 per month. The court will not further reduce John's net income to acknowledge the $300 per month automatic deduction which John takes in order to repay his credit union loan. The reason for this rule is that the law accords support payments a higher priority than other types of debts, and would rather see other debts not paid than to have a spouse or child go without adequate support.

When calculating a child support payer's living expenses, some states permit the court to consider the basic necessaries of life (such as rent or mortgage, food, clothing and health care), but not extraneous expenses such as school tuition, dining outside the home and entertainment. The reason for this is that courts consider that family support obligations should come before less critical personal expenses. In a growing number of states, all of the payer's personal expenses are considered to be irrelevant when calculating child support payments.

c. Ability to Earn

When a court computes the amount of child support to be paid by a parent, the judge usually factors both parties' ability to earn into the final decision. While actual earnings are an important factor in determining a person's ability to earn, they are not conclusive when there is evidence that a person could earn more if he or she chose to do so. For example, assume a parent with an obligation to pay child support leaves his current job and enrolls in medical or law school, takes a job with lower pay but good potential for higher pay in the future or takes a lower-paying job that provides better job satisfaction. In each of these situations, a court may base the child support award on the income from the original job (ability to earn) rather than on the new income level (ability to pay). In this situation, the court would likely have reasoned that the children's current needs take priority over the parent's career plans and desires.

d. Standard of Living

When a court sets child support, it often considers the family's predivorce standard of living and attempts to continue this standard for the children to the greatest possible extent. Courts, however, are aware of the difficulty of maintaining two households on the income that formerly supported one home. Arriving at a decision which will maintain the predivorce standard of living is, therefore, more of a goal than a guarantee.

2.   Tax Consequences of Child Support

Child support is tax-free to the recipient but not deductible by the payer. In the past, when ex-spouses had more flexibility in negotiating the amount of child support and alimony, many chose to pay more as alimony (which is deductible to the payer and reportable by the payee) and less as child support because of the resulting tax advantage to the payer. Since most states now determine the basic child support obligation by formula, however, shifting the amounts of child support and alimony to take advantage of tax deductions is increasingly difficult.

3.   Children May Not Be Traded or Withheld for Child Support

Some noncustodial parents equate their obligation to pay child support with the "right" to visit the child, while some custodial parents conclude that the payer loses the "right" to visit the child if he or she falls behind on support. In fact, neither position is accurate, and neither position reflects a consideration for the children's best interests.

Although some parents negotiate privately to trade child support for visitation with the children, no state condones this practice, and all states specifically prohibit parents from withholding visitation because the other parent owes support, or from withholding support because of disputes over custody or visitation. Quite simply, children need

financial physical and emotional support, but children are not to be traded or withheld for money.

4.   Modifying Child Support Orders

A child support obligation under a court order may be modified if financial circumstances have changed. You should note, however, that child support obligations are payable no matter what the payer's circumstances until such time as the court makes a new support order. For instance, consider Noah, who is required to pay $300 a month child support. If Noah loses his job, he will still be obligated to pay the $300 a month as long as the original court order stands. Importantly, if Noah does go to court to get the order modified on the basis of his decreased income, Noah will still be liable for all payments owed prior to the modification date because the courts will not take Noah off the hook retroactively. Even if Noah's ex informally agrees to let Noah pay less, Noah still technically owes the support because the underlying court order hasn't been modified.

Most child support orders can be modified upon a showing that the circumstances have changed. Some examples of these changes include:

- the existence of an additional financial burden (such as a medical emergency)
- additional income which becomes available because of remarriage
- changes in the law
- changes in employment
- increases in the cost of living
- increases or decreases in income
- disability
- medical or financial emergency
- hardship, and
- increases or decreases in the child's needs.

B. Understanding Alimony or Spousal Support

The following is a brief introduction to the subject of alimony (interchangeably called spousal support). If you want more detailed information, you can refer to Chapter 13, *Help Beyond the Book*, for a bibliography of resources.

Alimony is money paid by one spouse for the other's support as part of a court order or marital settlement agreement following divorce. Until the 1970s, alimony was a natural extension of the financial dependence in "traditional" marriages which wives had upon their husbands.

Traditional marriages presumed that the husband was the breadwinner and the wife stayed home, caring for the house and children but not earning any income. Alimony was paid only by the husband to the wife. The amount of alimony was determined by a number of factors, including the needs of the parties, their status in life, their wealth and their relative fault in causing the divorce. If a husband was committing adultery or treating his wife cruelly, he would generally pay more alimony than if the wife was having an affair or treating her husband cruelly. Today, except in marriages of long duration (roughly ten or more years), or in the case of an ill or ailing spouse, alimony usually lasts for a set period of time with the expectation that the recipient spouse will become self-supporting.

Alimony payments may be modified if the spouses so agree, or if the spouse wanting the modification petitions the court and the court agrees to change either the amount to be paid or duration of those payments. The only time alimony cannot be modified is when the spouses specifically agree that the alimony is nonmodifiable, or when alimony payments are part of an integrated property settlement agreement (that is, where alimony is paid as part of the property division. See "Integrated Property Settlement Agreement," below.)

When alimony and child support are combined into one payment without regard to which portion is alimony and which is child support, some states call this total payment "family support." Because of the increased concern over enforcement of child support orders, however, most courts require that child support and alimony be identified separately.

Courts typically use several basic criteria when setting alimony amounts:

- **Ability to pay.** Courts measure ability to pay based upon net income. Net income is calculated by first totaling the payer's gross income from all sources (such as wages, public benefits, interest and dividends on investments, rents from real property and profits from patents), and then subtracting any mandatory deductions (such as income taxes, Social Security, health care and mandatory union dues).
- **Ability to earn.** Some states calculate the spouse's ability to earn by comparing actual earnings and estimated earnings if there is evidence that a person could earn more if he or she chose to do so. Others, however, set alimony payments based only on actual earnings. For

example, Jane Doctor, who has earned $100,000 a year from the world of medicine for the past three years while married, quit her job when she and her husband separated in order to become a TV repairperson, with an annual income of approximately $20,000. During the divorce trial, Jane's husband, Lionel, requested alimony for himself. Because Jane abruptly changed her income, the court imposed a larger alimony obligation on Jane than she would normally pay given a salary of $20,000 a year. The court has reasoned that Jane can return to the world of medicine if she needs to and that her ex-husband should not be penalized because of her employment decision. In some states, however, the court would reason that ability to earn is too speculative and would set alimony on the basis of Jane's $20,000 income.

- **Ability to be self-supporting.** Courts normally calculate an ex-spouse's ability to support him- or herself by considering whether the ex-spouse possesses marketable skills and whether he or she is able to work outside the home (having custody of preschool children and not having access to day care could make this impossible). If a spouse has marketable skills and is able to work outside the home, but has chosen not to look for work, the court is very likely to limit the amount and length of alimony. In many states, courts do not award alimony if the marriage is of short duration or both spouses are able to support themselves. If, however, one spouse was dependent on the other for support during the marriage, the dependent spouse is often awarded alimony for a transition period or until he or she becomes self-supporting. If a spouse receiving alimony becomes self-supporting before the time set by the court for the alimony to end, the paying spouse can go to court and file a request for modification or termination of alimony based upon these changed circumstances. Although it is difficult to obtain, ex-spouses are sometimes awarded an extension of alimony if, at the end of the support period, they are still unable to support themselves.
- **Standard of living during the marriage.** When a court sets alimony, it often considers the family's pre-divorce standard of living and attempts to continue this standard for both spouses whenever feasible. This often means that alimony payments increase proportionately when the couple starts out with more

money. Whether or not both spouses worked outside the home during the marriage, it is often impossible to continue the same standard of living for both people after the spouses have gone their separate ways. This means that courts try, but cannot guarantee maintenance of the predivorce standard of living.

- **Length of the marriage.** When a marriage is relatively short, for example five years or less, and no children were born or adopted during the marriage, courts often refuse to award alimony. If there are children under school age, however, the court may award alimony in order to enable the primary custodial parent to provide full-time care for the children. For federal income tax purposes, alimony paid under a written agreement or court order is deductible by the payer and is taxable to the recipient. Child support, on the other hand, is tax-free to the recipient but not deductible by the payer.

- **Marital debts.** Upon divorce, the court considers who can pay any debts which have been accumulated as well as who benefits most from the asset attached to the debt, and allocates those debts accordingly. If the court orders a spouse to pay a large portion of marital debts, it often reduces the amount of alimony that spouse is ordered to pay.

- **Acquisition of a professional degree or license during the marriage.** Some spouses support their mates financially as well as emotionally through professional, graduate or trade school. When they divorce, alimony is rarely awarded to the spouse who supported the couple, even though he or she often made sacrifices, such as delaying his or her own education, in order to support the other. Some states, however, try to compensate the spouse who put the other through school in the alimony award.

- **Existence of an agreement before marriage.** Some couples enter into agreements concerning certain aspects of their relationship, including whether alimony will be paid in the event of divorce, prior to the marriage. Whether they are called antenuptial, prenuptial or premarital agreements, the agreements are usually upheld by the court unless one person shows that the agreement was likely to promote divorce, for example by including a large alimony amount in the event of divorce, was written and signed with the intention of divorcing or was inher-

ently unfair because, for example, the agreement provided that a spouse must give up all of his or her rights in his or her spouse's future earnings without the advice of an attorney.

INTEGRATED PROPERTY SETTLEMENT AGREEMENT

Upon divorce, couples commonly enter into a divorce agreement which divides marital property and may set alimony. This agreement is "integrated" if the property settlement and alimony payments are combined into either one lump-sum payment or periodic payments. Integrated agreements are often used when the marital property consists of substantial intangible assets (for example, future royalties, stock options or future pension plans) or when one party is buying the other's interest in a valuable tangible asset (for example, a home or business). In addition, if a spouse is entitled to little or no alimony, but is not financially independent, periodic payments may help that spouse gain financial independence.

C. Negotiating Child and Spousal Support

How should you approach your child or spousal negotiations? Quite simply, you should go back to the basics. This means understanding what makes these issues so difficult and finding ways to address each concern, one at a time, with the intent of finding child-focused solutions which both parents can accept.

Most parents resent the "principle" of paying child support—even more than they resent the dent it makes in their disposable income. Some of the ways parents express these objections include:

- "The money isn't being spent directly on the kids."
- "The receiving parent gains an undue benefit by being free to use child support monies to pay rent."
- "The parent receiving child support doesn't have to account for how the money is spent."
- "The child support allows the parent who receives it to be 'lazy' about supporting him- or herself and working to provide a living for the children."

MOTHERS FARE WORSE AFTER DIVORCE THAN DO FATHERS

Much has been made of the changed circumstances, financially, when families separate or divorce. Initially, both parents experience substantially reduced economic resources. Over time, this may change significantly as a result of new jobs, better pay, remarriage, public assistance, the sale of property or other factors. One disturbing fact, however, emerges consistently. Although the economic well-being of divorced mothers and their children increases over time, the income of mothers who do not remarry remains substantially below the father's income. By contrast, the economic well-being of divorced fathers (over time) remains substantially above preseparation levels. Despite this significant discrepancy, custodial mothers remain the primary support for their children in the years following the divorce. Even if paid in full, child support and alimony represent only a fraction of the mother's postdivorce household income.

Although child support issues are critically important for everyone, they are adult issues not to be shared with children. While it is often necessary for one parent to explain that they cannot provide the same things that the other parent can because of their finances, it is equally important that neither parent puts the children in the middle of financial issues.

Child support involves both getting the order and collecting the support. Although states offer child support recipients a number of techniques for collecting it, probably the most effective approach to enforcement is to prevent the problem from arising in the first place. As discussed, the recommendation to have both parents participating at a significant level in their children's lives is one of the most effective ways both to head off a dispute over child support—or repair a situation which has already deteriorated. If you are already in a dispute over child support, you can consider a number of different ways to approach this, including:

- talking to the other parent directly to find out why he or she isn't paying
- discussing how support payments are used, and the value of spending it in those ways

- asking whether the other parent wants a more substantial role in the children's lives
- assessing whether the paying parent's economic circumstances have changed, thereby warranting a change in the current order for support
- taking the matter to mediation and, if necessary, reviewing the entire parenting agreement to see whether changes there might make the parent feel better about paying
- investigating options for providing better support through medical, dental and vision care insurance, or
- investigating options for both parents to move to another area where both might be likely to find work, or work which pays better.

Happily, there is at least one way to approach negotiations over child support which tends to produce consistently superior results. This strategy is to make sure that both parents are actively involved with the children. There is a strong correlation between the amount of time a parent spends with his or her children and that parent's willingness to pay child support. Maccoby and Mnookin, in their book, *Dividing the Child* (Harvard Press), reported that most families opt for custody with the mother while the father pays child support. On average, fathers paid between two-thirds and three-fourths of the awarded support, but their compliance with support orders fell off over time.

Importantly, the researchers discovered that fathers tended to continue paying child support when they had regular and frequent visits, both daytime and overnight, with their children. The less involved with their children's lives they became, the less apt they were to keep paying support. A 1992 report by the Department of Health and Human services echoes this finding by emphasizing that "When the parents are involved (with their children), these payment problems will almost totally go away. Treating noncustodial parents as cash cows will doom our children to a continuing emotional and financial morass."

D. Dividing Jointly Owned Property

In all states, a divorce or separation involves the division of property that the spouses own jointly. In the community property states (California, Nevada, Arizona, New Mexico, Texas, Washington, Idaho and Wisconsin) this is usually considered to be property that was acquired after the marriage but before the spouses separated. Common exceptions to this rule are gifts and inheritances received by one spouse and kept in a separate account, and income earned on a spouse's separate property. In all other states, jointly owned property is property acquired jointly by both spouses.

Different types of property can raise different issues when it comes to dividing it in a divorce or separation. This is especially true when the property is a mix of a spouse's separate property and community or marital property. For instance, a house purchased with one spouse's separate property (assets) is that spouse's separate property upon divorce. However, if jointly owned property was used to increase the value of the house, figuring out who owns what can be tricky, especially if the house's value has appreciated significantly. Similarly, if one spouse owns a business as his or her separate property but both spouses work in the business, it can be difficult to decide how the appreciated value of the business should be divided.

These and other property division issues are covered in detail in *Divorce and Money,* by Woodhouse and Collins (Nolo).

RELEVANT ISSUES IN CHAPTER 5

Issue	Number
Medical, Dental and Vision Care	1
Surname	4
Making Decisions	11
Resolving Disputes When Making Decisions Together	12
Exchanging Information	14
Reinvolving a Previously Absent Parent	19
Moving	21
If Our Homes Are Far Apart	22
Holidays	23
Vacations	24
Special Occasions and Family Events	25
Improving Transition Times	29
When Parenting Styles and Values Are Very Different	31
Disparaging Remarks	33
Undermining the Parent/Child Relationship	34
Denying Access to the Children	35
When Nonrelatives Live in the Home	37
When Parents Have New Partners	38
Making Changes	41

■

CHAPTER

7

Making Mediation and Arbitration Work for You

Until recently, when parents could not agree on custody and visitation during or after a divorce, they would bring the case to court for a judge to decide. Now, many of these parents turn to a neutral third party who is trained to help people come to an agreement on their own. This process is called mediation, and the third party is known as a mediator.

Mediation has become such a well-accepted method of resolving custody and visitation disputes that most states encourage judges to order it in appropriate circumstances—indeed, a few states require it before a judge can even get involved. Even if a judge doesn't order mediation, you can voluntarily choose it if you need help in reaching an agreement. Although voluntary mediation usually requires that you pay the mediator, this cost is trivial compared to the cost of hiring lawyers to fight out custody and visitation issues in court.

You can use mediation in several different ways. Some parents use it to start the settlement process, and then stop mediation once they are able to negotiate on their own. Other parents use mediation now and then—an hour here, and an hour there—throughout the negotiation process to resolve various points of impasse. Still other parents mediate their entire parenting agreement. The point is this: View mediation as a flexible tool you can tailor to meet your family's needs as you design your agreement.

A. How Mediation Works

Mediators facilitate discussions so that parents can voice their concerns, identify important issues and focus their efforts on meeting their children's needs. Almost every mediation has the characteristics listed below:

- **The mediator is neutral.** The mediator has no personal or business ties with either parent, has no past knowledge of the family, is not aware (in advance) of the specific issues to be mediated and has no preconceived ideas about what parenting plan would be best for that family.
- **The process is confidential.** The mediator will not disclose to a court or anyone else what either parent says during the mediation. Furthermore, no one will know about the mediation or its results unless the parents agree or submit their agreement to a court to be incorporated into a court order. In rare circumstances, a mediator may be subpoenaed by a court and compelled to testify about the mediation if the mediator made a recommendation to the court and that recommendation is contested by a parent.
- **Mediation is focused on the future.** Most mediators ask parents to focus on what they'd like to happen in the future. This means that the mediator spends little time on who said or did what in the past, but significant time on what must be done to control or prevent these problems in the future. The mediator's goal is to help parents build agreements that are likely to succeed by avoiding past problems.
- **Agreements are voluntary.** An agreement is reached only when both parents say that the terms are acceptable.

B. Why Mediation Works

The reasons why mediation works and parents prefer mediation over litigation are many. Here are just a few:

- Mediation offers access to a trained neutral person who can help parents focus their attention on the issues to be resolved, as opposed to blaming each other for the problems they face.
- Mediation is confidential, which allows parents to freely discuss the issues and evaluate possible solutions without fear that the other parent can use the discussions or the mediator's statements to build a court case.

- Parents decide for themselves whether to accept or reject any particular agreement.
- Parents control the time, costs and acrimony associated with finding a resolution.
- Mediation helps parents improve their communication skills—an important part of successful separate parenting.

Mediators are especially skilled at generating ideas and helping parents overcome impasses. Mediators can also review a parenting agreement to point out such potential problems as:

- vague language—such as "reasonable visitation"
- vague action plans—for example, a plan that doesn't include specific pick-up and drop-off times for visits, vacations or holidays, and
- arrangements that might leave one parent feeling excluded from the children's lives—such as a sole custody arrangement with unspecified visitation.

Although mediators don't provide legal advice, they can often give general information about your state's custody and visitation laws, and suggest resources for information on child development and parenting theories. Especially if your mediator is also a family law attorney, you may be able to get the legal information you need if you want your agreement to best conform to what a court might want to see.

Even if your mediation sessions do not result in a complete parenting agreement, you probably will still benefit from the process. Partial agreements can narrow the issues to be negotiated or litigated later, and mediation can help open and improve lines of communication.

C. Proposing Mediation

For some families, the hardest task in mediation is getting it started. Many parents are reluctant to suggest to the other parent that they try mediation because they:

- are convinced the other parent will refuse, or
- fear they will appear weak to the other parent.

In fact, however, once you (or a mediator) explain mediation to the other parent, that parent is likely to see its obvious advantages over litigation and is likely to go along with it. And once mediation is underway, any suspicions of weakness in the position of the parent who initiated the mediation are usually rapidly dispelled.

Mediation can be suggested in several ways: by one parent, by a counselor, by a lawyer or by the mediator.

Following are sample conversations that illustrate how each person's proposal for mediation might sound:

ONE PARENT PROPOSES MEDIATION:

I have heard about a process called mediation that might help us get these things resolved. From what I understand, the mediator would help us to talk about our parenting situation—without fighting—so that we could see whether we can make the decisions on our own. We wouldn't have to spend any more time than we need to cover the issues and reach agreements. We could choose whether or not to involve attorneys, we might be able to avoid a court hearing and we wouldn't have to drag ourselves or the children through any more bitterness than is absolutely necessary. The mediator wouldn't tell us what to do, and each of us could decide for ourselves whether any particular agreement was fair before we agreed to, or signed, anything. If the mediation doesn't work, we can still try to negotiate things on our own or we can go to court—but at least we will have tried one more way to make our own decisions about how our children will be raised.

A COUNSELOR OR ATTORNEY PROPOSES MEDIATION:

At this point, I'd like to suggest that you consider a process called mediation. Mediation can be very effective for starting the dialogue on some of these difficult issues, and may allow both of you to find things that you can agree on. The mediator cannot impose a settlement on you—you and the other parent will be the ones to make all of the decisions. What the mediator can do is help you discuss your children's needs and how you plan to meet those needs—without allowing the discussion to deteriorate into an argument. When it works, and it works in the majority of cases, parents are in a better position to communicate and work together in the future. [Attorneys only:] After you reach an agreement, you can bring it back to me and I can review it. If mediation doesn't produce a full agreement, then you can go forward with negotiations on your own or through me, or you can take the matter to court.

THE PROSPECTIVE MEDIATOR PROPOSES MEDIATION:

_____ (name of parent, counselor or attorney) has asked me to contact you to discuss how mediation might help you and the other parent resolve custody and visitation decisions on behalf of your children. The focus of mediation is on your children, and making decisions in their best interests. If possible, we will work toward creating a com-

prehensive plan which describes all of the key elements of your parenting relationship. As a mediator, I am a neutral third party, which means that I have no previous relationship with either of you, and that I have no preconceived ideas about what decisions you should make. Although I will be happy to offer general information about the legal process and child development, I will not be making any recommendations about which options you should choose, and I will not provide legal advice of any kind. I will help the discussion to remain civil, even when you or the other parent is describing difficult or angry feelings.

As you begin to develop your parenting plan, I will help you make sure that it is clear, detailed and easy to understand and live with. Because mediation is confidential, you can be candid and don't need to worry that what you say will be repeated in court. Because an agreement results only when both parents say it is acceptable, mediated agreements generally last longer, and result in fewer arguments or court battles, than nonmediated agreements.

D. Understanding Basic Mediation Techniques

One of the best ways to understand why mediation works is to look at a sample mediation session.

FAMILY PROFILE

Matthew and Brenda are parents who live in neighboring communities and want to renegotiate their parenting plan, which has been in place for three years. Their children, Jason and Amy, are ages nine and seven, respectively.

1. The Mediator's Introduction

In addition to introducing themselves, mediators help parents articulate their own needs, interests and concerns, and focus their attention on how to best meet their children's needs, interests and concerns. This is also the time when the mediator sets the ground rules for discussion, and answers any questions which the parents might have.

MEDIATOR: *Now, I will ask each of you to describe your children, their needs, the current arrangements, any concerns which you have and your proposal for how you will share and divide your parenting responsibilities. As each of you speaks, I will ask that there be no interruptions, and that neither parent will make derogatory remarks about the*

other. Once we have done that, we will take each issue in turn, and discuss how it might be resolved so that you are meeting your children's needs. As you start discussing and evaluating your various options, I will be happy to offer information about some of the choices that other parents have considered, and will help you to generate ideas about solving difficult problems whenever it seems necessary. If either of you, or I, feel that discussion might be more productive if we meet separately, then I might take time to meet with each of you in private. Should either of you feel that you need advice from your attorney, just let me know and we will take a break.

2. Parents' Opening Statements

The parents' opening statements offer an ideal opportunity for each parent to hear how the other views the issues, and what they propose as a solution to meet their children's needs. Mediators use this time to learn about a particular family and to get an idea of what an agreement will have to achieve in order to be acceptable to both parents. By using techniques such as "reflective listening" (verifying that the listener has an accurate understanding of the speaker's meaning), mediators can be sure that they are developing a complete list of all the issues to be resolved.

BRENDA: *Right now, the children live with me during the week and they see their father on alternating weekends. We split all of the big holidays, like Christmas and Easter breaks, and alternate who gets the shorter holidays such as Thanksgiving, President's Weekend and Memorial Day. I think that everything is working just fine. So do the kids. Matthew is the one who wants to change this.*

MEDIATOR: *Can you tell me something about the children's activities, how they are doing in school and the things that you do together?*

BRENDA: *Both children are doing fairly well in school, they are involved in after-school sports, they do homework most days and they have soccer games on the weekends. I try to carpool with some of the other parents to get them to practices and games. I help them with their homework each evening.*

MEDIATOR: *Do both you and Matthew live in the same school district?*

BRENDA: *No—and I don't particularly like the schools in Matthew's district.*

MEDIATOR: *Thank you, Brenda. From what I understand, you and the children have developed some routines that accommodate their school work and sporting activities, and you are basically happy with the overall arrangements. Additionally, you don't see any advantages in considering a change in schools. Is this correct?*

BRENDA: *Yes.*

MEDIATOR: *Do you have anything that you'd like to add at this point?*

BRENDA: *No.*

MEDIATOR: *Now, Matthew, can you give me the same kind of information from your point of view?*

MATTHEW: *I feel like I'm losing touch with the kids. I want more time with them and Brenda refuses. I am a good parent, but I gave in last time and let the kids live with her. Now it's my turn. I want them to live with me, and they can see Brenda on alternating weekends. Jason says he wants to live with me, and Amy says that she doesn't care who she lives with, but I think that the kids should stay together.*

MEDIATOR: *Thank you, Matthew. As I see it, you feel that you would like to play a greater role in both children's lives, and that Jason, at least, has expressed a preference for living with you. You also feel that it would be best if the children stayed together—regardless of the actual living arrangements. What do you know about the children's activities and school performance?*

MATTHEW: *Not enough. I often don't hear about their soccer games if it's not my weekend, and I almost never hear about their school activities or performance—except for getting a copy of their report cards. I'd like to know more about both things. Although our school district may not offer all of the same programs as the one the children are in now, it is still a good school. Jason will be transferring into the middle school in two years, and the middle school in our area is just as good, if not better, than the one he would go to in his current district.*

MEDIATOR: *Clearly you would like to spend more time with Jason and Amy. Have you discussed this with them?*

MATTHEW: *Yes I have. Jason, especially, would like me to come to his games and practices. Amy has said that she'd like the same thing. If I at least knew something about the practice and game schedule, I could play a much bigger role in their lives—at least as far as sports goes. On the week-ends, they never bring home any school work, so I have very little information about how they're doing. I didn't want to sit in the same room as Brenda to have our parent/teacher conferences, so I missed out on that this year.*

MEDIATOR: *Have you asked the children whether they want to change schools?*

MATTHEW: *Yes, and they're not happy about it, but they would do it as long as it happened over the summer.*

MEDIATOR: *Okay. Are there any other issues that you'd like to bring up at this time?*

MATTHEW: *No.*

3. Negotiating the Agreement

Once a mediator has an idea of the issues each parent wants to address, he or she works with the parents to discuss each one to see whether it might be possible to find areas of agreement. From the conversation above, a list of issues might include:

- improving Matthew's access to information regarding school and sporting events
- increasing Matthew's time with the children
- evaluating how and when decisions should be made regarding which school the children will attend, and
- evaluating which should be the children's primary home during the week.

MEDIATOR: *Turning to one of the issues raised during your opening remarks, I am curious about what each of you thinks about finding ways that Matthew might increase the amount of time he spends with the children?*

BRENDA: *If Matthew wants to take over my turn in the carpool, he could get to know more of the children's friends and could attend some of the practices or games. In fact, I could give him a copy of the game schedule, and he could attend any of the games, whether I am there or not.*

MATTHEW: *I'd like to do that. What about school, though? I should get a copy of their school calendar, too, and maybe they should be bringing some of their work to me when they come to visit on the weekends.*

MEDIATOR: *Brenda, would you be willing to get this information to Matthew?*

BRENDA: *Sure.*

MEDIATOR: *Now, how about parent/teacher conferences? How do each of you suggest that these be handled?*

BRENDA: *I think that Matthew should take the time to set up his own conferences. I don't want to have them together. All he has to do is call the school and arrange to meet with each teacher.*

MEDIATOR: *Matthew, is this something that you'd be willing to do?*

MATTHEW: *Yes.*

4.   Turning Negative Feelings Into Positive Actions

Mediators recognize that it is hard to express negative feelings positively, and so a big part of their job is looking for ways to take anger, fears or problems and transform them into potential solutions. If mediators have a strong suit, it is turning "fighting words" into productive conversation.

> **EXAMPLE:** *A parent says something like: "He/She is such a flake that you can't expect him/her to follow through with any agreement." The mediator might help the parent to rephrase the objection as follows: "Do you mean that you don't trust him/her to follow through with agreements based on his/her past behavior? Can you describe the behavior that bothered you? What could he/she do to demonstrate trustworthiness in the future?"*

5.   Joint Versus Separate Meetings

Usually, the parents and mediator are in the same room. This approach is favored by most mediators because it helps the parents communicate with each other about their children—a skill they will need to work together in the future. If, however, the mediator feels that holding separate sessions may lead to an agreement, the mediator places the parents in separate rooms and shuttles back and forth.

Many mediations consist of a blend of same-room and separate-room sessions, depending on how high tension is, and whether the mediator perceives that a parent might be more forthcoming about an issue if the other parent isn't present. If there's a history of violence between the parents, the mediation may consist entirely of separate meetings between the mediator and each parent. This can help prevent intimidation of one parent by the other.

6.   Overcoming Impasses

Impasses, or seemingly unresolvable differences of opinion, need not bring mediation to a halt. Mediators have many "tricks of the trade" that they can and do use to help parents over the rough spots. Many of the strategies that were described in Chapter 4 have their parallel in mediation. Additional strategies are outlined below.

Some of the ways that parents can help each other, and the mediator, to understand what it would take for them to trust the other parent include:

- listing specific things the parent should do or not do, such as be on time or don't have the child deliver the child support check
- listing specific things the parent should say or not say, either during conversations between the parents, around the children or to friends or family members, and
- explain what "pushes their buttons" and how the other parent can avoid doing that

a.   Reframing Statements

When one parent makes a statement that seems to beg the other parent to respond aggressively, mediators can diffuse the tension by turning to the other parent and reframing the statement.

> **PARENT SAYS:** *If that is the way you are going to treat me, then you can just forget about seeing the kids for half of the*

summer—we can just stick to the alternating weekend schedule all year long!

MEDIATOR RESPONDS: *It seems that _____ (parent's name) has a difficult time feeling cooperative about finding ways to expand the amount of time that you and the children spend together when you make statements such as _____. Are there any other ways you could get that point across without it leading to conflict?*

b. Focusing the Discussion on the Children

When the level of tension rises, mediators can try to diffuse it by asking the parents to focus less on themselves and more on their children's best interests.

> **EXAMPLE:** *Matthew and Brenda are arguing heatedly over which home the children will live in during the school year. The mediator asks each parent to describe the school-age child's interests, attachment to friends, activities and special needs. The mediator then suggests that the parents analyze the relative advantages of each school and choose a residence that provides access to the school which best meets the children's needs.*

c. Insisting on Clarity

If a parent makes blanket statements about the other (such as, "He/she can't be trusted!"), the mediator can insist that this parent describe the events which led to a lack of trust, and ask what that parent could do to demonstrate trustworthiness in the future.

d. Balancing the Power

Sometimes an impasse is the result of a power imbalance between the parents. The power imbalance may be for any number of reasons, but is often evident when one parent:

- is more articulate than the other
- has traditionally dominated the other in making decisions
- has more experience in caring for the children, or
- has been violent, or has threatened to do harm to the parent, the children, friends or other family members or a family pet.

A mediator confronted with a power imbalance will try to "level the playing field" by:

- moderating one parent's dominating style and boosting the other parent's self-confidence
- allowing both parents equal time to speak, and

- insisting that parents take the time to be specific about their concerns and their proposals for the future.

Sometimes, the best way to balance power is to get outside help. A parent feeling at a disadvantage might turn to a counselor to improve self-esteem, consult a lawyer to understand his or her rights, speak with a child development specialist to understand the children's best interests or consult someone trained in domestic violence or child abuse to understand the impact of these events on all parties.

7. Recording the Agreement

When the parents reach agreement on a particular issue, the mediator takes careful notes. At the end of the sessions, the mediator will typically provide the parents with a summary of their entire agreement. It is each parent's responsibility to review that draft (with or without the help of an attorney) to make sure that it is accurate and complete.

E. Why Mediation Works in Very Difficult Cases

You may still be convinced that your conflicts with the other parent are unresolvable and that mediation will never work because:

- the conflicts are too intense
- each of you is entrenched in your position, or
- the conflicts involve domestic violence, child abuse or substance abuse.

First, understand that all family law mediators assume there is substantial conflict between you and the other parent, and are prepared to use their facilitation skills to diffuse the tension and to refocus you on determining and protecting your children's best interests. Be encouraged by the fact that disputing parents reach agreement in approximately 70% of all cases that go to mediation. To understand how serious conflict might be handled in mediation, consider a mediation between two divorcing parents, Joseph and Elizabeth.

FAMILY PROFILE
Joseph and Elizabeth are confronting the serious conflict, domestic violence, child abuse and substance abuse that were part of their marriage and separation.

MEDIATOR: *Now that we have agreed that there will be no interruptions while one parent is speaking, and that each of you will focus on the issues rather than on making derogatory remarks about the other, I'd like each of you to help me understand the situation from each of your points of view. First, I will need you to describe your children, and then I would like to hear how you propose to structure your parenting relationship to best meet your children's needs. Who would like to start?*

JOSEPH: *I'll start. Our kids have been through a lot. Joey and Mary are basically happy children, but this whole thing has been hard on them. Elizabeth's lifestyle has been so unstable. Her drinking problem ruined everything. First, she started hanging out at the bars, and had a few boyfriends. Then, she was upset at every little thing, and a few times she really took it out on the kids. Once, the kids ran away to a neighbor's house because they were afraid that she was really going to hurt them. I think that the kids should live with me and see their mother one afternoon a week until she can prove that she can take care of them.*

ELIZABETH: *My drinking! Big Joe has been an alcoholic ever since I've known him! When I wanted to separate, he beat me in front of the kids. That's when I knew for sure that I couldn't live with him any more. Now, I have my own life, and no one to beat me, and I want them to live with me. I may have had my problems in the past, but that's all over now. I'm going back to school to get myself to a point where I can earn a good living and support myself and my kids. Pretty soon, I'll be able to afford my own place. He can be the one to see the kids one afternoon a week. The kids have told me that they want to live with me, and I said they could.*

MEDIATOR: *Okay. It sounds as though both you and your children have been through some tough times and have been dealing with some difficult issues. What do each of you think would be important for your children as you make plans for the future?*

JOSEPH: *For the future? Well, I suppose that the most important thing is to make sure that the children aren't around Elizabeth or her friends when they are drinking and partying. They do miss her, I know that, but I just don't know how I can trust her to take care of them given the way she is behaving.*

ELIZABETH: *I agree that they shouldn't be around in the wrong situations, especially the violence. I'd like to find some way that we could be sure that they'd be safe and cared for in both homes.*

As this mediation progressed, the mediator helped the parents explore the issues that they had raised, and began looking for available resolution options. After some discussion, Joseph and Elizabeth disclosed that they had never tried to get help with substance abuse, domestic violence or parenting skills, but that each was willing to try if the other agreed to do the same.

Elizabeth conceded that while Joseph might benefit by learning new parenting techniques for disciplining the children, he had never beaten or abused them in any way. Both Joseph and Elizabeth agreed that her few episodes of "taking it out on the children" happened after Joseph had beaten her during the separation and were not part of her normal parenting style. Neither parent feared for the children's safety while they were in either parent's care, but Joseph felt strongly that Elizabeth's new friends and frequent partying created an unhealthy environment for the children.

Joseph and Elizabeth acknowledged that they did not want their children exposed to the violence, alcohol, partying or anger that they had experienced in the past. Elizabeth acknowledged that although she had come a long way in establishing a new life for herself, she still had some work to do before she would feel confident about caring for the children for more than short periods of time. Joseph agreed that he needed to get help in learning how to control his anger, but both agreed that for the moment at least, he was probably better able to care for the children for longer periods of time. Both parents planned to remain in the same community.

MEDIATOR: *To recap what you have decided so far, you would like to make a temporary agreement that will carry you through the balance of the school year. Each of you agrees to meet together again at the start of the summer vacation to review this agreement and to negotiate any necessary changes. Either of you may request mediation for your next meeting, but it is not required.*

Here is the agreement as I understand it: Elizabeth and Joseph agree to seek independent counseling or other support to deal with alcohol abuse. Each of you will continue with this counseling or support until such time as both you and your counselors agree that you can handle these issues on your own. Joseph agrees to seek counseling and support for dealing with anger. He will continue with this counseling until he and the counselor agree that he no longer needs this assistance. When his counseling has concluded, his counselor will write a letter to Elizabeth explaining the general issues covered in the counseling and that those issues have been dealt with or resolved. The children will be offered a chance to talk to a counselor, and may choose to continue counseling if they so desire. Both parents agree to identify at least one adult that the children can contact if they ever fear for their safety, or are concerned that their parent is too inebriated to provide adequate care. Neither child will be punished for contacting this "safe" adult— even if they misjudge the situation.

The children will live with Joseph during the week, and with Elizabeth two weekends out of the month. Elizabeth will arrange to take the children after school at least one afternoon a week, and will return them to Joseph's home by 7:00 p.m. Joseph will call Elizabeth each Monday evening between 4 and 6 p.m. to arrange for her midweek time with the children and a weekend visit, if appropriate, and to discuss the children's activities so that she can decide whether she will attend or otherwise participate. Each parent will be responsible for handling day-to-day decisions for the children when they are the primary caretakers, and each agrees to consult the other if important decisions are needed, and there is some lead time before the decision must be made. In the event of an emergency, either parent may seek whatever emergency attention is required, and will inform the other parent of the steps taken at the earliest practical time thereafter.

F.   What Mediators Don't Do

Although some courts will require mediators to make recommendations regarding how a custody or visitation dispute ought to be resolved when the parents can't agree (in California, especially), most mediators expect that only the parents can decide what kind of parenting plan they will accept. A mediator's sole mission is to help you and the other parent build your own agreement about how you will meet your children's needs. Sometimes, you may want to give in and have

someone else decide an issue for you. To get an outsider to make these decisions, however, you must choose a forum other than mediation. This usually means an expensive and divisive court hearing.

Mediators can offer general information, but they don't provide legal advice or counseling—even when they are also attorneys or mental health professionals. Legal advice can be offered by an attorney to only one parent, so each parent needs his or her own attorney. This is because each parent has his or her own separate legal interests, and one attorney cannot counsel a separating or divorcing couple on what is legally best for each of them.

If parents want to know what their legal rights are, they will have to consult with a good self-help law reference, do some legal research in a law library or pay for a consultation with an attorney.

 BE CAREFUL ABOUT TURNING YOUR CASE OVER TO A LAWYER

While each spouse can often benefit from talking to an attorney for an hour or two to get some advice and information, once one spouse is represented, the other spouse usually finds it necessary to also obtain representation. Once two attorneys are involved in the case, you run a high risk of a costly and adversarial process.

G. Choosing Between Court-Ordered and Private Mediation

Increasingly, parents cannot simply ask the court to resolve their custody or visitation dispute. Instead, a court orders a custody or visitation dispute to be mediated. Most states authorize, but don't require, their courts to order mediation. But a few states, including California, require it.

STATES IN WHICH A COURT MAY ORDER MEDIATION IN A CUSTODY OR VISITATION DISPUTE

Alabama	Kentucky	North Dakota
Alaska	Louisiana	Ohio
Arizona	Maine	Oregon
California	Maryland	Pennsylvania
Colorado	Michigan	Rhode Island
Connecticut	Minnesota	South Carolina
Delaware	Mississippi	South Dakota
District of Columbia	Missouri	Texas
Florida	Montana	Utah
Idaho	Nevada	Virginia
Illinois	New Jersey	Washington
Indiana	New Mexico	West Virginia
Iowa	North Carolina	Wisconsin
Kansas		

If you live in a state that authorizes or requires mediation, you have a choice. You can present the dispute to the court and accept what mediation the court orders, or hire a private mediator to help you reach agreement, thereby avoiding going to court in the first place.

The advantage to court-ordered mediation is that it is likely to be free or nominally priced. Private mediators, on the other hand, must earn a living and will probably charge a significantly higher fee. The advantages to using a private mediator, however, are many:

- You can shop for a mediator who suits both parents.
- You will have greater flexibility in scheduling.
- You can take as much time as you can afford.
- You can focus your full attention on the mediation without worrying about what the mediator will recommend to the court. (See Section H, below.)

As a general rule, if you are using mediation as a backup to negotiating your own parenting plan in Chapter 5, you will most likely want to use a private mediator. This is because most court mediation services are designed to settle only the basic custody and visitation questions that arise during a divorce or modification request, rather than to help parents draft a detailed parenting agreement.

If you want to first try court-ordered mediation and you live in a state where it is available, you must first file the appropriate legal papers setting out your dispute and asking

that it be resolved by the court. (See Chapter 13 for how to find an attorney or paralegal to help you do this.) You will then be informed of your requirement to participate in mediation, and may even be given a person to contact, or a date and time for your mediation hearing.

Mediators in court-based programs generally have a mental health, social service or probation department background. They are usually trained in the art and science of facilitating negotiations, and have general knowledge of family law and the principles of child development.

Court-appointed mediators are often limited to spending from one to six hours on any one case, depending on their caseload. Whenever possible, court-appointed mediators try to help parents find areas of agreement, and report that agreement to the court. If the parents are unable to reach an agreement through mediation, however, the court may ask the mediator, or a separate custody evaluator (see Section I, below), to assess the family's situation and make a recommendation about how the custody and visitation issues should be decided. When this happens, the mediator's or evaluator's recommendations are often the most important factor influencing the court's decision.

For more information about court-ordered mediation and evaluation, read Sections H and I. If you want more information about private mediation, skip ahead to Section J.

H. When the Mediator Makes a Recommendation to the Court

Most states that authorize court-ordered mediation do not ask the mediator to file a recommendation regarding custody or visitation with the court in the event the parents can't reach agreement. Instead, the court will make its own decision, perhaps based on an independent evaluation that the court orders to be conducted.

Alaska, California and Delaware are exceptions to this rule. In these states, judges may ask their court-appointed mediators to make a recommendation in the absence of an agreement between the parents. Regardless of your state, if you use court-ordered mediation, ask the mediator whether he or she will make a recommendation to the court if you and the other parent fail to reach agreement.

If your mediator will make a recommendation to the court, your strategy and focus during mediation will change. In this setting, you have two audiences—the other parent and the mediator who can influence a later court proceeding. Not only must you try to reach an agreement with the other parent, but also you must try to make a favorable impression on the mediator. Many mediators are impressed by parents who demonstrate the following qualities:

- a primary concern for understanding and protecting their children's best interests
- a willingness to consider a variety of settlement options, and
- a desire to facilitate contact between the children and their other parent.

To prepare for mediation that involves the possibility of a recommendation to the court by the mediator, you will want to research the factors your mediator will use in reaching a decision about what to recommend to the court and how the mediator's report will be treated by the court. You can get this information by talking to a person in the mediation program or by asking a knowledgeable attorney. (See Chapter 13.)

I.   Custody Evaluations

Many states allow judges to appoint a custody evaluator if the parents cannot reach an agreement on their own or through mediation. You may or may not be charged for this service. The evaluator, generally a mental health professional, spends time with the children and the parents to understand how the family currently functions, and to gain insights about what future arrangements might be in the children's best interests. Custody evaluations are often ordered when the parents disagree about custody and visitation, and:

- there is a history of domestic violence
- there is a history of child abuse or neglect
- there are allegations of substance abuse, or
- someone other than the biological or adoptive parents should perhaps be granted custody or visitation.

If an evaluation is conducted in your case, the evaluator will consider whether each parent has:

- a primary concern for understanding and protecting the children's best interests
- a willingness to consider a variety of settlement options, and
- a desire to facilitate contact between the children and the other parent.

As a general rule, a judge who orders an evaluation is very likely to adopt the evaluator's recommendation.

J.   Selecting a Mediator

As mentioned, mediators generally fall into two groups: court-connected and private practice.

1.   Court-Connected Mediators

If your state requires mediation whenever parents dispute custody and visitation issues, then the court will have a list of mediators or an in-house mediation program. You will have little, if any, choice over who actually conducts your mediation. If you need help in finding your local family conciliation or mediation court service, you can contact the court, ask an attorney or paralegal or contact one of the organizations listed in Chapter 13.

2.   Private Mediators

If you have a choice of mediators, because either the court gives you a choice or you are seeking private mediation, narrow your list of potential mediators to two or three candidates, and have each parent interview them. Ideally, the person you should choose is the one you agree is most likely to:

- be neutral—he or she has no preconceived ideas about how you should decide custody and visitation issues
- have expertise—he or she has had training and experience in dealing with custody and visitation issues
- focus on children—he or she understands general child development principles and knows how to identify children's interests, and
- have facilitation skills—he or she knows how to structure a mediation session so that each parent is heard and conflict is addressed and diffused, and he or she can assist you in overcoming impasses and planning for the long term.

When interviewing a mediator, you might ask questions such as:

- *What kind of training have you had?*
- *What subjects or skills did your training emphasize?*
- *How much experience have you had in working with individuals or families going through a divorce or separation?*
- *How much do you know about childhood development?*

- *How well versed are you in the effects of divorce and separation on children?*
- *Do you have any biases about how parenting issues should be settled, such as favoring custody with the mother or joint custody?*
- *What is your fee?*
- *How long do you think our mediation will take?*
- *What can I do to make mediation more productive?*

Although you may feel awkard in asking these questions, you should be able to get a good sense of whether you can trust the mediator by simply monitoring your reaction to the answers the mediator provides. That is, the answers themselves are not as important as how you feel about the mediators.

3. Finding a Private Mediator

If you need help in finding your local family conciliation or mediation court service, you can contact the court, ask an attorney or paralegal or contact the Association of Family and Conciliation Courts. The AFCC can be reached as follows:

> Association of Family and Conciliation Courts
> 329 West Wilson
> Madison, WI 53703-3612
> Voice: 608-251-4001
> FAX: 608-251-2231

If you want to find a mediator in private practice, you can check your telephone directory under "Mediation" or "Divorce Assistance," or you can contact:

- a community meditation program
- the court
- a paralegal
- a legal forms preparation service
- a public mental health agency, or
- the local Bar Association.

If none of these efforts generate a sufficient list of mediators, you can contact one of the following national organizations for a referral in your area:

- Conflict Resolution Center, Inc. publishes a directory of all kinds of ADR (Alternative or Appropriate Dispute Resolution) service providers. They can provide a list of mediators in your area and are available as follows:

> Conflict Resolution Center, Inc.
> 2205 E. Carson Street
> Pittsburgh, PA 15203-2107

> Voice: 412-481-5559
> FAX: 412-481-5601
> email: crcii@igc.apc.org

- The Academy of Family Mediators has approximately 2,000 members and requires that members meet certain basic training standards and complete a certain amount of continuing education each year. The Academy will give you a list of their members in your area and can be contacted as follows:

> Academy of Family Mediators
> 5 Militia Drive
> Lexington, MA 02421
> Voice: 781-674-2663
> Fax: 781-674-2690
> email: afmoffice@igc.apc.org

- The Society of Professionals In Dispute Resolution (SPIDR) is an association of all kinds of ADR service providers, including family and custody mediators throughout the country. They have chapters in each state and can give you a list of providers in your area. You can reach SPIDR through your state's local chapter (consult a telephone directory) or by contacting the national headquarters at:

> Society of Professionals In Dispute Resolution
> 1527 New Hampshire Ave., NW
> Washington, DC 20036
> Voice: 202-667-9700
> FAX: 202-265-1968

- The American Arbitration Association has begun developing its own panels of mediators. They have local area offices in most states (consult your telephone directory) and will give you local area information about their mediation services, or you can reach the national headquarters as follows:

> American Arbitration Association
> 335 Madison Ave. 10F
> New York, NY 10017-4605
> Voice: 212-716-5800
> FAX: 212-716-5905

K. Preparing for Mediation

To prepare for mediation, complete the worksheets in Chapter 3. By doing so, you and the other parent will have written down your individual views on your children and separate parenting, and will have some idea of the issues to be addressed during mediation. These worksheets can provide your mediator with a wealth of information.

Prior to your first mediation session, you should ask your court-appointed or private mediator about the availability of:

- informational brochures explaining the mediation process
- informational classes or video tapes on mediation or custody disputes, or
- materials that might be available in your public library to help you prepare for mediation. (Chapter 13 has titles of books or articles that might be helpful.)

As you prepare for mediation, keep in mind the following five points:

1. **Focus on your children.** The best preparation for mediation is to think about how you can meet your children's needs for high-quality care and meaningful ongoing relationships with both parents. This step is especially important if your mediation is with a court-appointed mediator who will make a recommendation to the court if you and the other parent can't agree. (See Section H, above.) You will want the mediator to know that your positions reflect your children's—not your own—needs and interests.

2. **Minimize conflict.** Your ability to work with the other parent with a minimum of conflict is crucial to a successful separate parenting relationship. Ongoing conflict between parents can be one of the most destructive forces in a child's life. In particular, explore ways to minimize the conflict by minimizing the contact you have, while maintaining the best possible relationship with your children. Issues to focus on in Chapter 5 are:

   - 11, Making Decisions
   - 14, Exchanging Information
   - 15, Where Our Children Will Live
   - 18, Maintaining Contact When the Children Are With the Other Parent
   - 25, Special Occasions and Family Events, and
   - 29, Improving Transition Times.

3. **Handle your anger.** Angry feelings and poor communication are common when parents separate or divorce. For some parents, the anger is so intense that they will go to great lengths to avoid reaching any agreement. Others will take great pains to make sure that their agreement inflicts humiliation, loss or significant

inconvenience on the other parent. If this situation continues over time, you may need professional help to put your feelings into perspective so that you can focus on making decisions for your children.

If you and the other parent cannot make these decisions on your own, through mediation or with the help of a counselor or attorneys, resolution will probably come via a court order. This is likely to cost a considerable amount of time, money and grief for everyone involved.

4. **Be positive.** Positive thinking reflects confidence in yourself, both in what you want to achieve and in your determination to find an acceptable solution. For some, this attitude comes naturally. For others, it requires a commitment to sort out their own thoughts and feelings so that they are certain of what they want. In either case, take a deep breath, put your "best foot forward" and see what happens!

5. **Be informed.** If you want to know your legal rights and obligations in a separation or divorce, you can consult with an attorney or hire one to represent you. (Various attorney-client relationships are described in Section M2, below.)

L. If You Can't Reach an Agreement

If you cannot reach an agreement resolving all parenting issues, you can:

- continue discussions on your own
- schedule further mediation sessions
- seek an independent evaluation and recommendation
- seek counseling
- submit the matter to arbitration, or
- litigate the issues in court.

M. Alternatives to Mediation

Many parents, attorneys and courts are confused about how mediation differs from counseling, attorney advocacy or arbitration. Following are some of the characteristics of each process. As you will see, counseling, legal advocacy and arbitration can be complementary to, but are fundamentally different from, mediation.

1. Counseling

The focus in counseling or other forms of therapy is on helping one or both parents explore, understand and resolve the personal and emotional aspects of a situation. Many parents use counseling to reduce or remove the anger, jealousy, bitterness and other feelings they have about the separation or divorce. This can help improve the working relationship with the other parent. In short, counseling explores "inner" space while mediation helps parents develop detailed plans for how they will parent separately.

Occasionally, a counselor who has worked with one or both parents may then attempt to mediate the parenting disputes. This practice is problematic. During therapy, patients disclose their thoughts, feelings and motivations to the therapist. Having this information makes it difficult, if not impossible, for the counselor to be a truly neutral facilitator.

2. Attorney Representation

Although many parents consider that divorce and attorneys go hand in hand, recent studies show that in nearly one-half of all divorces, at least one party is proceeding without a lawyer. Some go it alone because of the high cost of legal representation. Others choose to represent themselves to retain full control over their case. When parents complain about involving attorneys, it is usually because they feel that they have lost too much control over their cases, the decisions and the costs of finding a resolution.

You can use an attorney in one of two ways. First, an attorney can be a resource for legal information and ideas about how the law might affect your decisions. Attorneys can also negotiate on your behalf, examine your rights, represent your interests or advocate your position in court or during arbitration. (Arbitration is covered in Section 3, below.)

Lawyers, without representing either party, can serve as mediators. If a lawyer represents either parent, however, the lawyer must advocate for that parent. The lawyer can work to facilitate negotiations between the parents, but the lawyer cannot serve as a neutral mediator.

3. Arbitration

The process and results of arbitration are very similar to a court case, but less formal. You and the other parent (or, more likely, your attorneys) present your positions and requests for particular decisions to the arbitrator, who decides the dispute. Most parents choose to be represented by an attorney during arbitration.

There are two types of arbitration:
- **Binding arbitration** means you cannot appeal the arbitrator's decision to a court, unless you prove that the arbitrator abused the process.
- **Nonbinding arbitration** means that you can appeal the arbitrator's decision to a court, but may have to pay the other parent's court costs if you do not get a better result in court than you did in arbitration.

Only a few states specifically offer arbitration as an acceptable dispute resolution method in custody and visitation cases. (Chapter 12, Section C, contains a list of states that permit, prohibit or are silent on the subject of arbitrating custody and visitation disputes.)

a. Choosing an Arbitrator

In almost all cases, parents use a single arbitrator to settle their differences, and the arbitrator is generally an attorney. Occasionally, the arbitrator will be a mental health professional, but generally this happens only when the issues in dispute involve an assessment of the children's mental health. (More information about arbitrators is in Chapter 13.)

b. Arbitration Shouldn't Rise to a Court Trial

One of the dangers of arbitration is that it can turn into a miniature court trial. When this happens, arbitration becomes just as time-consuming and costly as a court trial, and the proceedings become just as adversarial. Discovery, the process by which each side finds out the other's evidence, can be just as extensive for arbitration as for a court trial.

One way to keep arbitration from turning into a court trial is to set limits in advance. For example, the parents can agree to share information rather than conduct extensive discovery. ■

CHAPTER

8

Dealing With Changes in Your Existing Agreements

Change is an almost inevitable part of any separate parenting arrangement. Any number of things might trigger a need for you to initiate, or respond to, requests for changes in your existing parenting agreement. First, because your children keep growing and changing, their needs, interests and activities will do so as well. Next, you and the other parent are both, presumably, moving on with your separate adult lives. New partners, new jobs or new homes can all mean changes—to a greater or lesser degree—in your existing arrangements.

Change—any change—offers both good news and bad news. The good news is that change provides both you and the other parent with an opportunity to either temper, or eliminate, things which the parents or children don't like in the existing arrangement. The bad news is that some of the things which one or more of you do like may also come up for discussion. All change brings a mixture of good and bad effects, and it takes a while to assimilate those changes— even if the overall effect is for the best. In short, change is difficult, and most people resist it—especially if they did not initiate the process.

For many, experience is a great teacher. While experience shows us what works and what doesn't, most of us have a limited range of individual experiences with which to generate new ideas for solving persistent problems. This book is intended to help you, regardless of whether this is your first parenting agreement. This chapter addresses the special concerns of parents who are faced with the need to make changes in their existing parenting agreements.

A. Why Changes Are Necessary—And What You Can Do About Them

Children are a study in transformation! Just when you have figured out how to handle one developmental stage, your child is on to the next one. If you are a diligent consumer of child development or parenting skills books, you may suspect that your child gets up in the middle of the night to read ahead and plan especially challenging "curves" which he or she can throw your way! As your child ages, and your boy or girl enters puberty, you may feel as though the steady rhythm of responding to developmental changes that surface every month or two has been replaced by a roller-coaster ride in which moods, interests and behavior change almost daily (or even hourly!). While consistency in your basic parenting style and principles is important, it is equally important that you recognize and fine tune that style to keep pace with your child's changing world.

Just as children change, so do their relationships with their parents. Children reach out to their parents differently throughout their various ages and stages, leaning toward one or the other according to their needs and wishes, and that parent's availability at a particular time. The routine and structure which your child demanded from you when he or she was younger may, predictably, give rise to a battle cry for "freedom from oppression" as he or she approaches puberty. "Daddy's little girl" may become uncomfortable with his way of doing things as she gets older, and prefer to live with her mother as she becomes a woman. "Mommy's little boy" may not accept her as an authority figure as he grows older, and thus he may prefer the company of his father as he tries to define himself as a man. Alternatively, mother/daughter and father/son relationships which once worked beautifully may now lead to constant conflict whose only solution appears to be a change in focus to the other parent.

Children, however, aren't the only ones who change. Parents change, too, especially as they reformulate their lives following a separation or divorce. Changes in marital status often mean changes in employment, friends, activities and residence—to say nothing of the changes in personal values, priorities and lifestyle. For some, being single again means that all elements of their lives are subject to review and possible change. For others, it means that they are now free to pursue the new life which they have planned for themselves for a long time.

Regardless of your particular circumstances, moving on with your life (whether it be immediately following the separation or divorce or some years later) can mean physically moving, finding new partners, creating or blending new families, seeking new employment, dealing with new money pressures and facing new challenges as you try to juggle your own life while continuing to meet your children's needs.

Given these seemingly endless opportunities to confront change, what's a parent to do? How can you balance your needs and desires with those of your children? The other parent? Your extended family? Once again, it pays to go back to the basics. Separation and divorce are solutions to adult problems. While it is vitally important for children that their parents be happy, financially stable, safe and secure, it is also important that, to the greatest possible extent, they have significant and ongoing relationships with both of their parents, have some sense of stability in their living arrangements, school and social settings, and be relatively free to concentrate on the important tasks of childhood and growing up. Your job, then, as you try to balance all of these various needs, wants and interests is to try to find solutions that put your children's interests in the forefront while still meeting your own needs.

RELEVANT ISSUES IN CHAPTER 5

Issue	Number
Making Decisions	11
Resolving Disputes When Making Decisions Together	12
Where Our Children Will Live	15
Maintaining Contact When the Children Are With the Other Parent	18
Moving	21
If Our Homes Are Far Apart	22
Holidays	23
Vacations	24
Special Occasions and Family Events	25
Transporting the Children	28
Treating Each Child as an Individual	30
Consistency in Raising Children	32
Undermining the Parent/Child Relationship	34
When Nonrelatives Live in the Home	37
When Parents Have New Partners	38

B. When You Are the One Initiating Change

When you are the one initiating change, you are (for a time at least) in the driver's seat. You are the one who first defines the issues, and you have the first opportunity to describe your preferred solutions. This somewhat enviable position, however, is not without its drawbacks. Once you put the subject of change on the table for discussion, you take the risk that you may not be completely satisfied with the final result.

Remember that for most of us, change is scary and that our "knee-jerk" reaction to this prospect is often an emphatic "NO!" The way you present the other parent with your request for changes is one important key to successfully achieving your objectives. The other critical factor is an understanding that your wishes are not the only ones to

be considered, and that productive and lasting changes allow everyone to gain at least something of what they want in the final outcome.

Before you make any formal proposal for change, consider the following:

- why the changes are necessary
- what you want to accomplish by making the changes
- who will be affected by these changes
- how each person will be affected by these changes
- what objections might be raised, and
- how you can respond to each of those objections.

After you have carefully thought through each of the points listed above, consider how you might best present your requests. For example, if you are the Mom and want the children to come and live with you during the school year, you may decide that:

- the change of residence is necessary because the children (ages 10, 12 and 14) say they want it
- you want to respond to the children's wishes to the greatest possible extent, and to provide more parent involvement and "follow-through" for their school-related activities
- the change in residence will be a positive change for you (because you will be able to get more involved with each child's classroom), for the children (because they will have the benefit of more parent involvement in school-related activities), for their father (because he will be able to focus on his work without worrying about short-changing the kids) and for their paternal grandparents (because they will not lose their relationship with the children)
- the father and paternal grandparents are sure to object, because they do not want to lose any of the influence which they currently have over the children's daily lives
- the list of objections which would be likely to arise include: Dad is feeling that the children are too young to have the deciding vote on this issue; the children are just complaining because they dislike the routine in his home and prefer the comparative freedom with you; and, there is no compelling reason to initiate a change since everything seems to be going well so far
- …you will answer these objections by pointing out that: the children should have an increasingly decisive voice in the custody and visitation arrangements; you want a more substantial role in their everyday lives

(including the discipline that is part of the bargain); the children have nothing to lose and everything to gain by being raised in both parents' homes; your school system offers more opportunities than the one they are attending now; the children will be able to continue their visits with their paternal grandparents during their traditional one-week vacation together each summer; and, the children will gain significant time with their maternal grandparents.

While this kind of preparation is good, and gets you a long way down the road toward an agreement, it doesn't guarantee success. What it does offer is a structure for organizing your thoughts, anticipating conflict and creating a setting within which the conflicts that do arise can be resolved. (To take this process further, consult Chapter 4, *How to Negotiate a Parenting Agreement.*)

C. When You Are the One Responding to a Request for Change

For many of us, the maxim "if it ain't broke, don't fix it" works well. Therefore, few of us react well when told that something needs to be fixed when we consider it to be working just fine. For some, change is so scary that it can even feel like a kind of assault when proposed by others. Parents who are notified that the other parent wants to make changes in an existing parenting arrangement commonly experience disillusionment, frustration and anger. Requests for changes in an existing parenting arrangement may even dredge up many of the thoughts, feelings and animosities associated with the marriage and its demise. This is especially true if the parent who feels that the existing arrangements are working well either did not initiate the divorce, or initiated the divorce after discovering his or her partner's infidelity.

While most requests for modification are initially considered to be unwelcome, they do happen, must be dealt with and may well be successful—even over your objections. The keys to your success in dealing with this situation are to curb your knee-jerk reactions, consider carefully and objectively what might be motivating the request and view this request as an opportunity to entertain discussion and accomplish changes which serve your children's best interests even better!

When presented with a request for modification of an existing custody and visitation agreement (or after being served with a court document which communicates this same information), you will need to step back, take a deep breath and develop as objective a perspective as possible on the following:

- why the changes are considered necessary by the other parent
- what the other parent wants to accomplish by making the changes
- who will be affected by these changes
- how each person will be affected by these changes
- what your, and other, objections to the proposed changes might be, and
- how you can respond to both the reasoning behind the proposed changes, as well as to the objections which are likely to be raised by the other parent to your position.

If we pursue the example cited in section B, above, and you are Dad, your response to Mom's position and proposals may well go something like this:

- Certainly the children should have an increasing level of input into the custody and visitation arrangements as they get older, the only question being, are 14-year-olds (let alone 12- and 10-year-olds) capable of making this kind of decision?
- You realize that Mom wants more involvement with the children, but that will be difficult given the distance between your homes—unless, of course, Mom wants to increase the number of calls, letters, care packages and trips out to see the kids.
- The ripple-effect of a change of this magnitude is significant. You recognize that the children don't like sticking to a routine at your home, but the allure of Mom's home would soon fade once she began imposing order, too. You are more than willing to find all sorts of ways in which maternal Grandma and Grandpa can be included in the kid's lives at your house.
- You counterpropose that making a change now is premature, especially with the 10-year-old just about to complete elementary school. Perhaps a change of custody in a year, when the 10-year-old would already be switching schools, would be preferable.

Again, this is only the start of a fairly lengthy dialogue, but in it and the approach are the seeds of an agreement. For more ideas about how to take this kind of discussion further, consult Chapter 4, *How to Negotiate a Parenting Agreement.*

D. When Tensions Are Running High

As with tension under any other set of circumstances, the first thing to do is to recognize its legitimate role in alerting you to a problem—then find ways to diffuse that tension. Perhaps the hardest, but most important, thing you can do in this particular circumstance is find a way to focus only on how this dispute relates to your children's best interests. In some cases, your soul-searching on this point will tell you that you must hold to your original position and your existing agreement "come Hell or high water." In many other situations, you will discover that at least some of the proposed changes have merit, and that you will have to find a way to get over your own hurt in learning to accommodate these changes. You will find a detailed discussion on de-escalating conflict in Chapter 4.

RELEVANT ISSUES IN CHAPTER 5

Issue	Number
Making Decisions	11
Resolving Disputes When Making Decisions Together	12
If Extended Family Members or Close Friends Are Fueling the Dispute	13
Separating the Adult Relationship Issues From Parenting Issues	40

E. What to Do After You Negotiate the Changes

RECORD THEM, RECORD THEM, RECORD THEM!

At a minimum, you and the other parent should record your new agreements on the parenting agreement form, which you will find in the appendix of the book. If you have already received a court order confirming your original arrangements, you should seek a modification of the order to reflect whatever changes you have negotiated.

The greatest problems you will confront when you do not have a court order that reflects your current agreement arise when an existing—and outdated—order is enforced in a moment of pique. This kind of conflict will not only wreak havoc on your existing, or future, positive relationship with the other parent, but it can also cause your children untold grief in trying to figure out what is happening to them and why.

RELEVANT ISSUES IN CHAPTER 5

Issue	Number
Making Changes	41
Making Substantive Changes to This Agreement	42
Explaining the Agreement to Your Children	43

CHAPTER

9

Understanding Your Children's Needs

Understanding and meeting your children's needs following a separation or divorce can be challenging, but it is certainly not impossible. To help you meet the challenge, this chapter includes the following:

- strategies for dealing with children of all ages and both sexes
- strategies for dealing with children at different ages and developmental stages (although your children may react differently at the ages and developmental stages described, the information may still help you to understand your children as time goes along), and
- strategies for dealing with children who have special needs.

The suggestions in this chapter refer to specific issue/option sets from Chapter 5 without duplicating the information contained in other parts of the book. Use the references to help you focus on your children.

A. Strategies for Your Children at Any Age

Children of all ages and both sexes usually share these three reactions to their parents' separation or divorce:

- they maintain a passionate desire to see their parents reunited
- they feel sad and angry, and
- they want their parents to stop fighting.

Therapist-researcher, Linda Bird Francke, author of *Growing Up Divorced* (Linden Press/Simon & Schuster, 1983), estimates that children need three years to get used to their parents' separation or divorce, and that the first year is the most difficult for them. During that time, children almost universally experience shock, depression, denial, anger, low self-esteem, shame and (especially among younger children) guilt—they think that they caused the divorce.

First and foremost, children need to know that their basic physical needs will be met. Despite the fact that in many households one parent provides considerably more child care than the other, most children feel cared for by both. A separation or divorce brings on feelings of loss, knowing that they will be cared for by only one parent at a time and fear that their needs won't be met.

Second, children want the conflict between their parents to lessen, if not end altogether. However difficult it may seem now, you and the other parent must find ways to work together without having your discussions deteriorate into arguments.

The seven strategies in this section suggest ways to reassure your children that they will continue to be loved and cared for. Each strategy identifies specific issue/option sets which apply in Chapter 5.

1. Reduce Conflict Between Parents

Ongoing conflict can be devastating for children of any age. Children burdened by ongoing conflict often have problems performing in school and relating to their friends, parents and other relatives. You will take an enormous amount of pressure off your children if you can work with the other parent without arguing regularly.

Managing conflict is difficult, but can be done. Chapter 4 suggests ways to manage conflict during your negotiations with the other parent. Chapter 13 has information on resources beyond the book which can help you understand, manage and resolve conflict.

RELEVANT ISSUES IN CHAPTER 5

Issue	Number
Making Decisions	11
Resolving Disputes When Making Decisions Together	12
Exchanging Information	14
Improving Transition Times	29
When Parenting Styles and Values Are Very Different	31
Disparaging Remarks	33
Undermining the Parent/Child Relationship	34
Denying Access to the Children	35

2. Help Children Maintain Good Relationships With Both Parents

Almost all children whose parents separate or divorce struggle at one time or another with how to be loyal to both parents. Some children have trouble showing that they love each parent equally. Others are pressured by one parent (directly or subtly) to love that parent more than the other. Parents who demand this of their children are putting them in an almost impossible situation. Dr. Isolina Ricci (*Mom's House, Dad's House*, Macmillan Publishing, 1980) offers an important insight into the tension that these feelings produce:

If we think of ourselves as part our mother and part our father, it may be easier to see how conflicting and frightening it can be to have one part inside of us hate the other part that is also inside.

To minimize any "loyalty" issues for your children, try to:

- balance the time that your children spend in each home
- be aware of what your children's lives are like in each home
- strengthen your children's relationship with each parent, and
- reduce your children's exposure to the conflict between you and the other parent.

RELEVANT ISSUES IN CHAPTER 5

Issue	Number
Exchanging Information	14
Where Our Children Will Live	15
Maintaining Contact When the Children Are With the Other Parent	18
Moving	21
If Our Homes Are Far Apart	22
Holidays	23
Vacations	24
Special Occasions and Family Events	25
Disparaging Remarks	33
Undermining the Parent/Child Relationship	34

3.　Establish a Sense of Family With Each Parent

It is common for both adults and children to worry about how parents and children will get along after the adults separate or divorce. Whether the parents remain single or have new partners, each parent must develop new ways to establish a consistent family environment for the children. Here are some suggestions that might work for you:

- establish a "normal" schedule with regular routines and special traditions that your children can share
- do not raise false hopes of reconciliation
- find a secure spot for your children to leave their things, and
- explore your new neighborhood with your children if you moved away from the family home.

RELEVANT ISSUES IN CHAPTER 5

Issue	Number
Resolving Disputes When Making Decisions Together	12
Maintaining Contact When the Children Are With the Other Parent	18
Improving Transition Times	29
When Parenting Styles and Values Are Very Different	31
Consistency in Raising Children	32
When Nonrelatives Live in the Home	37

4.　If a Parent Has a New Partner

Managing your life as a single parent will be quite challenging. It will be even more complex if you form a new relationship, especially when your children are living in your home.

Here are some ways to deal with a new partner:

Keep the relationship separate from your children until it becomes serious. Your children may develop a close attachment to your new partner and may have difficulty dealing with any break-up. One way to safeguard your children's feelings is to minimize contact between your new partner and your children. When your children and new partner do meet, keep it brief and casual until the relationship becomes serious. When your partner does stay over, be sure your children know there will be a guest at breakfast.

Be honest, but selective, in what you tell your children. Many parents are so pleased to have a new love interest that they are tempted to talk to their children as if they were adults. While your children may be flattered if you take them into your confidence, information about adult relationships can be overwhelming for children. For these reasons, openly acknowledge your new relationship and feelings when it becomes serious, but keep the details to yourself.

Decide what relationship your new partner will have with your children. If your relationship with a new partner becomes serious, you must consider what role your partner will have with your children. This subject will certainly be of interest to your children, and may cause some conflict between you and the other parent.

This decision may best be made after everyone involved is consulted. Among the questions you'll want to consider are your partner's role in:

- administering discipline
- providing child care

- sharing in household responsibilities
- participating in family events
- traveling on vacations, and
- making parenting decisions.

RELEVANT ISSUES IN CHAPTER 5

Issue	Number
Making Decisions	11
Resolving Disputes When Making Decisions Together	12
Special Occasions and Family Events	25
When Parenting Styles and Values Are Very Different	31
Consistency in Raising Children	32
Disparaging Remarks	33
Undermining the Parent/Child Relationship	34
When Nonrelatives Live in the Home	37

5. Keep Your Children From Growing Up Too Soon

Although everyone must assume new responsibilities after a separation or divorce, you must be careful not to overload your children. While most children are pleased to help when times get tough, some parents take this to an inappropriate extreme. For example, older children are sometimes asked to assume nearly all responsibilities for younger siblings, cooking and cleaning. Although you may not feel you have many options, your goal is to avoid turning your child into a full-time housekeeper and baby-sitter.

In addition, many parents experience intense emotional pressures from the changes that come after separation or divorce. The need to make more decisions, respond to your children's questions and support your children during their own adjustment period can leave you feeling overwhelmed. Although parents and children are natural sources of support for each other, parents should not rely heavily on their children for this support. Taking on the quasi-adult roles of confidante and comforter can cause serious psychological problems for your children later in life. Find another adult to confide in and relieve your own stress so you are ready and able to support your children.

You can address these concerns by including counseling or other emotional support in your parenting agreement, and by sharing more evenly the physical tasks of child-rearing.

RELEVANT ISSUES IN CHAPTER 5

Issue	Number
Psychiatric and Other Mental Health Care	2
Where Our Children Will Live	15
Undermining the Parent/Child Relationship	34
When a Parent Needs to Develop Parenting Skills	36

6. Help Children Who Are Having Difficulty Adjusting

Separation and divorce present difficulties for all children, but some have an unusually difficult time adjusting. Boys especially tend to become more aggressive, and girls often become depressed and withdrawn. No one expects children or parents to be happy with all aspects of a parenting arrangement; but children should be able to develop a generally positive attitude over time. If your children are having problems adjusting, you will need to intervene.

First, you need to know what's "normal" and what's not. Several resources can help you understand how children generally react to separation and divorce and how to recognize the symptoms of a truly troubled child.

Ask your librarian or public mental health department for a list of books, magazines and videos containing information on these issues. Three excellent books are:

- *Divorce and Your Child*, by Sonja Goldstein and Albert Solnit (Yale University Press, 1984)

- *How It Feels When Parents Divorce*, by Jill Krementz (Alfred A. Knopf, 1984), and
- *Mom's House, Dad's House*, by Isolina Ricci (Macmillan Publishing, 1980).

Chapter 13 and the bibliography include additional resources which might help you assess your children.

RELEVANT ISSUES IN CHAPTER 5

Issue	Number
Psychiatric and Other Mental Health Care	2
Religious Training	5
Driving and Owning a Car, Motorcycle or Off-Road Vehicle	7
Making Decisions	11
Exchanging Information	14
Domestic Violence, Child Abuse and Child Neglect	16
Alcohol or Drug Abuse	17
Maintaining Contact When the Children Are With the Other Parent	18
Reinvolving a Previously Absent Parent	19
Special Occasions and Family Events	25
Grandparents, Relatives and Important Friends	27
Improving Transition Times	29
When Parenting Styles and Values Are Very Different	31
Consistency in Raising Children	32
Disparaging Remarks	33
Undermining the Parent/Child Relationship	34
Denying Access to the Children	35
When a Parent Needs to Develop Parenting Skills	36
Explaining the Agreement to Your Children	43

7. Be Ready for Change

Parents commonly forget that their children grow up and perhaps will change dramatically over the years. When you negotiate your initial parenting agreement, you'll be tempted to assume that it will stand, unchanged, until your children reach adulthood. While it is possible that your first agreement will be your last, it's highly unlikely.

RELEVANT ISSUES IN CHAPTER 5

Issue	Number
Making Changes	41

B. Strategies for Your Children at Different Ages and Developmental Stages

Children seldom fall exactly into the age categories that psychiatrists, psychologists and other counselors use to describe them. Nevertheless, these categories are very useful because they describe the sequence of developmental changes most children follow. Furthermore, boys and girls may grow and develop somewhat differently, and these gender-related characteristics are noted as well.

Judith Wallerstein and Joan Kelly were the first researchers to systematically evaluate and document children's responses to divorce by age. Linda Bird Francke reaffirmed this research during interviews with 100 children of varying ages. In *Growing Up Divorced* (Linden Press/ Simon & Schuster, 1983), she concluded that:

- initially, both boys and girls experience high levels of stress and depression after the actual separation or divorce, and boys typically have more long-term adjustment problems following the separation or divorce
- girls whose fathers leave when they are very young and remain relatively uninvolved with the family are more likely than their counterparts whose fathers remain home to become sexually precocious
- single mothers often have more difficult relationships with their sons than they do with their daughters, and
- children between the ages of 9 and 15 have more difficulty handling a parent's remarriage than do children who are either younger or older.

1. Infants and Toddlers

Infants and children under the age of two must rely upon their parents and other care providers for almost all of their needs. Food, clothing, toilet training, entertainment, physical protection and emotional comfort are the most obvious.

In addition, children this age have fairly limited memory capabilities, and seldom understand that people and objects exist even though they cannot be seen and touched. Researchers know that children under two can form a number of relationships (or attachments) to their care providers, but suffer when there are too many differences in the way that care is provided and in the routines that are followed.

If your children are under two years old when you separate or divorce, consider the bird nesting option described in Issue 15, Where Our Children Will Live. If this isn't feasible, seriously consider designating one parent as the primary caretaker, while providing the other parent with frequent, if brief, visits.

If neither parent can provide the constant, demanding care required by very young children, you might turn to a relative or close friend to be your child's primary caretaker. Your children may feel somewhat insecure about what is happening, but it is preferable to your children receiving inconsistent care or being neglected.

2. Preschool Children

Preschoolers can, and do, accomplish some tasks on their own, but still rely heavily on care providers for most of their necessities. Children this age understand that people continue to exist even when they are not physically present. Because most preschoolers are used to viewing their parents as a unified team, separation from one often introduces a fear that the child will lose the other parent as well. Children this age can easily persuade themselves that the separation or divorce would not have happened if they had only behaved better, so you will need to pay attention and reassure them that this is not true.

Boys tend to have more trouble than girls dealing with the realities of a separation or divorce after their parents have parted company. Some speculate that this is because many parents provide their sons with minimal physical and emotional comfort. Parents may also expect their sons to get over their anger or pain—or at least hide them. These responses to sons may help your child handle a situation like a "little man," but are likely to lead to an inability to face and resolve painful emotional issues.

Children often formulate their sexual identities and preferences during this age period. For this reason, finding ways in which parents or other adults of both sexes can have a significant and ongoing relationship to your children is especially important.

As you plan for your preschooler's living arrangements, keep in mind the following:
- overnight visits can be started or increased at these ages
- parents should expand communication and cooperation between the households
- children should be encouraged to keep pictures of both parents at both homes
- children should have frequent contact with both parents, and
- parents need to explain their parenting agreement in terms that the children can easily understand.

RELEVANT ISSUES IN CHAPTER 5

Issue	Number
Psychiatric and Other Mental Health Care	2
Exchanging Information	14
Where Our Children Will Live	15
Maintaining Contact When the Children Are With the Other Parent	18
Reinvolving a Previously Absent Parent	19
Moving	21
If Our Homes Are Far Apart	22
Special Occasions and Family Events	25
Grandparents, Relatives and Important Friends	27
Treating Each Child as an Individual	30
Undermining the Parent/Child Relationship	34
Denying Access to the Children	35
When a Parent Needs to Develop Parenting Skills	36

3. Early Elementary School Children

Children in the early years of elementary school are moving into the larger world of relationships with friends and teachers, and so are better able than preschoolers to handle the changes that come with a separation or divorce. Preschoolers are still very closely tied to their parents, and separations from either parent are difficult to handle.

Early elementary school-aged children are generally fine with overnights, and can tolerate not seeing a parent for somewhat longer periods of time. Children in this age group, however, still have very strong wishes to see their parents get back together, and spend lots of time worrying that their behavior or misbehavior caused the separation or divorce. Children this age are keenly aware of how their parents are feeling, and often want to take care of each parent. For this reason, these children can become very skilled at hiding their worries so that they do not hurt their parents' feelings. Children this age may also be preoccupied with worries that they too will be left or "divorced," and will have no one to take of them. Professionals suggest that parents support these children by reminding them that separation and divorce is between adults and that each adult will continue to be a parent. Parents can also:

- create a calendar that allows the child to anticipate when he or she will spend time with each parent
- help children to choose and pack special books, toys or clothes he or she wants to take to the other parent's house
- establish a clear, frequent and regular schedule of visits
- set up or allow frequent telephone calls or other contact with an absent parent.

RELEVANT ISSUES IN CHAPTER 5

Issue	Number
Psychiatric and Other Mental Health Care	2
Education	3
Religious Training	5
Exchanging Information	14
Where Our Children Will Live	15
Maintaining Contact When the Children Are With the Other Parent	18
Reinvolving a Previously Absent Parent	19
Special Occasions and Family Events	25
Improving Transition Times	29
Treating Each Child as an Individual	30
When Parenting Styles and Values Are Very Different	31
Disparaging Remarks	33
Undermining the Parent/Child Relationship	34
Denying Access to the Children	35

4. Older Elementary School Children

Grade-schoolers are better able than younger children to deal with most parenting arrangements. They understand and can usually follow schedules in a parenting agreement, although transitions between homes can present a problem.

In general, calm children tend to handle the transitions better than irritable children.

Children in these middle years are busy forming their own identities and value systems, and lean heavily on their parents for guidance. Children need active participation by both parents in their daily lives, school and outside activities.

These children are also especially sensitive to both parents' feelings, and would do almost anything to avoid hurting either parent. As a result, some children are afraid to let their parents know if they are dissatisfied or angry. You may not know that your children are hurting unless you look hard. Here are some signs:

- inconsolable grief over their parents' breakup
- unhappiness, no matter where they are or what they are doing, and
- behavior that seems to be "too good to be true."

One ten-year-old who didn't want to hurt his parents, but was thoroughly unhappy with the arrangements, summed up all of his frustrations by saying, "I just wish I could grow up faster. It's better than being a kid."

Experts and parents alike recommend that you strive to achieve the following goals for separately parenting your elementary school-age children:

- tailor the schedule to meet your child's personality
- stick to the schedules you establish
- don't put children in the middle by asking them to carry messages to the other parent
- offer counseling or other emotional support, and
- support your children's participation in outside activities.

RELEVANT ISSUES IN CHAPTER 5

Issue	Number
Psychiatric and Other Mental Health Care	2
Education	3
Religious Training	5
Exchanging Information	14
Where Our Children Will Live	15
Maintaining Contact When the Children Are With the Other Parent	18
Reinvolving a Previously Absent Parent	19
Special Occasions and Family Events	25
Improving Transition Times	29
Treating Each Child as an Individual	30
When Parenting Styles and Values Are Very Different	31
Disparaging Remarks	33
Undermining the Parent/Child Relationship	34
Denying Access to the Children	35

5. Adolescents

Adolescence is a turbulent time for both boys and girls. In addition to the hormonal changes their bodies experience, adolescents increasingly become dependent on their peer group, have more activities independent of their parents and siblings and are trying to distinguish their values and attitudes from those of their parents.

A separation or divorce is difficult for most teens. As one 15-year-old said during mediation, "I wish that they (his parents) would just remember that they aren't the only ones going through this."

A teen's concerns can run the gamut. Some panic at the idea that they have to give their friends two phone numbers to call for social engagements. Others struggle with constant conflict with one parent and little or no contact with the other. The parenting arrangements that once worked may now be unrealistic given your teen's activities and preferences. Although adolescents are not yet legally capable of making all of their own decisions, parents should allow their teens more and more input into the decisions that shape the parenting agreement.

When you adjust your parenting agreement to meet your teen's interests and needs, consider:

- letting your teen decide where he or she wants to live

- strengthening your teen's relationship with one parent or another important adult if the teen and the other parent fight constantly
- involving your teen in identifying problems and developing solutions
- participating in parent-teen mediation, and
- guarding against forcing your teen(s) to grow up too soon.

RELEVANT ISSUES IN CHAPTER 5

Issue	Number
Education	3
Surname	4
Religious Training	5
Driving and Owning a Car, Motorcycle or Off-Road Vehicle	7
Military Service	8
Allowing Underage Marriage	9
Making Decisions	11
Where Our Children Will Live	15
Maintaining Contact When the Children Are With the Other Parent	18
Moving	21
If Our Homes Are Far Apart	22
Holidays	23
Vacations	24
Special Occasions and Family Events	25
Grandparents, Relatives and Important Friends	27
Treating Each Child as an Individual	30
Disparaging Remarks	33
Making Changes	41

C. Strategies for Children With Special Needs

Children with special educational, physical or emotional care needs require equally special consideration in your parenting agreement. Your needs for child care, ongoing medical or educational assessment and support will be substantial. Also, your agreement may have to stay in place longer than for other children. Rather than ending your parenting agreement when your children become adults or graduate from college, you may find that your separate parenting relationship lasts indefinitely.

As you consider each issue/option set in Chapter 5, you may have to add your own agreements to make sure you are meeting your child's needs. Here are some issue/option sets which may require your special attention, and some suggestions that go beyond what is in Chapter 5.

Issue 1: Medical, Dental and Vision Care

- Keep the number of health care providers down so there is consistency in your children's care.
- Any and all health care providers should be kept informed of your children's condition and progress.
- Be explicit about the kinds of ongoing assessment, therapy, medications or other treatment that may be necessary.
- Identify who will meet with doctors, therapists or other personnel to ensure that your children's ongoing care needs are met.

Issue 2: Psychiatric and Other Mental Health Care

- Plan how mental health support or assessment may be offered to your children.
- Plan how mental health or emotional support may be provided to other family members.

Issue 3: Education

- Be explicit about how any special education needs will be met.
- Identify who will be involved in meetings with teachers, administration or other school personnel to ensure that your children's ongoing educational needs are met.

Issue 10: Insurance

- Decide how your child's ongoing needs for health or other kinds of insurance will be met.
- Make sure that you incorporate your decisions into any agreements that provide for your children's financial future, such as a child support agreement.

Issue 11: Making Decisions

If your special-needs child will not be able to make his or her own decisions upon reaching legal adulthood, you may need to establish an adult guardianship and add language to that effect here.

Issue 15: Where Our Children Will Live

Because some special-needs children require intense, long-term care, consider including provisions which give the primary caretaker periodic breaks.

Issue 19: Reinvolving a Previously Absent Parent

A parent who has been uninvolved with a special-needs child because of the costs, time or special care required may need training, counseling or other support before providing any care.

Issue 20: Child Care

- Make sure the number of child care providers is kept to a minimum to provide consistency.
- Ensure that any child care providers are capable of caring for your special-needs children.

Issue 32: Consistency in Raising Children

- Make an effort to keep your expectations and standards for behavior consistent between both parents' homes.
- Make sure that any discipline is consistently applied in type and manner in both homes.

Issue 36: When a Parent Needs to Develop Parenting Skills

A parent who is not used to providing full-time care for a special-needs child may need training. ■

CHAPTER 10

Multiracial, Multicultural and International Families

Virtually all parents who separate or divorce experience conflict over some, if not many, child-rearing issues. Parents whose cultural, religious, ethnic or national identities differ often find that separate parenting presents even greater challenges. For example, you may have been attracted to your partner—at least in part—because of your cultural, religious, ethnic or national differences. These once-intriguing differences, however, may now be a source of conflict concerning your children.

Fortunately, diversity within a family need not be the source of unresolvable problems. Many parents find that by first acknowledging their different viewpoints on certain issues, they are able to address the following common concerns:

- accommodating differences in child-rearing practices
- encouraging the children to celebrate the traditions of both parents
- sorting out the role of power within the family
- accommodating religious differences
- working within the American legal system, and
- deciding if another country has authority over parenting (custody) issues.

A. Accommodating Differences in Child-Rearing Practices

In the United States, we have developed increasingly clear standards regarding how children must be raised and cared for, and the kinds of discipline which are, and are not, acceptable. These standards may conflict with the practices of other cultures or some religions, and may lead to serious disagreements. Sometimes the practices are so different from the generally accepted American norm that a parent is accused of child abuse or neglect.

Most frequently, practices acceptable in a particular culture which clash with American standards pertain to discipline in general and corporal punishment (such as spanking, caning or striking with an object) in particular. Some cultures and religions consider corporal punishment essential to properly mold a child's behavior. A nation's legal code or a religious doctrine may spell out the methods for inflicting this kind of punishment.

By contrast, corporal punishment is rarely acceptable in the U.S., especially in public schools and other public institutions. In fact, in some states, all forms of corporal punishment are illegal. Other states prohibit it after a certain age, such as 12.

RELEVANT ISSUES IN CHAPTER 5

Issue	Number
When Parenting Styles and Values Are Very Different	31
Consistency in Raising Children	32
When a Parent Needs to Develop Parenting Skills	36

Another area in which certain cultures or religions don't follow the dominant American norm is medical care. For example, parents of certain cultures or religions will refuse specific kinds of medical intervention on behalf of their children. Other parents distrust or reject Western medicine and instead follow Eastern practices such as acupuncture. Still other parents prefer holistic healing or other alternative medicines.

RELEVANT ISSUES IN CHAPTER 5

Issue	Number
Medical, Dental and Vision Care	1
Psychiatric and Other Mental Health Care	2

DON'T AGREE TO BREAK THE LAW
If you and the other parent are divorcing or legally separating, a court will probably review your parenting agreement. If any provision violates a state or federal law which governs the treatment of children, the court will reject your proposed parenting plan. It will probably also order a social worker to investigate both parents' homes and submit an evaluation to the court. The court will make whatever orders it deems necessary to protect your children's best interests, which will always be interpreted in accordance with the U.S. legal system.

B. Encouraging Children to Celebrate the Traditions of Both Parents

One way to minimize the child-rearing conflicts you experience because of cultural, religious, ethnic or national differences is to instill in your children a sense of specialness. Often children feel lost, angry and rejected after their parents separate or divorce, and the children's low feelings exacerbate the parental conflicts. You can help your children adjust to the separation or divorce, and therefore lessen your conflict with the other parent, by doing any of the following:

• teaching them who they are
• celebrating special traditions, and
• teaching them to respect (and embrace, if relevant) the ceremonies, rituals and traditions of their other parent.

For some parents, the core of their disagreement is about whose culture or religion is "better" or represents the "truth." You can hold firmly to your beliefs, but always remember that your children have two parents. Rather than trying to prove which culture or religion is better, try to find ways to equip your children to make their own decisions about both. One way to do this is to raise your children in both cultures or religions.

If those cultures or religions differ to the point that you cannot fully integrate your children into both, you can minimize your conflict—and differences—by finding a common principle, such as a commitment to family, and working from there. Perhaps mediators, elders or leaders within your particular communities can offer suggestions on living together peaceably.

Another suggestion is to teach your children about both cultures or religions, but to withhold certain ceremonies, rituals or traditions, such as initiations into a church or congregation, participation in funerals, undergoing religious communion or administering certain medical care. You might set limits because your children are not considered full members of the culture or group, or because certain functions might frighten or overwhelm your children.

RELEVANT ISSUES IN CHAPTER 5

Issue	Number
Religious Training	5
Holidays	23
Vacations	24
Special Occasions and Family Events	25
When Parenting Styles and Values Are Very Different	31

C. Sorting Out the Role of Power Within the Family

One feature of certain cultures, religions and ethnicities is that near absolute power is given to men, who make most of the substantive decisions that affect all family members. In such a situation, the bargaining power between the parents may be highly unequal, and you may seek certain specifics with your dispute resolution method. For example, in a culture in which men issue orders, fathers will seldom accept information or direction unless it comes from another male. These parents might purposely select a male mediator, and the mother might hire a male attorney to negotiate with the father or his attorney.

RELEVANT ISSUES IN CHAPTER 5

Issue	Number
Making Decisions	11
Resolving Disputes When Making Decisions Together	12
Disparaging Remarks	33
Undermining the Parent/Child Relationship	34

D. Working Within the American Legal System

The way that a culture describes conflict often indicates how that culture prefers to resolve it as well. In American society, conflict usually means there are two or more competing interests—one will win while the other(s) loses. For the most part, divorce or matrimonial litigation in our current legal system encourages each parent to confront the other and prove who will uphold the best interests of the children. Although litigation may be appropriate when a parent with a history of abuse, neglect or serious instability insists on significant unsupervised time with the children, litigation is usually unnecessarily costly and bitter. To parents from outside of the U.S., American litigation can be bewildering.

In some cultures, conflict is thought to result from inharmonious relationships. Once a relationship is found to be inharmonious, it is the community's responsibility to help the individual rediscover and fulfill his or her proper role. In many of these cultures, the best interests of the child are synonymous with the best interests of the group. The role that any one individual is therefore expected to fulfill within these communities is generally a function of his or her age, sex, social standing and economic resources.

Many of these communities are fairly cohesive, and the elders within the community or within the extended family are well regarded for their wisdom and leadership. When facilitators are needed to resolve conflict, elders are called upon because their status allows them to be persuasive problem solvers. Given this view of conflict and resolution, it is understandable why some parents are mystified when told that their decisions must hinge on the child's best interests as determined by state legislatures, the mental health profession and the courts.

Even mediation, which often is a versatile tool for resolving disputes, can be culturally biased. For example, selecting a mediator in the U.S. typically means finding someone totally neutral and unknown. In many cultures, however, parties are willing to participate in the process and reach agreement because the facilitator is well known to them. Additionally, the predominant mediation model in the U.S. today presumes that the parties will come to an agreement. In some other cultures, mediation is most effective when the facilitator suggests the solution and then persuades the parties to agree.

If you or the other parent comes from a background that is substantially different from the dominant Anglo-American culture, you may need to find attorneys, mediators, counselors or others sensitive to the issues and cultural differences. If you feel at a disadvantage because of language, either because you recently arrived in this country or because you don't understand the American legal system, you need to find knowledgeable support people from within your community who have the information you need.

To resolve your conflicts, look for people who can connect the priorities of each culture with the issues of disagreement.

RELEVANT ISSUES IN CHAPTER 5

Issue	Number
Psychiatric and Other Mental Health Care	2
Making Decisions	11
Resolving Disputes When Making Decisions Together	12
When Parenting Styles and Values Are Very Different	31

E. Deciding If Another Country Has Authority Over Parenting (Custody) Issues

If one or both parents are not U.S. citizens, your separate parenting may involve additional issues related to international borders. You—or the other parent—may justifiably fear that your children will be taken out of the U.S. without your knowledge or consent. Although protecting your children from a parent who truly wants to kidnap and hide his or her own children can be hard, laws do exist to help. (Chapter 12, Section F, has information on laws that can help you if your children are taken out of the country.)

RELEVANT ISSUES IN CHAPTER 5

Issue	Number
International Travel and Passports	6
Making Decisions (If there is any question over which country actually has jurisdiction, consider adding specific language.)	11

Although not located on foreign soil, American Indian nations have a special legal standing within the United States. Section 1911 (a) of the Indian Child Welfare Act states:

An Indian tribe shall have jurisdiction exclusive as to any state over any child custody proceeding involving an Indian child who resides on or is domiciled within the reservation of such tribe, except where such jurisdiction is otherwise vested in the State by existing Federal law. Where an Indian child is a ward of a tribal court, the Indian tribe shall retain exclusive jurisdiction, notwithstanding the residence or domicile of the child.

This Act covers the termination of parental rights, foster care and adoptive placements as well as custody proceedings. If you are unsure whether or not you must resolve your differences within a tribal court, see an attorney. ∎

Nontraditional Families

The traditional image of a family is a mother, a father and their children. Millions of American families, however, look very different, and are often referred to as "nontraditional families." Some of these families consist of childless couples—married or unmarried, gay or straight—although most include children. Nontraditional families—as we define them below—make up the substantial majority of U.S. families.

A. What Are Nontraditional Families?

Nontraditional families fall into one of the following categories:

Stepfamilies. In a stepfamily, a single parent establishes, usually by marriage, a new long-term relationship. The children usually refer to the new partner as a stepmother or stepfather. The partner calls the children his or her stepchildren.

Blended families. A blended family consists of at least two, and as many as four, stepfamilies. At its core, it's a former couple, their children, the new relationships entered into by the members of the former couple and the children of those new relationships. Dr. Constance Ahrons describes these families as binuclear families in her book *The Good Divorce* (Harper Collins, 1994). Here is an example of a blended or binuclear family: Mark and Evelyn marry and have a daughter, Lisa. They get a divorce, sharing custody of Lisa. Mark marries Shauna, who is divorced herself with a child from her previous marriage. Mark and Shauna have a son Rueben. Evelyn comes out as a lesbian after divorcing Mark, and forms a relationship with Cindy. Together they adopt a child.

Single parents. Many people—through circumstance or choice—are single parents. Obviously, the separate parenting issues in this book are not relevant, unless the single parent has involved another adult in raising the children. For example, a single mother may get help from her own parents or from a close friend in raising her children.

Grandparent-headed families. Some parents go beyond "getting help" from their own parents in raising children. In many families, especially those torn apart by violence or drugs, the grandparents have custody of, or guardianship over, their grandchildren—either formally (by court order) or informally (by agreement of the parents).

Unmarried couples. Many unmarried heterosexual couples have children together.

Same-sex-parent-headed families. Current estimates indicate that more than 15,000 lesbians and gay men have had or adopted children during the lesbian and gay "baby boom" of the 1980s and 1990s. Many, if not the majority, of these children are being raised by two mothers or two fathers.

Open-adoptive families. In general, a legally married husband and wife who adopt a child do not fall into the category of a nontraditional family. This changes, however, if the couple maintains a relationship with the birth mother—meaning the child is raised by the adoptive parents but has visits with the birth mother.

B. The Legal Relationship of a Nontraditional Parent and His or Her Children

Probably the greatest challenge faced by nontraditional families is the lack of societal and legal recognition. Despite the fact that fewer and fewer American families consist of the traditional mother, father and their children, the institutions—including the legal system—that deal with families are still geared for the traditional family model. Nontraditional families often feel left out, ignored and unsupported. These problems are exacerbated when the adults in that family divorce or separate. Sometimes, a person who has spent years raising children now finds himself or herself shut out because he or she is not considered a legal parent.

In a nontraditional family, it is imperative that when the adults raising the children split up, they continue to look out for the best interests of their children. If that means maintaining contact with all the adults involved in raising the children, then the parenting agreement must explicitly provide for this. Don't expect a court to do it—a court will usually order continuing contact only when the adult is a recognized "legal parent." (Some courts will order contact between children and a "psychological" parent, but often only if the legal parent doesn't object.)

Parents generally fall into one of four categories:

- legal parents
- biological, nonlegal parents
- psychological parents, and
- legal guardians.

Depending on the category, a parent may or may not have the legal right to custody or visitation with, or the legal responsibility to care for or support, the children.

As you read about the various categories of legally recognized and unrecognized parents, remember that you are not obligated to follow the strict letter of the law. As mentioned, if it's in the best interests of your children for them to maintain contact with the adults who have been raising them, then by all means continue that contact.

1.   Legal (Biological and Adoptive) Parents

Legal parents have both the authority and the obligation to provide basic care and comfort for their children. They are charged with making the decisions that affect their children's health, education and welfare. They are further charged with providing for their children's financial support. Recognizing a child's legal parent can differ for men and women.

The legal mother is usually, but not always, the woman who conceives and gives birth to the child (see Section 2, below) or who legally adopts the child.

The legal father is a man who legally adopts a child, or was married to the mother when the child was conceived or born, or declared the father in a paternity action. In addition, a man may be presumed to be the legal father if he:

- attempted to marry the mother (even if the marriage wasn't valid) and the child was conceived or born after the attempt
- married the mother after the birth and agreed either to have his name on the birth certificate or to support the child, or
- welcomed the child into his home and openly held himself out as the father.

A legal parent's obligations and rights end *only* if a court issues an order terminating parental rights. If you are the biological father of a child you have not seen for a while, you are still considered a parent unless a court says otherwise. This means you have the right to seek custody of or visitation with your child and you can be sued to pay child support.

2.   Biological, Nonlegal Parents

In a number of situations, a person is biologically related to a child but nevertheless is not considered the child's legal parent.

a.   Birth Mothers

The most common biological, nonlegal parent is a birth mother who gives up her child for adoption. A birth mother traditionally severs all ties (if she had any) with the child—and adoptive parent(s)—following an adoption.

In recent years, however, a number of adoptive parents have chosen to retain an ongoing relationship with their child's birth mother. This arrangement is usually called an open adoption. In some families, the relationship is little more than an exchange of holiday and birthday cards. In others, it includes regular visits and attendance at family celebrations.

b.   Surrogate Mothers

A surrogate mother is a woman who bears a child for someone else. Most surrogate mothers become pregnant with the semen of a man wishing to become a father. A few others have an already-fertilized egg of another woman implanted in their uterus, in which case the surrogate mother is not genetically related to the child. In either case, upon the birth of the child, the surrogate mother relinquishes all rights and responsibilities for the child and turns the child over to either the man (in the former situation) or the man and/or woman (in the latter situation).

Surrogate mothers offer infertile and gay male couples a way to become parents. The process is not without risk, however. Surrogacy carries with it a risk that the surrogate mother will change her mind and refuse to relinquish the child. Some states have passed laws regulating surrogacy contracts. Most states are silent on the issue.

A few highly publicized cases in which the surrogate mother changed her mind have drawn attention to the issue. In general, courts have ruled that a surrogate mother has the rights of a legal parent if she contributed genetic material to the child—that is, she became pregnant with the semen of a man wanting to become a father. If, however, an already-fertilized egg of another woman is implanted in her uterus, the donor generally has no parental rights.

Robin Leonard and Stephen Elias, in *Nolo's Pocket Guide to Family Law* (Nolo), summarize the New Jersey Supreme Court's holding in the first, and most famous surrogacy case, the *Matter of Baby M.* (537 A.2d 1227):

> *The surrogate mother changed her mind after the baby was born and decided that she wanted to keep the baby. The baby's father and his wife sued the surrogate mother to enforce the contract. The trial court declared the contract valid, terminated the surrogate mother's parental rights and allowed the father's wife to adopt the baby. The New Jersey Supreme Court reversed that decision, ruled that surrogate motherhood contracts are unenforceable and then treated the case like any other disputed custody case, awarding custody to the father and visitation rights to the surrogate mother.*

Some parents who have obtained their children through a surrogacy arrangement have chosen to retain an ongoing relationship with the surrogate mother, similar to the open adoption described above.

c. Semen Donors

Artificial insemination (also called alternative insemination) is the process in which a woman is inseminated by a means other than sexual intercourse. If the semen comes from the woman's husband, the man is considered the legal father of the child.

In the majority of cases, the semen comes from someone other than the woman's husband. This type of artificial insemination offers infertile and lesbian couples a way to become parents. The process is not without risk, however, because a semen donor who is known to the couple might change his mind and sue for paternity.

If the woman is married when the insemination and birth occur, her husband, not the donor, is considered the legal parent. If the woman is unmarried when the insemination and birth occur, whether the donor is considered the legal father depends on a number of factors, including the procedure and the state. In Oregon and New Jersey, for

example, the woman and the donor may enter an agreement spelling out their intentions, including that the donor not be considered the legal father. In California, if the insemination of a married woman is performed by a doctor, the donor is not considered the legal father. If no doctor is used, the donor may be considered the legal father.

As with open adoptions and some surrogacy arrangements, a few legal parents maintain an ongoing relationship between the semen donor and the child.

d. Ova Donors

In one of the newest reproductive techniques, a woman donates an egg, which is fertilized in vitro and then implanted in the uterus of a different woman who wishes to become a mother. Usually, the egg is fertilized with the semen of the husband of the woman into whom the egg is implanted.

This is such a new procedure that the legal relationship of the ova donor and the child is unknown. In the long run, the donor will probably not be considered a legal parent for two reasons. First, the ova donor is legally similar to a surrogate mother, even though the ova donor shares genetic material with the child, while the surrogate mother does not. Second, the ova donor can be equated to a semen donor, who usually is not considered a legal father.

3. Psychological Parents

"Psychological parent" is a general description of an adult who has formed a significant emotional bond with a child by contributing substantially to the child's care and upbringing. Psychological parents are not legally responsible for the care or support of a child; nor are they automatically entitled to custody of, or visitation with, the child.

In some situations, a court will grant visitation between a child and a psychological parent if the court believes it would be detrimental to the child for the relationship to end.

a. Stepparents

A stepparent is the new spouse of a legal parent. In general, the stepparent and stepchild have no legal relationship. This means that unless the stepparent legally adopted the child, the stepparent is not obligated to care for or support the child and is not entitled to seek custody or visitation. Of course, many stepparents are instrumental in the upbringing and support of their stepchildren.

In a few states, including Michigan and Wisconsin, some stepparents have been granted the status of "equitable" parent. Most often, this occurs when the stepparent and child consider themselves to be parent and child, or when the legal parent has encouraged the relationship. Equitable parents are often granted shared custody of, or visitation with, the children, and are ordered to pay child support.

b. Co-Parents

A co-parent is the unmarried partner of a biological or adoptive parent. The concept of co-parent has become extremely important for lesbian and gay couples. Because no state allows same-sex couples to legally marry, the partner of a lesbian mother or gay father cannot adopt the parent's child under a state's traditional stepparent adoption statute. This means that when a lesbian or gay couple raise a child together, usually only one partner (the biological or adoptive parent) is recognized as the legal parent.

In such a situation, the co-parent has few legal rights if the couple splits up. Tragically, the co-parent is not entitled to visitation or custody; nor is the co-parent obligated to provide financial support. In a few states, a lesbian co-parent has sued for visitation after the couple separated and the legal parent barred the co-parent from seeing the child. In only one state—New Mexico—did the court grant the co-parent visitation, based on an agreement the couple had giving the co-parent visitation. The court said that a parent "may enter into an agreement with another person concerning the custody of a child" and that "sexual orientation, standing alone, is not a permissible basis for the denial of shared custody or visitation."

CO-PARENTS WHO ARE ALSO LEGAL PARENTS

Until 1985, gay and lesbian couples (and their lawyers) assumed that state laws were written so that adoptions were available only to married couples and single people. If a "single" person—such as the partner of a biological parent—sought to adopt, the biological parents' rights would first have to be terminated, hardly the result a lesbian or gay couple wanted.

Then the lawyers got smart and began reading the text of the state adoption statutes. Most laws, they realized, authorize adoptions by married couples and single people, but don't expressly exclude unmarried couples. Similarly, the stepparent adoption statutes expressly authorize adoptions by the new spouse of a legal parent if the other legal parent is dead, had his parental rights terminated, abandoned the child or consented to the adoption, but don't forbid an unmarried partner from becoming a stepparent.

Now, joint adoptions by gay and lesbian couples or second-parent (the equivalent of stepparent) adoptions have been granted in the District of Columbia and several states including Alaska, California, Illinois, Massachusetts, Michigan, Minnesota, New Jersey, Oregon, Pennsylvania, Texas, Vermont and Washington. In New York, the courts are split—some have granted the adoptions while others have denied them. When a court grants a joint or second-parent adoption, both mothers or both fathers are considered legal parents.

c. Other Important Adults

Grandparents, aunts and uncles and adult friends of legal parents often form significant emotional bonds with children. In all states, grandparents (and in some states, aunts and uncles) can ask the court to grant them visitation with their grandchildren following a divorce or separation. It's up to the court whether or not to grant the visitation, but many will, recognizing the special relationship children often have with their grandparents.

4. Legal Guardians

A legal guardian is an adult given the legal right—either by the parents or by a court—to care for and control a minor child. Formal legal guardianships (those ordered by a court) tend to be set up for children who lack stable parenting. For instance, grandparents (or aunts and uncles) are often appointed legal guardians of their grandchildren (or nieces and nephews) when the parents are unable to care for the children because of drug abuse, imprisonment or lack of basic parenting skills. A legal guardian often needs a court order so that schools, hospitals and other institutions have an adult to turn to when a decision about the child needs to be made.

If the legal guardian has completely taken over the parenting role, a court may grant custody of the children to the guardian. The court may also order that the legal guardian allow the parents to visit with the children. Some legal guardians have a more limited role because they are only asked to care for a child who is away at school. When this happens, the legal guardian is there to make quick decisions in the event of an emergency.

C. Recognizing the Nontraditional Parent's Role

If your children have a close relationship with a biological, nonlegal parent, a psychological parent or a legal guardian, you will want to provide for the continuation of that relationship in your parenting agreement unless you believe your children are being harmed.

You have several ways to handle this, depending on your children's relationship with the adult. If your children haven't been living with the adult, as might be the case with a close friend or nearby relative, you can either incorporate a regular visitation schedule or allow your children to initiate contact in your parenting agreement.

If, however, your children have been living with the adult and for all intents and purposes that adult is another parent to your children, do what you can to minimize the harm to them. You may be angry and want that person out of your life. And that person may have no legal standing whatsoever to claim "parenthood." But if your children know that person as a parent, put your anger and the legal labels aside and fill out the parenting agreement in Chapter 5 as if you were a legally married couple getting a divorce, both entitled to continuing contact with your children.

RELEVANT ISSUES IN CHAPTER 5

Issue	Number
Making Decisions	11
Grandparents, Relatives and Important Friends	27
When Parents Have New Partners	38

D. Resolving Conflict in a Way That Meets Your Family's Needs

Most nontraditional families need to find ways to resolve disputes outside of the courtroom. The court system is geared to working with traditional families. This does not necessarily mean that nontraditional families suffer discrimination within the court system, although lesbian and gay couples often justifiably feel that way.

In most situations, however, the dynamics of nontraditional families require more effort and understanding than the legal system can give. Court calendars are overcrowded and court personnel are overworked; judges cannot take the time to thoroughly investigate your children's relationship with their stepsiblings, their grandparents, your partner and all the other important people in their lives.

When adults who have raised (or at least lived together with) children in a nontraditional family decide to live apart, they often find mediation helpful for defining the role the nonlegal parent will have in the children's lives and for developing a plan to carry it out. If mediation isn't an option or doesn't work, consider arbitration—where you can obtain a resolution without having to negotiate with the other person. (Chapter 7, *Making Mediation and Arbitration Work for You*, has information on how each process works and how to select a mediator or arbitrator.)

No matter which process you use, it is imperative that the facilitator understands the issues that are important to you and structures the process so that it will meet your needs. You may need to go beyond the suggestions in Chapter 7 for finding the right facilitator. For example, if you're a lesbian couple splitting up, consider contacting a gay community center, support group, religious organization or other gay or lesbian institution for help in finding someone to mediate your parenting issues.

E. Creating New Relationships After the Divorce or Separation

You may be reading this chapter because, while your traditional family divorced or separated a while ago, you or your children's other parent have formed a new relationship, creating a nontraditional family. A new relationship can bring joy to the new couple and anguish for the still-single parent. Depending on who is now coupled and who is still single, you or your ex may be jealous or suspicious of the new partner. Or, you or your ex may be scared that your children will want to live in the other household, especially if the new mate has children of similar ages to yours.

Similarly, your children might feel awkward when a parent has a new partner. If you form a new relationship, you must find ways to maintain the existing parent-child relationship while creating and cementing new bonds. One highly effective way to do this is to find times when just you and your children can spend time with each other. Don't use the excuse that "everyone is too busy." If you don't spend quality time with your children, they may begin to feel left out, especially if your new partner has children or you and your new partner have a child together. Occasional lunch dates, trips to the park or video parlor or other one-on-one activities can make all the difference in the world.

With your new family in place, you often have the perfect excuse to start building some new family traditions that can give your children a sense of belonging to your new family. These rituals can be simple or elaborate, but must happen consistently to become routine. If your new family has established a family activity night, then setting aside one night a week or month will be a priority. If your new tradition is a holiday (either real or invented), then be sure to celebrate it annually.

Finally, remember that language is powerful and finding names or descriptions for new relatives can be challenging. Some children call a parent's new partner something like Mom or Dad (or Mother or Father); other children use the new partner's first name. Still others invent a name, or use a word from a language other than English. Describing stepsiblings can present similar problems and solutions (such as inventing a name or using a non-English word). Other children simply describe the stepsiblings as "new" brothers or sisters in order to avoid a lengthy explanation.

RELEVANT ISSUES IN CHAPTER 5

Issue	Number
Maintaining Contact When the Children Are With the Other Parent	18
Holidays	23
Special Occasions and Family Events	25
Treating Each Child as an Individual	30
When Parents Have New Partners	38

CHAPTER

12

State and Federal Laws Affecting Child Custody

Note: The information and charts in this chapter highlight certain legal issues that often come up in child custody and visitation cases. They are not intended to be a treatise on child custody law, or to offer definitive legal advice about how to handle your individual case. Statutes are often repealed or amended, and court cases interpreting statutes can be difficult to understand and track. If you want complete and up-to-date information on a specific law for your state, either do your own research or consult an attorney. (See Chapter 13, *Help Beyond the Book.*)

Most custody and visitation laws are enacted by state legislatures, not Congress. Nevertheless, state laws include some basic similarities and trends when it comes to raising children whose parents divorce or separate and helping parents resolve disputes about these issues. Most fundamentally, unless a court is convinced that harm will come to the children or to a parent, courts in every state generally:

- prefer that the parents share in parenting their children
- place a value on children maintaining frequent and continuing contact with both parents
- insist that both parents have access to medical, educational, religious and other relevant information about their children, and
- recommend or order mediation before deciding custody and visitation disputes.

A. Custody and Visitation

The term *custody* generally refers to:

- the legal authority to make decisions about a child—sometimes called *legal custody*, and
- maintaining physical control over a child—sometimes called *physical custody*.

Visitation describes the time that a noncustodial parent, grandparent or other important person spends with a child. All states specifically provide grandparents the right to ask for visitation as part of a court order.

DIFFERENTIATION BETWEEN LEGAL AND PHYSICAL CUSTODY

In the states listed below, a court may make different awards for legal custody and for physical custody. In all other states, a custody award encompasses both legal and physical custody.

Alabama	Idaho	New Jersey
Arizona	Indiana	Ohio
California	Iowa	Pennsylvania
Colorado	Massachusetts	Utah
Connecticut	Minnesota	Virginia
District of Columbia	Mississippi	West Virginia
Georgia	Missouri	Wisconsin
Hawaii	New Hampshire	

In about 20 states, the court may differentiate between legal and physical custody—that is, make one decision regarding legal custody and another decision regarding physical custody. For example, Lorraine may be awarded primary physical custody while Lorraine and Justin together are awarded legal custody. In the other states, the court simply makes a custody award that encompasses both legal and physical custody. The trend is toward differentiating between the two.

Depending on the state and the situation, a court can award *sole custody* to just one parent or *joint custody* to both parents. A joint custody award can be for legal and physical custody or for legal custody only. Rarely would a court order joint physical custody but give only one parent legal custody.

Because the general goal is to keep both parents actively involved in raising their children, courts try to award joint legal custody. Joint physical custody is a bit trickier. While joint physical custody doesn't necessarily mean that the children will spend exactly half of the time with each parent, it does require coordination so that the children spend significant amounts of time with both parents.

The following are the types of questions courts ask when considering a joint custody arrangement:

- Do both parents demonstrate a willingness and ability to cooperate in advancing their children's welfare?
- Do the children have a close relationship with each parent?
- Can both parents communicate and make joint decisions regarding child care and education, or has child-rearing become a battleground?

- Are the parents' homes sufficiently close to each other to accommodate the practical considerations of shared parenting?
- How much time does each parent have available for the children?
- Will each parent encourage sharing of love, affection and time with the other parent?
- Will joint custody promote more frequent and continuing contact with both parents?

JOINT CUSTODY

Only Arkansas, New York, North Dakota and Rhode Island have no statutes relating to joint custody. In these states, joint custody may be allowed under court decisions.

Joint custody required:
Louisiana

Joint custody permitted if parents don't agree to the arrangement:

Alabama	Iowa	New Hampshire
Alaska	Kansas	New Jersey
Arizona	Maryland	New Mexico
Colorado	Massachusetts	North Carolina
Delaware	Michigan	Ohio
Florida	Minnesota	Oklahoma
Hawaii	Mississippi	South Dakota
Idaho	Missouri	Vermont
Illinois	Montana	Wisconsin
Indiana		

Joint custody available if both parents agree:

California	Nebraska	Texas
Connecticut	Nevada	Utah
District of Columbia	Oregon	Virginia
Georgia	Pennsylvania	Washington
Kentucky	South Carolina	West Virginia
Maine	Tennessee	Wyoming

Virtually every state has specific statutes allowing judges to order joint custody. In some states, judges can even order joint custody over the objections of the parents. This might happen in cases where, for example, the judge believes that parents seem equally qualified, their homes are not too far apart and they seem able to resolve their differences outside of court.

Split custody is the unusual situation in which a court grants custody of one or more children to one parent and grants custody of different children to the other parent. While only a few states have laws expressly discouraging judges from splitting children between their parents' homes, the practice is generally criticized by mental health professionals and child advocates and is rarely ordered by a court.

Most states prevent judges from considering the gender of the parents when awarding custody. These laws are meant to eliminate the automatic preference of awarding custody, especially custody of very young children, to their mother.

GENDER OF PARENT CANNOT BE A FACTOR

Judges are prohibited from favoring one parent over the other when awarding custody.

Alabama	Indiana	North Dakota
Alaska	Kansas	Oklahoma
Arizona	Kentucky	Oregon
Arkansas	Maine	South Dakota
California	Maryland	Utah
Colorado	Missouri	Vermont
Delaware	Nebraska	Virginia
District of Columbia	Nevada	Washington
Florida	New Hampshire	Wisconsin
Georgia	New Mexico	Wyoming
Hawaii	New York	

B. Best Interests of the Child

The standard used by courts in making custody and visitation rulings is called the *best interests of the child*. Courts typically will place a higher value on protecting a child's best interests than on any other factor when deciding custody and visitation.

Nearly every state has specific statutes listing factors that a court should consider when assessing the best interests of the children. But those lists are not meant to be exhaustive. Judges have the discretion to consider virtually all relevant information when deciding on the best interests of the child.

The kinds of considerations found in state statutes follow, with examples.

Parent's ability to meet the child's emotional and financial needs. A judge will consider a parent's ability and willingness to meet each child's needs for love, guidance and education as well as food, clothing and medical care. The court will also consider::

- the amount of time each parent has available for the child
- the time a parent has spent caring for the child before and during the divorce or separation proceedings , and
- the understanding and commitment that each parent has to helping the child develop emotionally and physically into a responsible adult.

Example: *Eight-year-old Sara's father arranged his career so that he would be available to care for Sara before and after school, fix dinner, follow an evening routine and reading her a bedtime story. Because of her career, her mother was much less available to provide this kind of daily care. The judge decided that Sara would live primarily with her father during the school year and spend part of her summer living with her mother. The judge reasoned that Sara would experience the fewest possible disruptions by living most of the time with her father.*

Every state allows a judge to order one parent to pay child support to the other parent. The idea behind this policy is to make sure that children are able to have a roughly comparable standard of living at each home.

While it is certainly important for children to have access to some of the stability, security and advantages that money can buy, poverty or living on welfare is not a sufficient reason to deprive the poorer parent of custody.

Example: *Chris and David are seven- and ten-year-olds whose father has dedicated his life to his career, making quite a substantial salary, and who recently moved out of the family house. Their mother has not worked outside of the home since they were born, but has been a caring and loving full-time mom. The judge awards custody to the mother and orders the father to pay child support.*

Moral fitness and conduct of the parents. Some states allow a judge to consider parent conduct—including lifestyle, living accommodations and other factors—in deciding their moral fitness. Moral fitness is a fairly subjective term and can mean different things to different judges. To many judges, parents are considered morally fit when they are focused on the child, provide a safe, secure and nurturing environment and are a generally good role model.

Many judges consider a parent to be morally unfit if that parent has a series of short-term, live-in relationships or allows the children to be around a new partner, roommate or friend who is involved in drugs or illegal activities. For these reasons, it is possible that judges may look beyond one parent's adultery, as long as they seem to be a good, caring parent and the circumstances surrounding the adultery did not appear to have harmed the child. Where a parent's misconduct affects a child's health, safety or welfare, some states require a judge to explain a decision that allows a violent parent to win custody or unsupervised visits.

The sexual habits and living arrangements of a parent may or may not be used to judge moral fitness, depending on the state and circumstances. For instance, in most states, a judge will probably not decide that a parent is unfit if he or she lives, unmarried, with a responsible, long-term partner. A judge will probably not consider poor behavior from many years ago, as long as the parent has shown that he or she is presently a good parent and appears to be capable of continuing that pattern into the future.

SEXUAL ORIENTATION AND CUSTODY

Only the District of Columbia has a law on the books stating that a parent's sexual orientation cannot be a factor in a custody or visitation award. In a few other states—including Alaska, California, New Mexico and Pennsylvania—courts have ruled that a parent's homosexuality, in and of itself, cannot be grounds for an automatic denial of custody.

In reality, a lesbian or gay parent faces a difficult struggle trying to gain custody in most American courtrooms. This is true even if the parent's gay or lesbian partner has been involved in parenting for much or all of the child's life. Because not all states allow gay or lesbian parents to adopt, it can be difficult to get the same legal rights to custody and visitation as heterosexual parents.

It is fair to say that many, if not most, judges are ignorant about, prejudiced against or suspicious of gay and lesbian parents. Only a few judges understand that a parent's sexual orientation, alone, does not affect the best interests of the children. But judges often use the best interests standard to deny a gay or lesbian parent custody.

Physical safety of the child. Because the safety of a child is a primary concern of the courts, assuring that a child will not be physically neglected or subject to or exposed to violence or abuse is of utmost importance. Most states do allow parents to physically discipline their child within reason. Most states have laws that prevent a parent or potential caretaker with a history of abuse against another parent or a current spouse, cohabitant or companion from gaining custody of a child. Withholding custody from a parent who has abused his or her spouse is not considered punishment against the parent, but is done in the best interests of the child because of the profound impact that seeing, hearing or knowing about violence between parents can have on a child.

Quite a few disputed custody cases involve the children's exposure to tobacco smoke. Most states now recognize the virtually undisputed evidence that environmental tobacco smoke is harmful to children. Courts will weigh this factor against all the others in making a deci-

sion. For instance, while a court might prefer to grant custody to a nonsmoking parent if a child has respiratory problems, that same court might grant custody to the smoking parent if the nonsmoking parent was found to be violent.

While a judge cannot decide the comparative merits of the parents' religions in deciding custody, religious beliefs can also be taken into account if they are potentially dangerous to the child's chance for a good education or general welfare. For instance, if a parent's religious beliefs prevent him or her from giving the child immunizations or blood transfusions, the court may determine that this is potentially harmful and give decision-making authority for these issues to the other parent.

Quality of child's relationships with others. Another factor that courts consider when trying to protect a child's best interests is maintaining that child's relationship with brothers, sisters, grandparents and the extended community within which they live. Deciding the quality of the child's relationships can include how the child gets along with family members, the amount and nature of time spent together, and which parent or caretaker has taken a greater responsibility for meeting the child's emotional and practical needs.

Example: *Tawila is 11 years old. Her father is seeking custody and would be able to provide an emotionally supportive home for her, but Tawila has not been getting along at all with her father's new wife, and her school work has been suffering. In this situation, the judge might order that Tawila live primarily with her mother, recommend or order family counseling between Tawila, her father and stepmother, allow increasing amounts of time for visits or change the structure of the living arrangements if Tawila's relationship with her stepmother improves.*

Courts also consider sibling bonds to be extremely important. Because divorce or separation causes such disruption in a child's life, courts try to keep all other relationships in a child's life unchanged, if possible. For that reason, as mentioned earlier, most states will not order split custody—where close siblings are separated—except for compelling reasons. A judge will consider splitting siblings more readily if, for example, there has been violence or other serious problems between the children, or if they are of dramatically different ages or have different parents.

Example: *Lisa, 17, wants to stay with her father so she can finish high school at her current school. Lisa's mother and father agree, however, that her mother should be the primary caretaker of Lisa's three-year-old twin brothers. In this situation, the court might support splitting the children up for much of the year. But the judge might also order that the children spend significant amounts of time together at both parents' homes.*

Continuity and household stability. Courts consider continuity and household stability—staying with the same parent or caretaker and/or living in the same residence—as an important factor in deciding child custody disputes. Stability is important because it means that the child can count on some aspects of his or her life remaining the same after the separation and divorce of his or her parents. Courts prefer, therefore, to allow children to remain in the family home or the same community, as long as there are no safety concerns.

Continuity is also an important factor that judges consider if parents want to change their custody and visitation arrangements after the first custody order is made. In general, unless a parenting plan has been scheduled for review by the court, parents can only file for a change in their custody and visitation order if there has been a significant change in circumstances. But the definition of "significant" is a little vague. For example, a change in one parent's employment may be significant or insignificant, depending on many factors. For example, a change from one 9-to-5 job to anther might have little impact on visitation. But if the new job requires lots of travel, it may be hard to maintain the old visitation schedule.

Maintaining continuity if one parent wants to move away. While the court does not have the ability to prevent a parent from moving, a judge can order custody to shift from the moving parent to the remaining parent in order to preserve a child's contact with the remaining parent, family members, schools, friends and community. Different states and different judges will balance the needs of children and their parents using different criteria. In some states, courts require the moving parent to justify why the move will have a beneficial effect on the child. Other courts shift the responsibility to the remaining parent to show why the move would be against the best interests of the child.

Other factors that judges will consider when making these kinds of decisions include the amount of time the child spends with each parent, the quality of life and relationship the child has with each parent and the relative advantages and disadvantages of moving or remaining with one or the other parent.

Other life changes may also affect custodial or visitation rights. A judge won't modify an existing custody arrangement, however, unless it is essential and appropriate to the circumstances. If a custodial parent begins abusing drugs or neglecting the child's welfare, for example, the court is likely to remove the child from the situation. Often, however, a judge will consider increasing the amount of time a parent has with his or her child once he or she has proven he or she can remain clean and sober and committed to providing a stable and nurturing environment for the child.

Continuity of residence and caretaking has received great recognition in the courts, especially when a party seeking custody is a nonparent. For instance, when a child has lived with a grandparent for a significant period and is well adjusted and happy, the importance of keeping this stable setup may mean that the child will remain with the grandparent while gradually rebuilding a relationship with his or her birth parent or parents. The process of rebuilding a healthy parenting relationship might include supervised visits, an order that the parent attend one or more parenting classes or a shared custody arrangement that ensures the child will be able to keep close ties to his or her grandparent.

Child's preference. Most states consider where and with whom an older child would rather live. At most, however, the child's wishes are one factor in deciding custody, and the court can follow or ignore them. In many cases, the child's preference will act as a tie-breaker when both parents or potential custodians are equally fit.

A judge will consider the preference only of a suitably mature child. Usually, the older a child is, the more weight is given to the child's wishes. While some states require that a child of a certain age—usually 12—be able to state his or her preferences for where he or she will live and how often he or she will spend time with the other parent, the judge still must make sure that choice is in the child's best interests. Often, a judge will either ask the child directly, or will order a child custody investigation or evaluation to understand the reasoning behind the child's preferences and to make a recommendation that would be in the child's best interests. The court will most likely give serious weight to the child's choice if it is based on sound reasoning and achieves the child's long-term best interests. The court will probably ignore the preference if it has been influenced by one of the parents, is based on promises of indulgences or may lead to only present happiness or enjoyment.

Example: *Onoke is a 12-year-old boy who wants to stay with his father after his parents divorce so he can stay at a junior high where he has been doing well and has a circle of friends. The judge will give Onoke's choice more weight than if he chose to live with his dad because he gets to stay up later and eat fast food more often than at his mom's.*

Friendly parent. Because courts believe that a child needs the love and guidance of both parents if possible, judges will make an effort to preserve the child's relationship with both parents. Thus, judges consider very strongly the ability of a parent to foster a positive relationship with the other and to support frequent and meaningful contact with the other parent. A parent must demonstrate an ability to set angry feelings aside and encourage his or her children to have a loving relationship and frequent contact with the other parent. Courts take interference with the other parent's visitation rights or attempts to undermine the child's relationship with the other parent very seriously. In short, a judge will consider this fundamental question: In whose custody will the child have a better chance of contact with both parents? For example, a judge may take away custody from a parent who repeatedly cancels scheduled visits for punitive or vindictive reasons.

CAN RACE PLAY A ROLE IN CUSTODY DECISIONS?

Palmore v. Sidoti, 466 U.S. 429 (1984) is a U.S. Supreme Court decision in which the court ruled that it was unconstitutional for a court to consider race when a noncustodial parent petitions a court for a change of custody. In the case, a white couple had divorced, and the mother had been awarded custody of their son. She married an African-American man and moved to a predominantly African-American neighborhood. The father filed a request for modification of custody based on the changed circumstance that the boy was now living with an African-American man in an African-American neighborhood. A Florida court granted the modification. The U.S. Supreme Court reversed, ruling that societal stigma, especially a racial one, cannot be the basis for a custody decision.

C. Mediation

By now, if you have read the earlier chapters, you should have a good grasp of child custody mediation. Just a reminder—mediation is a nonadversarial process in which a neutral person (called a mediator) meets with disputing persons to help them settle a dispute. (It is discussed in depth in Chapter 7.)

In nearly every state, parents can be ordered to participate in mediation before bringing a custody or visitation dispute to court. At the same time, however, when domestic violence is an issue, many courts either will not make the victim mediate the dispute, or will at least allow the parent to meet with the mediator separately and at separate times.

Courts make different use of the mediation. For example, in a few states, the judge can ask a mediator to make a recommendation regarding custody and visitation if the parents cannot settle the issues during the mediation.

In more than one-half of the states, mediation is considered confidential—the mediator cannot testify in court about anything said during mediation. If the parents cannot reach agreement in mediation, then the matter will either be referred to a child custody evaluator or investigator, or taken to court for a hearing so that the judge can make the decision.

In just under one-half of the states, child custody mediators must possess certain education, training and experience in order to participate in court-sponsored mediation. Of course, if you are not required to mediate the custody and visitation issues but you choose to anyway, you're free to select whomever you want as the mediator—as long as the other parent agrees.

OTHER TECHNIQUES FOR RESOLVING CUSTODY AND VISITATION DISPUTES

Mediation isn't the only way to resolve custody and visitation disputes outside of litigation. In about one-half of the states, a judge has the authority to appoint an investigator—usually a social worker—to look into the homes of both parents, to talk to the children and parents and to make a recommendation about custody and visitation.

A handful of states permit disputing parents to use arbitration to resolve custody and visitation issues. Arbitration is a process similar to court because the parties, or more likely their attorneys, present a "case" and the arbitrator resolves the issues. But it is often quicker and less expensive than a court trial. For more difficult cases, or cases that have been in the court system for a long time, the judge may appoint a special master to review the case and make whatever decisions may be necessary to resolve the parents' ongoing disagreements in a way that will implement the court order. (Arbitration is discussed in Chapter 7, and the role of the special master is discussed in Chapter 13.)

PARENTS CAN BE ORDERED TO PARTICIPATE IN MEDIATION BEFORE BRINGING A CUSTODY OR VISITATION DISPUTE TO COURT

Alabama	Kansas	Ohio
Alaska	Louisiana	Oregon
Arizona	Maine	Pennsylvania
Arkansas	Maryland	Rhode Island
California	Minnesota	South Carolina
Colorado	Mississippi	South Dakota
Connecticut	Missouri	Texas
Delaware	Montana	Utah
Florida	Nevada	Virginia
Idaho	New Jersey	Washington
Illinois	New Mexico	West Virginia
Indiana	North Carolina	Wisconsin
Iowa	North Dakota	

PARENTS CAN BE EXCUSED FROM COURT-ORDERED MEDIATION IF THERE IS A HISTORY OF DOMESTIC VIOLENCE

Alaska	Montana	North Dakota
Florida	Nebraska	Ohio
Hawaii	Nevada	Pennsylvania
Iowa	New Jersey	Utah
Maryland	New Mexico	Washington
Minnesota	North Carolina	Wisconsin

PARENTS CAN BE EXCUSED FROM COURT-ORDERED MEDIATION IF THERE IS A HISTORY OF CHILD ABUSE

Iowa	New Jersey	Pennsylvania
Maryland	New Mexico	Utah
Minnesota	North Carolina	Virginia
Montana	North Dakota	Washington
Nebraska	Ohio	Wisconsin
Nevada		

PARENTS CAN BE EXCUSED FROM COURT-ORDERED MEDIATION IF IT IS FOUND TO BE INAPPROPRIATE UNDER THE CIRCUMSTANCES

Indiana	New Jersey	Utah
Kansas	North Carolina	Virginia
Maine	Ohio	Washington
Maryland	Texas	Wisconsin
Nevada		

JUDGES CAN ASK A MEDIATOR FOR A RECOMMENDATION ON CUSTODY AND VISITATION IF THE PARENTS CAN'T SETTLE THE ISSUES DURING MEDIATION

California	Delaware	South Dakota

MEDIATION IS CONSIDERED CONFIDENTIAL—THE MEDIATOR CANNOT TESTIFY IN COURT ABOUT ANYTHING SAID DURING MEDIATION

If both parents expressly waive this or let the mediator conduct a subsequent investigation or evaluation regarding custody, the mediator may testify in court.

Alabama	Maryland	Oklahoma
Alaska	Minnesota	Oregon
Arizona	Montana	Rhode Island
Arkansas	Nebraska	South Dakota
California	Nevada	Tennessee
Connecticut	New Hampshire	Utah
Florida	New Jersey	Virginia
Idaho	North Carolina	Washington
Indiana	North Dakota	Wisconsin
Kansas	Ohio	Wyoming
Louisiana		

A COURT CAN ORDER A CUSTODY INVESTIGATION OR EVALUATION TO HELP IT MAKE A DECISION

Arizona	Kansas	New Mexico
California	Kentucky	New York
Colorado	Michigan	North Dakota
Delaware	Minnesota	Ohio
Florida	Missouri	South Dakota
Georgia	Montana	Utah
Hawaii	Nevada	Washington
Illinois	New Jersey	Wisconsin
Indiana		

CHILD CUSTODY MEDIATORS MUST POSSESS CERTAIN EDUCATIONAL, TRAINING AND EXPERIENCE QUALIFICATIONS

California	Montana	Oregon
Idaho	Nebraska	South Dakota
Indiana	Nevada	Texas
Kansas	New Jersey	Utah
Louisiana	North Carolina	Washington
Maryland	North Dakota	West Virginia
Minnesota	Ohio	Wisconsin

ARBITRATION IS SPECIFICALLY PERMITTED TO RESOLVE CUSTODY AND VISITATION DISPUTES

Arbitration is a process similar to court because the parties, or more likely their attorneys, present a "case" and the arbitrator resolves the issues. (Arbitration is discussed in Chapter 7.)

New Mexico	Oklahoma	Texas
North Dakota	South Carolina	Washington

D. Interference With Custody

Custodial interference occurs when a parent or guardian keeps a child away from a person who has a legal right to custody. In most states, it is a crime to take a child from his or her parent or guardian with the intention of depriving that person of custody. In many states, depriving a parent or guardian of custody is a felony if the child is taken out of state. Also, in most states, the parent or guardian deprived of custody may file a suit for damages against the person who took the child.

Many states recognize good-cause defenses to custodial interference. In most cases, a defense negates the charge; in other situations, it reduces the charge from a felony to a misdemeanor. Commonly-accepted defenses include the following:

- taker has or seeks legal custody (accepted in about a dozen states)
- taker is protecting child or self from bodily harm (accepted in about one-half of the states), and
- taker reported taking of the child to police or parent and promptly returned child (accepted in slightly more than a dozen states).

DEFENSE TO CUSTODIAL INTERFERENCE: TAKER HAS OR SEEKS LEGAL CUSTODY

Alabama	Iowa	Rhode Island
Alaska	Missouri	South Dakota
District of Columbia	New Jersey	Wisconsin
Illinois	Pennsylvania	

DEFENSE TO CUSTODIAL INTERFERENCE: PROTECTING CHILD OR SELF FROM BODILY HARM

California	Michigan	Pennsylvania
Colorado	Minnesota	Rhode Island
District of Columbia	Missouri	Vermont
Florida	Nevada	Washington
Idaho	New Jersey	West Virginia
Illinois	New York	Wisconsin
Louisiana	Ohio	Wyoming
Maryland		

DEFENSE TO CUSTODIAL INTERFERENCE: REPORTED TO POLICE OR PARENT; CHILD RETURNED PROMPTLY

Arizona	Missouri	Pennsylvania
California	Montana	Rhode Island
District of Columbia	Nevada	Tennessee
Idaho	New Jersey	Texas
Illinois	New Mexico	Washington
Kentucky	Ohio	

E. Interstate Custody Disputes

All states and the District of Columbia have enacted a law called the Uniform Child Custody Jurisdiction Act, or UCCJA, which sets standards for when a court may make a custody determination and when a court must defer to an existing determination from another state. In general, a state may make a custody decision about a child if one of the following is true. The conditions are stated in order of preference.

1. The state is the child's home state—this means the child has resided in the state for the six previous months, or was residing in the state but is absent because a parent has removed the child from or retained the child outside of the state.
2. There are significant connections with people—such as teachers, doctors and grandparents—and substantial evidence in the state concerning the child's care, protection, training and personal relationships.
3. The child is in the state and either has been abandoned or is in danger of being abused or neglected if sent back to the other state.
4. No other state can meet one of the above three tests, or a state can meet at least one of the tests but has declined to make a custody decision.

If a state cannot meet one of these tests, even if the child is present in the state, the courts of that state cannot make a custody award. Also, a parent who has wrongfully removed or retained a child in order to create a home-state jurisdiction or significant connections will often be denied custody. In the event that more than one state meets the above standards, the law requires that only one state award custody. This means that once the first state makes a custody award, another state can neither make another "initial" award nor modify the existing order.

Having the same law in all states helps achieve consistency in the treatment of custody decrees. It also helps solve many of the problems created by kidnapping or disagreements over custody between parents living in different states.

Example: *Sam and Diane met and married in Missouri. They moved to Delaware where their child (Sam Jr.) was born. Sam, Diane and Junior lived in Delaware until Junior was ten. At that time, Sam took Junior to Missouri in an effort to divorce Diane and raise Junior himself. When Sam went to court in Missouri and requested custody, his request was denied because Delaware is Junior's home state, the state within which he has significant connections, and Sam removed Junior from Delaware in an effort to create home-state jurisdiction in Missouri. (Diane should go to court in Delaware and request custody, even though Junior is in Missouri.)*

In 1997, the Uniform Law Commission, the organization that drafted and proposed the UCCJA, drafted a similar law known as the Uniform Child Custody Jurisdiction and Enforcement Act, or UCCJEA. The Uniform Law Commission wants each state to replace the UCCJA with the UCCJEA, which contains the jurisdiction provisions of the UCCJA and additional laws concerning the enforcement of existing child custody decrees issued by the state where the child resides, another state, an Indian court or a foreign country.

A law called the Parental Kidnapping Prevention Act, or PKPA (28 U.S.C. §1738A and 42 U.S.C. §§654, 663), is a federal statute that addresses kidnapping by noncustodial parents and inconsistent child custody decisions made by state courts. The law provides penalties for kidnapping and requires states to recognize and enforce the custody decisions of courts in other states, rather than make a second, and possibly inconsistent, decision.

F. International Custody Disputes

"Comity" is a legal doctrine under which countries recognize and enforce the other countries' legal decrees. Under the Uniform Child Custody Jurisdiction Act and the Uniform Child Custody Jurisdiction and Enforcement Act (see Section E, above), courts in the U.S. must recognize properly-entered-into custody decrees of other nations. In turn, many other countries recognize U.S. custody orders.

The International Child Abduction Remedies Act (12 U.S.C. §§601 through 610) is a federal U.S. law that enables the Hague Convention on the Civil Aspects of International Child Abduction to be followed in the U.S. This Hague Convention is an agreement among the U.S. and over 60 other nations. Its purpose is to provide the prompt return of children wrongfully removed or retained in any participating country, and to ensure that the rights of custody and access under the law of one country are effectively respected in another. It addresses jurisdictional questions and provides common rules and procedures to determine child custody in a dispute that crosses international borders.

Most countries in the world have signed the Convention on the Rights of the Child. The United States has not signed it. This Convention describes an international commitment to children, and is relevant for children of divorced parents of different nationalities. Specifically, this convention provides that:

- both parents have responsibilities, rights and duties in common for the upbringing and development of their children
- all signatory nations have an obligation to support parents in providing their children the necessary protection and care to sustain a minimum quality of life
- children have the right to regular and sustained contact with both parents even across national borders
- decisions affecting children should preserve the best interests of the child, and
- children should be given a voice in the legal decisions which affect them.

You can learn more about the Convention on the Rights of Children—and what you can do to get the U.S.

to ratify the Convention—by visiting the website UNICEF-USA at http://www.unicefusa.org/infoactiv/rights.html.

If a child is abducted from the U.S. to another country or a child is abducted from another country and brought to the U.S., you can contact the U.S. State Department Office of Citizen and Counselor Services for help.

Finally, to prevent a child from being taken out of the U.S. without the custodial parent's consent, that parent can do the following:

- provide the State Department with a copy of a custody order showing who is the custodial parent, and
- request that the State Department withhold a child's passport unless it is requested by the custodial parent.

G. Custody and the IRS

The following tax benefits are available to parents to offset the cost of raising children:

- earned income credit
- child care credit
- medical expense deductions, and
- head of household filing status.

Only a custodial parent is entitled to claim the child care tax credit. In general, employed custodial parents of a dependent child under the age of 13 are eligible for the credit for child care expenses incurred so that the parent can earn an income. As the custodial parent's income increases, however, the credit phases out.

Both parents can claim a deduction for medical expenses actually paid, but only if those medical expenses exceed 7.5% of their adjusted gross income. If your total medical expenses are high enough, you may want to allocate them to the lowerwage earner so that that parent can take the deduction.

Only a parent with physical custody (meaning custody more than half of the time) can file as head of household. If the parents have joint legal and physical custody (and physical custody is divided 50-50), neither can file as head of household because the dependent child resides with neither parent for more than 50% of the year. If you have more than one minor child and share physical custody, you can specify your arrangement as 51% for one child with one parent and 51% for the other child with the other parent. Because each parent has a dependent child in the home more than 50% of the year, each parent can file as head of household. ■

Help Beyond the Book

Understanding and resolving child custody and parenting issues can be a challenge, but by reading this book and completing the various worksheets, you and the other parent have gone a long way toward building a successful separate parenting relationship. You now have more information, problem solving skills and insights than most parents who separate or divorce—and your children are the lucky beneficiaries of your efforts!

Many parents find that child custody and separate parenting issues are too difficult, emotional or technical to handle completely on their own. If this is true for you, consider taking any of the following courses of action:

- do some legal research
- research nonlegal issues, or
- work with any number of professionals, including mediators, counselors, attorneys, arbitrators, paralegals or child custody evaluators.

A. Researching Legal Issues

This brief discussion tells you how to use a reference from this book to look up a state or federal statute or court decision.

1. Finding a Law Library

To look up state or federal statutes or court decisions, go to your county law library (usually in the county courthouse) or the library of a law school that is open to the public. (Most law school libraries open to the public are ones at state universities. A private university law library must let members of the public in, too, if that library is a "federal depository." This means that it houses all federal government documents.) Some, but not all, large public libraries also have collections of state or federal statutes; call before you go.

2. Finding Background Materials

Before turning to statutes and cases to answer a legal question on child custody, it is often helpful to use a background resource. This will not only help you narrow your question, but will also, more often than not, get you to the right statute and case as well.

Three excellent books for researching state laws on child custody and visitation are:

- *Handling Child Custody, Abuse, and Adoption Cases,* by Ann M. Haralambie (Shepard's/McGraw-Hill)

- *Child Custody and Visitation Law and Practice* (Matthew Bender)
- *Joint Custody and Shared Parenting,* edited by Jay Folberg (Guildford Press).

3. Finding Statutes

When you look up a statute, try to use what is called an "annotated" version of the statutes. Annotated statutes include not only the texts of the statutes themselves, but also brief summaries of court cases and legal articles that have discussed each statute. After you look up a statute, you may want to read the cases listed, also, to see how courts have construed the language of the statute.

Federal statutes. Federal statutes are organized by subject in a set of books called the *United States Code* (U.S.C.), which is probably available in every law library. Libraries often have one or both annotated versions of the U.S.C.—either *United States Code Service* (U.S.C.S.) or *United States Code Annotated* (U.S.C.A.). If you know the statute's common name or its citation, you should be able to find it easily.

> EXAMPLE: You want to read some of the provisions of the International Child Abduction Remedies Act, 12 U.S.C. §601 and following. You would look in Title 12 of the U.S.C., U.S.C.S. or U.S.C.A. (the numbers are on the spine of the book) and find section 601. The statute begins with section 601 and includes many sections.

State statutes. State statutes, which fill many volumes, are often organized into "codes." Each code covers a separate area of law, such as Marriage and Divorce or Husbands and Wives. Although you probably won't have a citation from this book, you can look up the subject of the law you want to read in the index to the code or statutes.

4. Making Sure You Have the Most Recent Version of the Statute

Each year, state legislatures and Congress pass hundreds of new laws and change (amend) lots of existing ones. When you look up a statute, it's crucial that you get the most recent version.

To do that, always look for a pamphlet that is inserted in the back of the hardcover volume of statutes. It's called a pocket part, and it contains any changes made to the statute in the hardcover book since the hardcover was printed. Pocket parts are updated and replaced every year—it's much cheaper than producing a whole new hardcover volume every year.

Look up the statute again in the pocket part. If there's no entry, that means the statute hasn't been changed as of the date the pocket part was printed. If there is an entry, it will tell you what language in the statute has been changed.

To check for changes that are even more recent—made since the pocket part was printed—you can check something called the Advance Legislative Service. It's a series of paperback pamphlets that contain the very latest statutory changes.

5. Finding Cases

If you want to look up a case (court decision) and have the citation, all you need to do is decipher those strange numbers and abbreviations.

The proper citation for the case holding that it is unconstitutional for a court to consider race in a custody dispute is *Palmore v. Sidoti*, 466 U.S. 429 (1984).

The name of the case includes the name of the plaintiff (Palmore) followed by a v. (meaning versus) followed by the defendant's name (Sidoti). 466 is the volume number where the case is found in the series called *United States Reports* (abbreviated by U.S.) at page 429. The case was decided in 1984.

Only cases decided by the U.S. Supreme Court are published in the *United States Reports*. (They are also published in the *Supreme Court Reports*.) Most of the cases you'll want to read will have been decided by courts within your state, and published in volumes entitled something like *[name of your state] Reports* or *[name of your state] Appellate Reports,* or possibly in a reporter for a region of the U.S., such as the *Atlantic Reporter.* A law librarian can help you figure out exactly which series of reports contain the case you are looking for.

6. Making Sure the Case Is Still Good Law

Judges don't go back and change the words of earlier decisions, like legislatures amend old statutes, but cases can still be profoundly affected by later court decisions. For example, any state's highest court, usually called the Supreme Court, has the power to overrule a decision of a trial court or an appellate court. If it does, the trial court's or an appellate court's written decision no longer has any legal effect.

There are several ways to check to make sure a case you're relying on still represents valid law. The most common is to use a collection of books called *Shepard's*, which lets you compile a list of all later cases that mention the case you're interested in. Unfortunately, the *Shepard's* system is too complicated to explain here. If it's important to you, consult one of the legal research tools mentioned below.

7. More Legal Research

Legal research is a subject that can (and does) easily fill a whole book of its own. Here are some good resources if you want to delve further into the subject:

- For a thorough, how-to approach to finding answers to your legal questions, see *Legal Research: How to Find and Understand the Law*, by Stephen Elias and Susan Levinkind (Nolo, 1998).
- For an entertaining and informative video presentation of the basics of legal research, take a look at *Legal*

Research Made Easy: A Roadmap Through the Law Library, by Professor Robert Berring of the University of California-Berkeley (Nolo/LegalStar).

B. Researching Nonlegal Issues

The bibliography at the end of this chapter (Section F) lists a wide range of books and articles that discuss both the legal and nonlegal aspects of separate parenting. What follows are citations to books and articles that are particularly strong in certain areas. To find additional possible titles, browse in your public library or local bookstore.

1. Children and Divorce

- *Boys and Girls' Book About Divorce*, by Richard A. Gardner, M.D. (Jason Aronson, Inc.)
- *Divorce and Your Child: Practical Suggestions for Parents*, by Sonja Goldstein, LL.B., & Albert Solnit, M.D. (Yale University Press)
- *Growing Up Divorced*, by Linda Bird Francke (Linden Press/Simon & Schuster)
- *How It Feels When Parents Divorce*, by Jill Krementz (Alfred A. Knopf)
- *Mediation and the Special-Child Family*, by Jeff Davidson (Jossey-Bass), particularly pages 79-83.
- *My Parents Are Divorced Too*, by Bonnie Robson, M.D. (Everest House)

2. Conflict Resolution

- *Divorce and Decision Making: A Woman's Guide*, by Christina Robertson (Follett Publishing Company)
- *The Eight Essential Steps to Conflict Resolution*, by Dudley Weeks, Ph.D. (Jeremy Tarcher, Inc.)
- *Fighting Fair*, by Robert Coulson (The Free Press)
- *Getting to Yes: Negotiating Agreement Without Giving In*, by Roger Fisher & William Ury (Harvard Negotiation Project/Penguin Books)
- *A Guide to Divorce Mediation*, by Gary Friedman, J.D. (Workman Publishing)
- *You and Divorce Mediation*, by Richard H. Millen (Richard H. Millen)

3. Shared Custody

- *The Joint Custody Handbook: Creating Arrangements That Work*, by Miriam Galper Cohen (Running Press)

- *Mom's House, Dad's House: Making Shared Custody Work*, by Isolina Ricci, Ph.D. (Macmillan Publishing Co.)

4. Parenting Skills

- *Divorce and Your Child: Practical Suggestions for Parents*, by Sonja Goldstein, LL.B., & Albert Solnit, M.D. (Yale University Press)
- *Mom's House, Dad's House: Making Shared Custody Work*, by Isolina Ricci, Ph.D. (Macmillan Publishing Co.)

5. General Information About Divorce and Related Topics

- *Divorce and Child Custody*, by Deanna Peters & Richard L. Strohm (Layman's Law Guides)
- *Divorce and Decision Making: A Woman's Guide*, by Christina Robertson (Follett Publishing Company)
- *Effects of Divorce on the Visiting Father-Child Relationship*, by Judith S. Wallerstein, Ph.D., & Joan B. Kelly, Ph.D. (American Journal of Psychiatry, 1980)
- *Nolo's Pocket Guide to Family Law*, by Robin Leonard & Stephen Elias (Nolo)
- *Uncoupling: Turning Points in Intimate Relationships*, by Diane Vaughan (Oxford University Press)
- *You and Divorce Mediation*, by Richard H. Millen (Richard H. Millen)

C. Research on the World Wide Web

The following World Wide Web sites may have material that will be useful or help answer any questions you have.

Child Support Resources

Federal Office of Child Support Enforcement, Home Page
http://www.acf.dhhs.gov/ACFPrograms/CSE/index.html

General Divorce and Custody Resources

Dean Hughson's Divorce Page: Index of Resources
http://www.divorcesupport.com

Legal Dot Net: Family Law, An Overview
http://www.db.legal.net

Divorce Help Directory of Self-Help Services
http://www.divorcehelp.com/dir/dol.html

Divorce On-Line
http://www.divorceonline.com

Divorce Talk Newsletter
http://www.divorcetalkusa.com/divorcetalk.html

Mediate.com
http://www.mediate.com

Newsgroups
http://alt.support.divorce
usenet.alt.support.single-parents

Mental Health Resources

American Academy of Child and Adolescent Psychiatry Homepage
http://www.aacap.org

American Psychiatric Press, Inc.
http://www.appi.org/

American Association for Marriage and Family Therapy
http://www.9amft.org

Legal Information and Research

Nolo.com Self-Help Law Center
http://www.nolo.com

Law Around the Net
http://law.net/roundnet.html

U.S. Divorce Law
http://www.law.cornell.edu/topics/divorce.html

Law Group Network
http://www.llr.com/

Fathers' Rights

Fathers' Rights and Equality Exchange
http://www.vixcom/free/

Fathers' Resource Center
http://www.parentsplace.com/readroom/frc/index.html

General Parenting Support

Positive Parenting News
http://www.fishnet.net/~pparents/news.html

Parent's Place Reading Rooms
http://www.parentsplace.com/readroom/

D. Finding Professionals Who Can Help

Often, a human being can be a great help if you hit a road-block in negotiating or carrying out your parenting arrangements. Below are some suggestions on finding professionals who can help and what to expect of them. Because your relationship with any helping professional will be a deeply personal one, whenever possible, meet with two or three different people to see whose education, experience and style best match your needs.

Each section below includes a few questions you might use to structure your initial meeting with a professional. Use these questions only as one tool as you make a decision. More important in making your decision is your instinct, the professional's answers and any personal referrals you've received. The key is feeling comfortable working with the person. This means that you want someone who can:

- understand and identify with your general situation
- learn about your particular circumstances, and
- communicate effectively so you can make appropriate decisions.

1. Mediators

Mediators can help parents resolve separate parenting issues. The goal of mediation is for you and the other parent to develop an agreement which protects your children's best interests and is acceptable to both of you. Parents can use mediation to resolve some or all of their parenting issues or as a tool for reopening lines of communication and improving information exchanges. (Detailed discussion on mediation and mediators is in Chapter 7.)

When interviewing a mediator, you might ask questions such as:

- What kind of training have you had?
- What subjects do you usually help parents with in handling parenting disputes?
- How much experience have you had working with parents who are separating, divorcing or renegotiating an existing parenting plan?
- Are there any issues that might come up that you do not deal with (such as money or property issues)?
- How do you approach mediation?
- Will you make a recommendation regarding how we should resolve a problem if we cannot resolve it on our own?
- Will everything we discuss in mediation be confidential?

- Do you have any preferences for ways that parents should structure their parenting plans (such as having joint custody)?
- What are your fees?
- How long should this process take?

2. Counselors, Therapists and Other Mental Health Professionals

Counseling, therapy or other mental health assistance can be an important part of dealing with separation, divorce and separate parenting issues—for both parents and children. For example, if parents find that they cannot discuss any issue without arguing, dealing with the underlying feelings about themselves, each other or the end of the relationship can help. (Information about the role of counseling is in Chapter 7.)

Mental health professionals are fairly easy to find. You may be able to get referrals from friends or relatives, the local mental health department, a battered women's shelter, a school counselor, your religious advisor or your family physician. If none of those lead to possible candidates, you can look in your Yellow Pages directory under:

- Counseling
- Mental Health
- Psychiatrists
- Psychologists
- Psychotherapists, or
- Social Workers.

When interviewing a mental health professional, you might ask questions such as the following:

- What kind of training have you had?
- What subjects or skills did your training emphasize?
- How much experience have you had in working with individuals or families going through divorce or separation?
- How much do you know about childhood development?
- How well versed are you in the effects of divorce and separation on children?
- Do you have any biases about how parenting issues should be settled, such as favoring custody with the mother or joint custody?
- What is your fee?

- How long do you think I will need to spend with you to resolve the issues we've talked about?

3. Child Custody Evaluators

Most child custody evaluators are mental health professionals, but may not advertise these evaluation services. To get a list of potential evaluators, you can contact your court, a court-connected mediation program, a local mental health department, a family law or matrimonial law attorney or the local bar association.

When interviewing a child custody evaluator, you might ask all but the last question listed in Section 2, above, for counselors, therapists and other mental health professionals, as well as the following:

- How long does a child custody evaluation take?
- What kinds of information will you be looking for from me, the other parent and our children?
- How can I help make the evaluation process go smoothly?

4. Professionals With Training in Domestic Violence

Not every mental health professional or health care worker has the training and experience to understand and effectively deal with domestic violence issues. To find someone who does, be specific about what you are looking for. Many public mental health departments and all battered women's shelters have access to volunteer or paid staff members who know how to recognize and respond to families who have experienced domestic violence. Additional resources may be available through local police departments, hospitals and schools (especially in larger cities and metropolitan areas).

When interviewing a domestic violence support professional, you might ask questions such as:

- What kind of training have you had?
- What are the different ways you could help me?
- Do you have experience in working with children?
- Have you ever accompanied someone to mediation?
- Have you ever accompanied someone to a court hearing?
- Who else do you work with to support victims of domestic violence?

5. Professionals With Expertise in Dealing With Child Abuse

Assessing the nature and extent of child abuse or neglect often requires special training and expertise. Depending on the type of abuse that is suspected, doctors can help detect physical assaults, and psychologists or pediatric psychiatrists can help to discover and document emotional, sexual or other forms of abuse.

To find a professional with training in these areas, contact:

- the child protection division of your local welfare department
- your local police department
- your doctor
- a hospital
- your religious advisor
- the school your children attend, or
- a battered women's shelter.

When interviewing a professional who will be helping your child deal with issues associated with child abuse, you might ask questions such as:

- What kind of training have you had?
- What subjects or skills did your training emphasize?
- How much experience have you had in working with children whose parents are separated or divorced?
- How do you work with children my child's age?
- Who else do you work with once you have a clearer picture of what happened and how it has affected my child?

6. Attorneys

If you choose to work with an attorney and you have read some or all of this book, you will probably want someone who is willing to work with you rather than take over your case. More and more family and matrimonial law attorneys offer their clients a large role in shaping their own cases. Nevertheless, choosing the right attorney for your particular case is critically important.

Traditional lawyering tends to be highly adversarial. But only a handful of cases merit this kind of attention. Most separate parenting issues need a cooperative problem-solving approach rather than a contest to assign blame or guilt and declare who is a "better" parent.

If you decide that you need an attorney's advice, you will be happier if you first decide exactly what kind of help you need. For example, you may want:

- general information on certain issues of law
- information on how courts in your area tend to decide certain questions, or
- an analysis of what might happen if you took your case to trial.

Attorneys are very easy to find. You may be able to get referrals from friends or relatives, a battered women's shelter or a paralegal. If you are gay or lesbian, are from another country, are a member of a religious or ethnic minority, have a physical disability or are in some other way considered a minority, you need a lawyer particularly sensitive to your needs. Try contacting a local support group or legal organization for your community for names of possible attorneys. If none of those lead to candidates, you can contact your local bar association or look in your Yellow Pages directory.

What is most important is that you find an attorney whose skills and experience are adequate, whose style is compatible with the job you want performed and who will let you keep control over your case. Finding someone with a lot of family or matrimonial law experience will be attractive, but keep looking if that person opposes mediation (if you want to use it) or wants to take over your case entirely.

To find the right attorney for your situation, make a list of exactly what kind of help you want from an attorney, figure out how much you can afford and then interview two or three possible candidates. Start your initial meeting by explaining your needs and then by asking the following questions:

- Do you have any specialized training other than your legal education? (Some attorneys have advanced legal degrees, such as in tax law, which can be very helpful if you are going through a divorce; other attorneys are considered specialists in particular fields; still others have mediation training.)
- How many custody cases have you handled?
- How much do you know about childhood development?
- How well versed are you in the effects of divorce and separation on children?
- Do you have any biases about how parenting issues should be settled, such as favoring custody with the mother or joint custody?
- What legal issues do you anticipate will need resolving?

- How do you feel about resolving parenting disputes outside of court, such as through mediation or arbitration?
- How long do you think it will take to settle the issues we've discussed?
- What is your fee?

Each question defines a slightly different role for your attorney. Shopping for legal assistance in this way can be discouraging, because many attorneys hesitate to give any advice without full authority over all aspects of the case. If you persevere, however, you'll find an attorney willing to work with you in the way you have defined, and you'll be very happy with the overall results.

7.   Legal Typing Services (Independent Paralegals)

Thirty years ago, people who didn't want to hire a lawyer to help with a legal problem had two choices: handle the problem themselves or not have it handled at all. Now, businesses known as "typing services" or "independent paralegals" exist in many places to assist people in filling out the forms necessary to complete their own legal work. Independent paralegals often can help in routine family law matters, including the preparation and filing of a separate parenting agreement in the appropriate court on the appropriate form.

Independent paralegals are very different from lawyers. They cannot give legal advice or represent you in court—by law, only lawyers can do those things. When you consult an independent paralegal, it will still be up to you to decide what steps to take in your case, and to gather the information needed to complete necessary court forms. Independent paralegals can, however:

- steer you to appropriate written instructions and legal information you need to do your own legal work
- provide the appropriate court forms, and
- type your papers in a format acceptable to a court.

The following statement, posted in Divorce Centers of California, a prominent typing service near San Francisco, summarizes its services well:

WE ARE NOT ATTORNEYS

We are pro per assistants. Attorneys represent people. We assist people to represent themselves. If you want someone to represent you, you will need to hire an attorney. If you want to "do it yourself," we can help. We believe that representing yourself is the only way to gain, and keep, control over your own life and your own legal problems. You don't need legal training to use the courts or manage your own legal affairs. You have a constitutional right to represent yourself without an attorney. Let us assist you!

A recommendation from someone who has used an independent paralegal is the best way to find a reputable one in your area. Failing that, services often advertise in classified sections of newspapers under Referral Services, usually immediately following attorneys. Also check the Yellow Pages under Divorce Assistance or Legal Help. A local legal aid office may provide a reference, as will the occasional court clerk. Also, many offices advertise in local throwaway papers.

When interviewing a typing service or independent paralegal, you might ask questions such as:

- What kind of training have you had?
- Do you have experience filing forms in the court I will be using?
- Do you have experience filing all of the forms I will be using in my case?
- Who can answer your legal questions about filling out the forms I will be submitting?
- What happens if the court sends a form back saying it is not filled out properly, or that I need more forms prepared?

8.   Arbitrators

Arbitration is fairly uncommon in custody and visitation cases, but might be considered to obtain access to specialized expertise. For example, parents with a special-needs child might ask a specialist to evaluate and decide (which is what an arbitrator does) a particularly difficult legal custody or physical custody issue. (Arbitration is discussed in Chapter 7.)

Several organizations offer arbitration services. Perhaps the best known is the American Arbitration Association.

You can find a local chapter in the telephone directory, or you can contact the national headquarters, listed below, for referrals to local providers.

> American Arbitration Association
> 335 Madison Ave., 10F
> New York, NY 10017-4605
> Voice: 212-716-5800
> FAX: 212-716-5905
> Website: www.adr.org

The Conflict Resolution Center, listed below, publishes a directory of all kinds of ADR (Alternative or Appropriate Dispute Resolution) service providers, including arbitrators.

> National Institute for Dispute Resolution
> 1726 M Street NW, Suite 500
> Washington, DC 20036
> Voice: 202-466-4764
> FAX: 202-466-4769
> Website: www.nidr.org

The Society of Professionals In Dispute Resolution (SPIDR) is a national association of ADR service providers, including arbitrators. SPIDR has chapters in every state. You can contact a state or local chapter (look in a telephone directory) or the national headquarters:

> Society of Professionals In Dispute Resolution
> 1527 New Hampshire, #300
> Washington, DC 20005
> Voice: 202-667-9700
> FAX: 202-265-1968
> Website: www.spidr.org

In addition to these national organizations, arbitrators are listed in the Yellow Pages directory under Arbitration. You might also get referrals to arbitrators from a community mediation program, your court, your local mental health agency or the local bar association.

E. Additional Resources

Bill of Rights for Children of Divorce, by Vance Packard, 87 Mill Road, New Canaan, CT 06840. Vance Packard is a severe critic of the effects of divorce on children, and a staunch advocate of the child's right to remain whole in spite of his or her parents' divorce. His views are contained in his "Bill of Rights for Children of Divorce," which is printed below. Mr. Packard has given permission for parents to tear this out and keep it for their own use.

BILL OF RIGHTS FOR CHILDREN OF DIVORCE

1. Children of divorce are entitled to parents who set aside at least 20 minutes every month to discuss, in person or on the phone, the progress and problems of the children—and only the children. There should be no recriminations about any other topic, such as money. The children's schoolwork, health, mental state, activities and apparent reaction to the divorce should be the focus of such talks.
2. Children of divorce are entitled to parents who go out to dinner together with them, if desired by the child, on their birthdays or other important holidays. The parents should also both go to school events important to the children.
3. Children are entitled to have separated parents who do not belittle the other parent in front of the children.
4. Children of divorce are entitled to have parents who refrain from any action that would seem to force the children to take sides.
5. Children of divorce are entitled to be free from any sense of pressure from either parent to serve as informants about the ex-partner's spending, dating or other activities. If children freely choose to chat about the other parent, that is another matter.
6. Children of divorce are entitled to have complete freedom to phone either parent. If distances are involved, the calls will be collect. The children's parents will also agree that it is permissible for the noncustodial parent to call his or her children at least once a week.
7. Children of divorce are entitled to have parents who agree to notify each other in all emergencies or important events involving the children.
8. Children of divorce are entitled to have parents who by agreement are civil and avoid recriminations when they are in the presence of the child.

1. National Support Organizations

Step Family Foundation
(Assists stepfamilies)
333 West End Ave.
New York, NY 10023
Voice: 212-877-3244
FAX: 212-362-7030

ABA Center on Children and the Law
(Studies how courts deal with children and children's issues)
750 15th St. NW
Washington, DC 20005
Voice: 202-662-1720
FAX: 202-662-1755
Website: www.abanet.org

National Center for Youth and the Law
(Studies how courts and legislatures deal with children's issues)
114 Sansome St., Suite #900
San Francisco, CA 94104
Voice: 415-543-3307
FAX: 415-956-9024

Joint Custody Association
(Advocacy for joint custody arrangements and assistance to joint custodial parents)
10606 Wilkins Ave.
Los Angeles, CA 90024
Voice: 310-475-5352

Equality Nationwide for Unwed Fathers
(Advocacy and assistance for unwed fathers)
10606 Wilkins Ave.
Los Angeles, CA 90024
Voice: 310-475-5352

Kayama
(Assistance with obtaining a Jewish divorce)
1202 Avenue J
Brooklyn, NY 11230
Voice: 800-932-8589
FAX: 718-692-2044

Childfind Mediation Program
(Assistance for parents who have taken or are considering taking their child in violation of existing court orders)
P.O. Box 277
New Paltz, NY 12561
Voice: 800-AWAYOUT
FAX: 914-255-5706

Lambda Legal Defense and Education Fund
(Legal informational and referral for gay and lesbian parents)
120 Wall St., Suite 1500
New York, NY 10005-3904
Voice: 212-809-8585
FAX: 212809-0055

Custody Action for Lesbian Mothers
P.O. Box 281
Narbeth, PA 19072
215-667-7508

Gay & Lesbian Advocates & Defenders
(Legal informational and referral for gay and lesbian parents)
294 Washington St., #740
Boston, MA 02108
Voice: 617-426-1350

Lesbian Mothers' National Defense Fund
(Fundraising and advocacy for lesbian mothers)
P.O. Box 21567
Seattle, WA 98111
Voice: 206-325-2643

National Center for Lesbian Rights
(Legal informational and referral for gay and lesbian parents)
870 Market St., Suite 570
San Francisco, CA 94102
Voice: 415-392-6257
and
462 Broadway, Suite 500A
New York, NY 10013
Voice: 212-343-9589

2. Domestic Violence Resources

Domestic violence tends to carry forward from one generation to the next. Do yourselves and your children a favor—get help now and try to break the cycle.

You can get a referral to professionals with experience in domestic violence from many sources, including the following:

- battered women's shelters
- local mental health departments
- hospitals
- doctors
- school counselors

- religious institutions
- police departments
- social service agencies
- women's groups, and
- community organizations.

Many books and videos provide real and practical insights into managing anger and frustration more productively. A librarian, local mental health department or private practice counselor, psychologist or psychiatrist may be able to suggest materials or offer information about how to help your children deal with the issues.

3. Alcohol or Drug Abuse Organizations

Perhaps the best-known programs for alcohol and drug abuse are Alcoholics Anonymous, Al-Anon and Narcotics Anonymous. To find a local group, contact one of the national organizations as follows:

Alcoholics Anonymous
475 Riverside Dr.
New York, NY 10015
Voice: 212-870-3400
FAX: 212-870-3003

Al-Anon Family Groups
(For friends and families of alcoholics)
1372 Broadway
New York, NY 10018
Voice: 888-425-2666
FAX: 212-869-3757

Narcotics Anonymous
16155 Wyandotte St.
Van Nuys, CA 91406
Voice: 818-359-0084
FAX: 818-785-0123

Other ways to find alcohol or drug treatment programs or support groups include contacting your local mental health department, police department, hospital, family physician or library or consulting your Yellow Pages directory under the following headings:

- Alcoholism Information and Treatment, or
- Drug Abuse and Addiction.

F. Bibliography

- Ahrons, Constance R., Ph.D., *The Good Divorce*, Harper Collins Publishers, 1994.
- Brown, Neil D., Samis, Michelle D.C., "The Application of Structural Family Therapy in Developing the Binuclear Family," *Mediation Quarterly*, 1987, pp. 51–69.
- Bryant, Suzanne, "Mediation for Lesbian and Gay Families," *Mediation Quarterly*, 1992, pp. 391–395.
- Burbano, Maria Elena, Cordona, Ray, "Cross-cultural Issues In Mediation," *Mediation Quarterly*, 1992.
- Campbell, Linda E.G., Johnston, Janet R., "Multifamily Mediation: The Use of Groups to Resolve Child Custody Disputes," *Mediation Quarterly*, 1987, pp. 137-162.
- Charlesworth, Stephanie, "The Acceptance of Family Mediation in Australia," *Mediation Quarterly*, 1991.
- Cloke, Kenneth, "Shared Custody: A Case Study in Mediation," *Mediation Quarterly*, 1988, pp. 31–35.
- Cohen, Miriam Galper, *The Joint Custody Handbook: Creating Arrangements That Work*, Running Press, 1991.
- Corcoran, Kathleen O'Connell, Melamed, James C., "From Coercion to Empowerment: Spousal Abuse and Mediation," *Mediation Quarterly*, 1990, pp. 303–316.
- Coulson, Robert, *Fighting Fair*, The Free Press, 1983.
- Davidson, Jeff, "Mediation and the Special-Child Family," *Mediation Quarterly*, 1987, pp. 79–83.
- Davis, Albie M., Salem, Richard A., "Dealing With Power Imbalances in the Mediation of Interpersonal Disputes," *Mediation Quarterly*, 1984, pp. 17–26.
- Edelman, Joel, Crain, Mary Beth, *The Tao of Negotiation*, Harper Business Press, 1993.
- Emery, Robert E., Jackson, Joanne A., "The Charlottesville Mediation Project: Mediated and Litigated Child Custody Disputes," *Mediation Quarterly*, 1989, pp. 3–18.
- Erickson, Stephen K., Erickson, Marilyn S. McKnight, "Dan and Linda: A Typical Divorce Mediation Case," *Mediation Quarterly*, 1988, pp. 3–21.
- Fisher, Roger, Ury, William, *Getting to Yes: Negotiating Agreement Without Giving In*, Harvard Negotiation Project, Penguin Books, 1981.
- Francke, Linda Bird, *Growing Up Divorced*, Linden Press/Simon & Schuster, 1983.
- Friedman, Gary J., J.D., *A Guide to Divorce Mediation*, Workman Publishing, 1993.

- Gadlin, Howard, Ouellette, Patricia A., "Mediation Milanese: An Application of Systemic Family Therapy Approach to Family Mediation," *Mediation Quarterly*, 1987, pp. 101–118.
- Gardner, Richard A., M.D., *Boys and Girls' Book About Divorce*, Jason Aronson, Inc., 1983.
- Garwood, Fiona, "Divorce and Conciliation in Sweden and Scotland," *Mediation Quarterly*, 1991, pp. 293–301.
- Goldstein, Sonja, LL.B., Solnit, Albert, M.D., *Divorce and Your Child: Practical Suggestions for Parents*, Yale University Press, 1984.
- Haynes, John M., "John and Mary: Sharing Parenting After Divorce," *Mediation Quarterly*, 1988, pp. 23–29.
- Haynes, John M., "The Process of Negotiations," *Mediation Quarterly*, 1983, pp. 75–92.
- Heitler, Susan M., Ph.D., *From Conflict to Resolution: Strategies for Diagnosis and Treatment of Distressed Individuals, Couples and Families*, W.W. Norton & Co., 1990.
- Hurt, Barbara J., "Gentle Jeopardy: The Further Endangerment of Battered Women and Children in Custody Mediation," *Mediation Quarterly*, 1990, pp. 317–330.
- Ihara, Toni, Warner, Ralph, *The Living Together Kit*, Nolo Press, 1990.
- Kaplan, Nancy M., "The Development and Operation of the Northwest Mediation Service," *Mediation Quarterly*, 1984, pp. 47–58.
- Kelly, Joan B., "Mediation and Psychotherapy: Distinguishing the Differences," *Mediation Quarterly*, 1983, pp. 33–44.
- Kirkpatrick, Gary, "The Good, The Bad, The Indifferent," *Mediation Quarterly*, 1988, pp. 37–45.
- Kirkpatrick, Martha, M.D., Smith, Catherine, Roy, Ron, M.D., *Lesbian Mothers and Their Children: A Comparative Survey*, American Orthopsychiatric Association, Inc., 1981.
- Krementz, Jill, *How It Feels When Parents Divorce*, Alfred A. Knopf, 1984.
- Leitch, M. Laurie, "The Politics Of Compromise: A Feminist Perspective On Mediation," *Mediation Quarterly*, 1987, pp. 163–175.
- Lemmon, John Allen, Ed.D., "Dimensions and Practice of Divorce Mediation," *Mediation Quarterly*, 1983.
- Leonard, Robin, Elias, Stephen, *Nolo's Pocket Guide to Family Law*, Nolo Press, 1994.
- LeResche, Diane, "Comparison of the American Mediation Process With a Korean-American Harmony Restoration Process," *Mediation Quarterly*, 1992, pp. 323–339.
- Levy, Bert, *Trust—The Main Ingredient for a Successful Mediation*, Bancroft Whitney, 1993.
- Lutker, Eric R., Ph.D., Wand, Carl F., Esq., *Do It Yourself Divorce*, The Forms Man, 1992.
- Maccoby, Eleanor E., Mnookin, Robert H., *Dividing the Child: Social and Legal Dilemmas of Custody*, Harvard Press, 1992.
- Maxwell, David, "Gender Differences in Mediation Style and Their Impact on Mediator Effectiveness," *Mediation Quarterly*, 1992, pp. 353–364.
- Mayer, Bernard, "Mediation in Child Protection Cases: The Impact of Third-Party Intervention on Parental Compliance Attitudes," *Mediation Quarterly*, 1989, pp. 89–106.
- McIsaac, Hugh, "Toward a Classification of Child Custody Disputes: An Application of Family Systems Theory," *Mediation Quarterly*, 1987, pp. 39–50.
- Mehren, Elizabeth, "Lesbian Mothers: Two New Studies Shatter Stereotypes," *Los Angeles Times*, June 1, 1983.
- Melton, Gary, *Families and the Courts in the Twenty-first Century*, University of Nebraska, 1992.
- Millen, Richard H., *You and Divorce Mediation*, Richard H. Millen, 1991.
- Miller, Brian, "Gay Fathers and Their Children," *The Family Coordinator*, 1979.
- National Center for State Courts, *National Symposium on Court-Connected Dispute Resolution Research*, State Justice Institute, 1994.
- Oshiro, Donna A., O'Donnell, Clifford R., *A Culturally Competent Legal System: Cultural Factors in Family Court Cases in Hawaii*, University of Hawaii, 1992.
- O'Toole, Kathleen, "Joint Custody Can Work," *Academy of Family Mediation News #10.4*, 1992.
- Pagelow, Mildred Daley, "Effects of Domestic Violence on Children and Their Consequences for Custody and Visitation Agreements," *Mediation Quarterly*, 1990, pp. 347–363.
- Peters, Deanna, Strohm, Richard L., *Divorce and Child Custody*, Layman's Law Guides, 1993.
- Plesent, Emanuel, "Mediation for Reconciliation," *Mediation Quarterly*, 1988, pp. 47–50.
- Ricci, Isolina, Ph.D., *Mom's House, Dad's House: Making Shared Custody Work*, Macmillan Publishing Co., 1998.
- Robertson, Christina, *Divorce and Decision Making: A Woman's Guide*, Follett Publishing Company, 1980.

- Robson, Bonnie, M.D., *My Parents Are Divorced Too,* Everest House, 1980.
- Rogers, Susan J., "The Dynamics of Conflict Behavior in a Mediated Dispute," *Mediation Quarterly*, 1987, pp. 61–71.
- Samis, Michelle D.C., Saposnek, Donald T., "Parent-Child Relationships in Family Mediation: A Synthesis of Views," *Mediation Quarterly*, 1987.
- Saposnek, Donald T., "Aikido: A Systems Model for Maneuvering in Mediation," *Mediation Quarterly*, 1987, pp. 119–136.
- Saposnek, Donald T., "Strategies in Child Custody Mediation: A Family Systems Approach," *Mediation Quarterly*, 1983, pp. 29–54.
- Saposnek, Donald T., "The Value of Children in Mediation: A Cross-Cultural Perspective," *Mediation Quarterly*, 1991, pp. 325–342.
- Sargent, George, Moss, Bleema, "Eriksonian Approaches in Family Therapy and Mediation," *Mediation Quarterly*, 1987, pp. 87–100.
- Sherman, Ed, *Practical Divorce Solutions*, Nolo Press Occidental, 1994.
- Stern, Marilyn, Van Slyck, Michael R., Newland, Lori M, "Adolescent Development and Family Dynamics: Delineating a Knowledge Base for Family Mediation," *Mediation Quarterly*, pp. 307–322.
- Stuart, Richard B., Jacobson, Barbara, "Principles of Divorce Mediation: A Social Learning Theory Approach," *Mediation Quarterly*, 1987.
- Vaughan, Diane, *Uncoupling: Turning Points in Intimate Relationships*, Oxford University Press, 1986.
- Walker, Janet A., "Family Mediation in England: Strategies for Gaining Acceptance," *Mediation Quarterly*, 1991.
- Wallerstein, Judith S., Ph.D., "Children and Divorce," *Pediatrics in Review*, 1980.
- Wallerstein, Judith S., Ph.D., "Psychodynamic Perspectives on Family Mediation," *Mediation Quarterly*, 1987, pp. 7–21.
- Wallerstein, Judith S., Ph.D., "The Impact of Divorce on Children," *Psychiatric Clinics of North America*, 1980.
- Wallerstein, Judith S., Ph.D., Kelly, Joan B., Ph.D., "Effects of Divorce on the Visiting Father-Child Relationship," *American Journal of Psychiatry*, 1980.
- Weeks, Dudley, Ph.D., *The Eight Essential Steps to Conflict Resolution*, Jeremy Tarcher, Inc., 1992.
- Yahm, Howard, "Divorce Mediation: A Psychoanalytic Perspective," *Mediation Quarterly*, 1984, pp. 59–63.
- Zaidel, Susan, "Challenges Facing the Development of Family Mediation in Israel," *Mediation Quarterly*, 1991, pp. 281–292. ■

Appendix: Tear-Out Forms

Worksheet 1: Describe Your Child

Worksheet 2: Describe Your Relationship With Your Child

Worksheet 3: Adding the Details

Worksheet 4: Checklist of Issues for Your Parenting Agreement

Parenting Agreement

WORKSHEET 1: DESCRIBE YOUR CHILD

Child's name: _____

1. What kind of person is this child?

    _____

    _____

2. What makes this child special?

    _____

    _____

3. How does this child like the current parenting arrangements?

    _____

    _____

    _____

    _____

4. How has this child's behavior changed since the separation or divorce?

    _____

    _____

    _____

    _____

5. Has this child expressed any preferences regarding the future?

    _____

    _____

    _____

6. How does this child react to change?

    _____

    _____

7. What makes change easier for this child to accept?

    _____

    _____

8. How does this child let you know that something is wrong?

    _____

    _____

    _____

9. Who else is important in this child's life?

    _____

    _____

WORKSHEET 2: DESCRIBE YOUR RELATIONSHIP WITH YOUR CHILD

Child's name: _____

1. What do you and this child like to do together?

   _____
   _____
   _____

2. What are your plans and wishes for this child's future?

   _____
   _____
   _____

3. What do you think are the most important things for this child to achieve?

   _____
   _____
   _____

4. How do you and this child handle and resolve conflict?

   _____
   _____
   _____

5. How do you handle discipline with this child?

   _____
   _____
   _____

6. How did you share parenting responsibilities and time with this child during the time you were married or living together?

   _____
   _____
   _____

7. How do you and the other parent share parenting responsibilities and time with this child now?

   _____
   _____
   _____
   _____

8. Are you happy with the current arrangements? (Please explain)

   _____
   _____
   _____
   _____

9. Is this child happy with the current arrangements? (Please explain)

_____

_____

_____

10. If changes are in order, what would you suggest?

_____

_____

_____

_____

_____

_____

_____

WORKSHEET 3: ADDING THE DETAILS

1. List of existing court documents, orders or agreements. (Note that the terms listed here might be different in your state. See Chapter 12 for the terms used in your state.)

_____

_____

_____

_____

2. Parent's name, occupation and work schedule.

_____

_____

3. Schedule of children's activities (such as school, religious training and after-school activities).

_____

_____

_____

_____

4. Children's special needs or interests.

_____

_____

_____

5. Religion.

_____   _____

_____   _____

6. Where do you live now?

_____

_____

7. Do you have any plans to relocate from the area? (Please explain)

_____

_____

_____

8. Do you have any plans for remarriage?

_____

_____

9. Are there any adult relatives or friends with whom the children should or should not have close contact?

_____

_____

_____

10. Counseling for children.

_____
_____
_____

11. Counseling for parents.

_____
_____
_____

12. Do you want to address domestic violence issues in your parenting agreement? If yes, why?

_____
_____
_____
_____

13. Do you want to address the use or abuse of drugs or alcohol in your parenting agreement? If yes, how do you think these issues should be handled in your parenting agreement?

_____
_____
_____
_____

14. Do you have any special concerns about your parenting arrangements?

_____
_____
_____

15. Do you have any special concerns about your relationship with the other parent?

_____
_____
_____
_____

WORKSHEET 4: CHECKLIST OF ISSUES FOR YOUR PARENTING AGREEMENT

1. Existing court documents, orders or agreements which must be changed to accommodate your parenting agreement.

2. Existing agreements to consider while negotiating this parenting agreement.

3. Steps you will have to take to resolve legal or religious issues such as divorce, legal separation, annulment, etc.

4. Any concerns or recommendations made by a counselor, school teacher, therapist or other interested adult regarding your children's emotional, spiritual or physical well-being.

5. Each child's current relationship with each parent.

6. Each child's feelings, reactions or concerns about separation or divorce.

7. Changes you think would be good in each child's current relationship with each parent.

_____
_____
_____
_____
_____
_____

8. Changes that may be necessary in each child's current relationship with each parent.

_____
_____
_____
_____
_____

9. Current problem areas for children.

_____
_____
_____
_____
_____

10. Current areas of conflict between the parents.

_____
_____
_____
_____
_____

11. Changes either parent would like to see in current parenting relationship.

_____
_____
_____
_____
_____

12. Times when either parent is available to care for children: _____
_____

13. Times when only _____ is available to care for children: _____

14. Times when only _____ is available to care for children: _____

15. Other adults children will be spending time with.

_____
_____

16. Adults or minors the children should not spend time with (or be alone with).

_____

_____

17. Any problems with violence, abuse or neglect that would have to be accommodated.

_____

_____

_____

_____

_____

_____

_____

18. Other comments or issues to be included.

_____

_____

_____

_____

_____

_____

_____

_____

_____

_____

_____

PARENTING AGREEMENT

A. Parties. The following is a mutually acceptable agreement between _____
_____ and _____
_____ regarding how we will share parenting responsibilities for our children [list names]:

_____   _____

_____   _____

_____   _____

_____   _____

B. How Long This Agreement Lasts. The term of this agreement is _____ [period of time].

If this is a temporary agreement, we will negotiate a new agreement on or before _____ [date].

C. Terms of the Agreement.

#_____ **Medical, Dental and Vision Care**

_____ Our children's medical, dental and vision care providers will be [choose one]:

    _____ We will use only the following health care providers:

      _____ [medical].
      _____ [dental].
      _____ [vision].

    _____ We will each choose health care providers. We will exchange names, addresses, phone numbers and releases so that our providers can share records and information.

_____ _____ [parent] will see to it that our children receive their routine care.

_____ Our children's special health care needs will be met as follows [specify]:

_____
_____
_____

_____ In a medical emergency [choose one]:

    _____ Either parent may seek medical treatment and must inform the other parent as soon as possible thereafter.

    _____ Either parent may seek medical treatment, except for the following procedures or interventions:

    _____
    _____

_____ _____ [parent] is the only person who may seek medical treatment.

_____ If our children develop an ongoing medical condition or have other special health care concerns, we will assure consistency in their care as follows [choose all that apply]:

    _____ We will share all medical records.
    _____ We will include the medications with our children as they travel between our homes.
    _____ We will each fill all prescriptions and dispense the medications when caring for our children.
    _____ We will exchange written instructions on needed care.
    _____ We will each keep whatever physical supports or enhancements our children need in our home.

_____ Our children will receive the following dental care [specify]:

_____
_____
_____

_____ Our children will receive the following vision care [specify]:

_____
_____
_____

_____ We further agree that [specify]:

_____

_____

_____

#_____ **Psychiatric and Other Mental Health Care**

_____ Our children may undergo psychiatric or other mental health care as follows [choose all that apply]:

    _____ If either parent feels it is necessary.

    _____ If it is recommended by a school counselor or other health care provider.

    _____ Only if we agree.

    _____ Only if it is made available through the school.

    _____ Only if it is available at low or no cost to us.

_____ Either of us may undergo psychiatric or other mental health care as follows [choose all that apply]:

    _____ If either parent feels it is necessary.

    _____ If it is recommended by a school counselor or other health care provider.

    _____ Only if we agree.

    _____ Only if it is made available through the school.

    _____ Only if it is available at low or no cost to us.

_____ Our children's other mental health issues, such as _____ [specify],

will be addressed as follows [specify]:

_____

_____

_____

#_____ **Education**

_____ Our children will attend [choose one]:

    _____ public school.

    _____ private school.

    _____ home school.

_____ We will pay for any private or home school as follows [specify]:

_____

_____

_____

_____ Any decision to change schools will be made as follows [choose all that apply]:

    _____ If we agree.

    _____ After consulting our children.

    _____ After consulting with _____ [parent].

    _____ Only _____ [parent] may change our

    children's enrollment in a particular school.

_____ Any decisions to support our children's special educational needs or talents will be made as follows [choose all that apply]:

    _____ If we agree.

    _____ After consulting our children.

    _____ After consulting with _____ [parent].

    _____ Only _____ [parent] may decide

    how to support our children's special education needs.

_____ We will participate in parent associations as follows [choose one]:

    _____ Either parent may participate.

    _____ Only one parent may participate at a time.

    _____ _____ [parent] will participate.

_____ We will participate in the classroom as follows [choose one]:

     _____ Either parent may participate.

     _____ Only one parent may participate at a time.

     _____ _____ [parent] will participate.

_____ We will participate in parent-chaperoned events as follows [choose one]:

     _____ Either parent may participate.

     _____ Only one parent may participate at a time.

     _____ _____ [parent] will participate.

_____ We will attend parent-teacher or other school conferences as follows [choose one]:

     _____ Both will attend.

     _____ Each will schedule a meeting with the teacher or other school official.

     _____ _____ [parent] will attend and will inform the other of the matters discussed.

     _____ _____ [parent] will attend and will not inform the other of the matters discussed.

_____ Any emergency contact information needed by a school will be completed as follows [choose one]:

     _____ We both will be listed in the following order:

     _____

     _____

     _____ Only _____ [parent] will be listed.

     _____ Others to be listed will be [list names]:

     _____

     _____

     _____

_____ Good school performance means:

_____

We will encourage good school performance as follows [choose all that apply]:

     _____ After discussion and agreement.

     _____ After consultation with our children.

     _____ With the following rewards:

     _____

     _____

_____ Poor school performance means:

_____

We will discourage poor school performance by [specify]:

_____

_____

_____

_____ Our children [check one] ☐ may ☐ may not attend sex education classes at school.

     _____ _____ [parent] will notify the school of this decision.

_____ Our children's post-secondary education will be paid for as follows [specify]:

_____

_____

_____ Any decisions regarding our children's options for post-secondary education will be made as follows

[choose all that apply]:

     _____ By agreement between parents and children.

     _____ Based on the children's interest and ability to be accepted at a particular school.

     _____ Based on what we can afford.

     _____ Other [specify]:

     _____

     _____

     _____

_____ We further agree that [specify]:

_____
_____
_____

#_____ **Surname**

_____ Our children's surname is _____.

Any decision to change that surname will be made as follows [choose all that apply]:
_____ Our children will keep this surname until they become legal adults.
_____ Our children may choose their surname.
_____ Our children may choose their surname after age _____.
_____ We will discuss and agree on any change of surname.
_____ _____ [parent] has the authority to change our children's surname.

_____ We further agree that [specify]:

_____
_____
_____

#_____ **Religious Training**

_____ Our children's religious beliefs and training will be as follows [choose all that apply]:
_____ Our children will be raised _____ [specify].
_____ Our children will be taught about both of our religions: _____
and _____.
_____ Our children may choose their religious training as long as it generally conforms to the principles of the
_____ religion.
_____ Our children may choose their religious training. _____ [parent]
will supervise such training.

_____ We further agree that [specify]:

_____
_____
_____

#_____ **International Travel and Passports**

_____ Our children may obtain a passport under the following conditions [choose one]:
_____ Either parent may obtain a passport if it is necessary for travel.
_____ Either parent may obtain a passport, but our children may travel out of the country only if the other parent
approves of the itinerary and the dates of the trip.
_____ Either parent may obtain a passport, but our children may not travel out of the country unless _____
_____ [adult's name] travels with them.
_____ A passport may not be issued to our children under any circumstances.
_____ Only _____ may obtain a passport for the children.

_____ We further agree that [specify]:

_____
_____
_____

#_____ **Driving and Owning a Car, Motorcycle or Off-Road Vehicle**

_____ We will permit our children to own a car.
_____ We will not permit our children to own a car.
_____ We will permit our children to drive a car under the following conditions [choose all that apply]:
_____ After completing a certified training course.
_____ With the consent of _____ [one or both parents].
_____ With adult supervision.

_____ Driving only on unpaved roads.
_____ Using a family car.
_____ After buying a car.
_____ After being given a car.
_____ After paying their own car insurance.
_____ They must pay for any tickets received while operating the car.

_____ We will permit our children to own a motorcycle.

_____ We will not permit our children to own a motorcycle.

_____ We will permit our children to drive a motorcycle under the following conditions [choose all that apply]:
_____ After completing a certified training course.
_____ With the consent of _____ [one or both parents].
_____ With adult supervision.
_____ Driving only on unpaved roads.
_____ Using a family motorcycle.
_____ After buying a motorcycle.
_____ After being given a motorcycle.
_____ After paying their own motorcycle insurance.
_____ They must pay for any tickets received while operating the motorcycle.

_____ We will permit our children to own an off-road vehicle.

_____ We will not permit our children to own an off-road vehicle.

_____ We will permit our children to drive an off-road vehicle under the following conditions [choose all that apply]:
_____ After completing a certified training course.
_____ With the consent of _____ [one or both parents].
_____ With adult supervision.
_____ Driving only on unpaved roads.
_____ Using a family off-road vehicle.
_____ After buying an off-road vehicle.
_____ After being given an off-road vehicle.
_____ After paying their own off-road vehicle insurance.
_____ They must pay for any tickets received while operating the off-road vehicle.

_____ We further agree that [specify]:

_____
_____
_____

#_____ **Military Service**

_____ Our children may enter military service if they are under the legal age as follows [choose all that apply]:
_____ If they so choose.
_____ In the event of a war.
_____ If they are at least age _____.
_____ If we both agree.
_____ If _____ [parent] consents.
_____ Never.
_____ We further agree that [specify]:

_____
_____
_____

#_____ **Allowing Underage Marriage**

_____ Our children may marry if they are under the legal age as follows [choose all that apply]:
_____ If they so choose.

_____ In the event of a pregnancy.

_____ If they are at least age _____ .

_____ If we both agree.

_____ If _____ [parent] consents.

_____ Never.

_____ We further agree that [specify]:

_____

_____

#_____ **Insurance**

_____ Our children's medical insurance will be provided as follows [choose all that apply]:

_____ We both will obtain coverage if it is available through an employer at low or no cost.

_____ We will share the costs of any uncovered expenses as follows [specify]:

_____

_____

_____ _____ [parent]

will obtain coverage up to $ _____ under the following conditions [choose all that apply]:

_____ Type of coverage: _____

_____ Named beneficiaries: _____

_____ Insurance claims submitted by: _____ [parent].

_____ Our children's dental insurance will be provided as follows [choose all that apply]:

_____ We both will obtain coverage if it is available through an employer at low or no cost.

_____ We will share the costs of any uncovered expenses as follows [specify]:

_____

_____

_____ _____ [parent]

will obtain coverage up to $ _____ under the following conditions [choose all that apply]:

_____ Type of coverage: _____

_____ Named beneficiaries: _____

_____ Insurance claims submitted by: _____ [parent].

_____ Our children's vision care will be provided as follows [choose all that apply]:

_____ We both will obtain coverage if it is available through an employer at low or no cost.

_____ We will share the costs of any uncovered expenses as follows [specify]:

_____

_____

_____ _____ [parent]

will obtain coverage up to $ _____ under the following conditions [choose all that apply]:

_____ Type of coverage: _____

_____ Named beneficiaries: _____

_____ Insurance claims submitted by: _____ [parent].

_____ We will obtain life insurance coverage as follows [choose all that apply]:

_____ We both will obtain coverage if it is available through an employer at low or no cost.

_____ We will share the costs of any uncovered expenses as follows [specify]:

_____

_____

_____ _____ [parent]

will obtain coverage up to $ _____ under the following conditions [choose all that apply]:

_____ Type of coverage: _____

_____ Named beneficiaries: _____

_____ Insurance claims submitted by: _____ [parent].
_____ We will obtain _____ insurance as follows [choose all that apply]:
    _____ We both will obtain coverage if it is available through an employer at low or no cost.
    _____ We will share the costs of any uncovered expenses as follows [specify]:

_____

_____

_____ _____ [parent]
will obtain coverage up to $ _____ under the following conditions [choose all that apply]:
    _____ Type of coverage: _____
    _____ Named beneficiaries: _____

_____ Insurance claims submitted by: _____ [parent].

#_____ **Making Decisions**

_____ Choose all that apply:
    _____ Whenever possible, we will discuss the issues and attempt to reach an agreement.
    _____ We both will make an effort to remain aware of our children's interests, activities, school performance and overall health.
    _____ _____ [parent] will make an effort to keep _____ [other parent] aware of our children's interests, activities, school performance and overall health.
    _____ _____ [parent], as the primary caretaker, will be responsible to make [most/all] of the decisions on behalf of our children and will inform _____ [other parent] as soon as possible thereafter.
    _____ _____ [parent], as the primary caretaker, will be responsible to make all of the decisions on behalf of our children and need not inform _____ [other parent] of these decisions.
    _____ _____ [other adult/guardian] will be given authority to make decisions on behalf of our children.

_____ We further agree that [specify]:

_____

_____

_____

#_____ **Resolving Disputes When Making Decisions Together**

_____ If disagreements arise regarding this Parenting Agreement or our general parenting arrangements, we agree as follows [choose all that apply]:
    _____ _____ [parent] has authority to make final decisions when we can't agree.
    _____ Before this parent makes a final decision which resolves a disagreement, he/she will consult with _____ [other adult] for advice.
    _____ _____ [parent] has authority to make final decisions regarding _____ [specify] and _____ [other parent] has authority to m1ake final decisions regarding _____ [specify].

_____ We will participate in the following, at either parent's request [choose all that apply]:
    _____ counseling
    _____ mediation
    _____ arbitration
    _____ meeting with attorney[s]
    _____ other: _____ [specify]

_____ We further agree that [specify]:

_____

_____

_____

#_____ **Exchanging Information**

_____ We will not ask our children to carry messages between us.

_____ We will share information about the children [choose all that apply]:

 _____ at least every _____ [specify interval of time].

 _____ with each exchange of our children.

 _____ the day or evening before an exchange.

 _____ as needed.

_____ (Parent)/We will assume the responsibility to establish contact with the appropriate sources of information

regarding our children's [choose all that apply]:

 _____ health care

 _____ school

 _____ sports

 _____ other: _____ [specify]

_____ We will communicate with each other [choose all that apply]:

 _____ in person

 _____ by telephone

 _____ by letter

 _____ by email

 _____ other: _____ [specify]

_____ We further agree that [specify]:

_____

_____

#_____ **Where Our Children Will Live**

_____ Our children shall live primarily with _____ [parent] and live with

_____ [other parent] as follows [specify; include days and times of exchanges]:

_____

_____

_____

_____ Our children will alternate between our homes as follows [choose one]:

 _____ Alternating weekends (Friday 6 pm to Sunday 6 pm)

 _____ Alternating weekends (Friday 6 pm to Monday am)

 _____ Alternating weekends (Friday 6 pm to Sunday 6 pm), weekly midweek visit

 (Wednesday 5 pm to 8 pm)

 _____ Alternating weekends (Friday 6 pm to Sunday 6 pm), weekly midweek overnight

 (Wednesday 5 pm to Thursday, start of school)

 _____ Alternating weekends (Friday 6 pm to Monday at school), weekly midweek overnight

 (Wednesday 5 pm to Thursday 7 am)

 _____ Two to three weekly contacts for two to three hours each; Saturday or Sunday visits gradually expanded to

 six hours each as the child gains security; overnight visits added approximately six to 12 months after

 visitation starts as child is secure

 _____ Live in _____'s (parent's name)

 home except for alternating weekends, alternating holidays and a portion of the summer.

 _____ Live in _____'s (parent's name)

 home except for midweek overnights, most weekends, alternating holidays and a portion of the summer.

 _____ Live in _____'s (parent's name) home and

 visit _____ for short or daytime visits only.

_____ Monday afternoon to Wednesday am with _____

(parent's name), Wednesday pm to Friday am with _____

(parent's name), alternating weekends, Friday to Monday am with each parent.

_____ Monday am to Wednesday am with _____

(parent's name), Wednesday am to Friday am with _____

(parent's name), each weekend is split (Friday pm to Saturday pm with _____

_____ (parent's name), Saturday pm to

Monday am with _____ (parent's name).

_____ Tuesday and Thursday 4 pm to 7 pm and Saturday 10 am to Sunday 10 am with _____

_____ (parent's name), and the balance

of the week with _____ (parent's name).

_____ Tuesday 4 pm to Wednesday 9 am, Thursday 4 pm to 7 pm and Saturday 5 pm to Sunday 5 pm with

_____ (parent's name), and the balance

of the week with _____ (parent's name).

_____ Children will alternate living in each home every:

    _____ week

    _____ two weeks

    _____ month

    _____ six months

    _____ other: (describe) _____

_____ Children live in _____'s (parent's name) home

during the week and in _____'s (parent's

name) home on the weekends.

_____ During the school term, the children live in _____'s

(parent's name) home during the week and in _____'s

(parent's name) home on the weekends. During the summer, the children will live in _____

_____'s (parent's name) home during the week and

in _____'s (parent's name) home on weekends.

_____ Our children's schedule for each month will be as follows [specify; include days and times of exchanges]:

Week 1: _____

Week 2: _____

Week 3: _____

Week 4: _____

Week 5: _____

_____ Our children will not live with either of us, but with _____ [other adult].

We will spend time with our children as follows [specify; include days and times of exchanges]:

_____

_____

_____ Our children will reside at _____ school

and spend time with each of us as follows [specify; include days and times of exchanges]:

_____

_____

_____ Our children will remain in one home. We will take turns living there as follows [specify; include days and times

of each parent's arrival and departure]:

_____

_____

_____ We further agree that [specify]:

_____

_____

_____

#_____ **Domestic Violence, Child Abuse and Child Neglect**

_____ If events such as _____ [specify] occur,

_____ [parent] may seek a restraining order from the court which will [specify]:

_____

_____

_____

_____

_____ Anyone providing care for our children other than a parent will be told about any existing restraining orders.

_____ [parent] will seek counseling from _____

_____ [provider] regarding _____

_____ [specify]; also [choose all that apply]:

_____ Parent and provider will be permitted to determine when the need for counseling has concluded.

_____ At the conclusion of parent's counseling, provider will send a letter to _____
[other parent] indicating that counseling has concluded to the parent and provider's satisfaction.

_____ We will offer counseling and emotional support to our children as indicated in issue # _____ [Psychiatric and Other Mental Health Care].

_____ If our children are exposed to a violent or otherwise dangerous situation, the parent in whose care they are will remove them from the situation and, if necessary, find another adult to provide care for them.

_____ Our children may call _____ [adult's name]

if they fear for their safety while in _____ 's [parent]

care. This adult will care for the children until he/she receives different instructions from the other parent.

_____ We will seek an independent evaluation regarding _____

_____ [specify] for help in how we might best address this situation.

_____ The time the children are with _____ [parent] will be supervised by

_____ [other adult]

to ensure the children's safety and well-being. The supervised visits will continue until [choose all that apply]:

_____ our children feel ready to spend time alone with _____ .

_____ a counselor indicates that the supervision is unnecessary.

_____ other: _____ [specify]

_____ From _____ until _____ ,

_____ [parent] will not spend time with our children.

_____ During that time, _____ [parent]

will maintain contact with our children via [choose all that apply]:

_____ phone

_____ letter

_____ email

_____ other: _____ [specify]

_____ We further agree that [specify]:

_____

_____

_____

_____

#_____ **Alcohol or Drug Abuse**

_____ _____ [parent] will attend a 12-step or similar program.

_____ _____ [parent] will seek counseling from _____

_____ [provider] to deal with the substance abuse; also [choose all that apply]:

_____ Parent and provider will be permitted to determine when the need for counseling has concluded.

_____ At the conclusion of parent's counseling, provider will send a letter to _____
[other parent] indicating that counseling has concluded to the parent and provider's satisfaction.

_____ _____ [parent] will modify his/her behavior around
our children so that he/she is "sober" as follows [choose all that apply]:

    _____ Will not operate a motor vehicle within _____ hours of consuming drugs or alcohol.

    _____ Will not consume drugs or alcohol for at least _____ hours before visits with the children.

    _____ Will submit to a drug and alcohol screening test performed by _____

    _____ [name of organization].

    _____ The time the children are with _____ [parent] will be supervised

    by _____ [other adult] to ensure
the children's safety and well-being. The supervised visits will continue until [choose all that apply]:

        _____ our children feel ready to spend time alone with _____ .

        _____ a counselor indicates that the supervision is unnecessary.

        _____ other: _____ [specify]

    _____ _____ [parent] will prevent others
from consuming drugs or alcohol while our children are in [his/her] care.

    _____ During that time, _____ [parent]
will maintain contact with our children via [choose all that apply]:

        _____ phone

        _____ letter

        _____ email

        _____ other: _____ [specify]

_____ We further agree that [specify]:

_____

_____

_____

#_____ **Maintaining Contact When the Children Are With the Other Parent**

_____ Our children and _____ [parent] will make an
effort to talk at least every _____ [specify frequency] as follows:

    _____ _____ [parent or children] will initiate each call.

    _____ Calls will be made between _____ and _____.

    _____ If either _____ [parent] or children
will be unavailable at the usual time, the unavailable person will arrange a new time by:

        _____ calling the other parent

        _____ sending a note

        _____ email message

        _____ other: _____ [specify]

_____ Our children and _____ [parent] will not call back and forth more than every
_____ [specify] unless something unusual happens or it is a special occasion.

_____ Our children will be given their own telephone line.

    _____ _____ [parent] will be responsible to teach telephone rules.

    _____ _____ [parent or children] will be responsible for telephone bills.

_____ _____ [parent] and the children can also communicate by:

    _____ letter

    _____ audio or video tapes

    _____ email or electronic conferencing

    _____ other: _____ [specify]

_____ Visits with _____ [parent] will include
a midweek dinner on _____ [day of week] as follows [specify time for exchange]:

_____

_____

_____

_____ We will arrange for our children to communicate with _____ [parent] while our children are away on vacation.

_____ We further agree that [specify]:

_____

_____

_____

#_____ Reinvolving a Previously Absent Parent

_____ _____ [parent] has been absent from our children's life for _____ [period of time], and now wishes to become reinvolved. To make this transition easier for all of us, we agree as follows [choose all that apply]:

_____ We will both seek counseling.

_____ Our children will receive counseling.

_____ We will focus our attention and conversations on our children.

_____ We will build up the amount of time _____ [parent] spends with our children as follows:

_____

_____

_____ _____ [parent] will retain the support systems and schedules he/she established while _____ [parent] was absent, as follows:

_____

_____

_____ To make sure that _____ 's [parent] reentry into our children's lives is for the long term, we will make necessary modifications to this agreement on or before _____ [specify date].

_____ We further agree that [specify]:

_____

_____

_____

#_____ Child Care

_____ In securing child care, we will proceed as follows [choose all that apply]:

_____ Any child care provider will [choose all that apply]:

_____ be a licensed child care provider.

_____ be over the age of _____.

_____ be a relative or close friend.

_____ not care for more than _____ children at any time when our children are there.

_____ come into the home.

_____ other: _____ [specify]

_____ Each parent has the discretion to select the child care provider, but may not use [list names or traits unacceptable]:

_____

_____ Each parent will call the other first to care for the children in that parent's absence.

_____ We will try to share child care responsibilities with neighbors and friends.

_____ Our children can care for themselves, but _____ [other adult] will check in with them.

_____ Our children can care for themselves as long as they follow these rules:

_____

_____

_____

_____ We further agree that [specify]:

_____
_____
_____
_____

#_____ **Moving**

_____ We agree that in the event either parent plans to relocate from _____

_____ [describe community, county, state], that parent will provide

the other parent with at least _____ days' notice in order to allow us to assess the impact that this

move will have on our current parenting arrangements, and to renegotiate or modify the agreement accordingly.

_____ We agree that neither parent plans to relocate now, but in the event either parent wishes to relocate in the future,

we will consider the following [choose all that apply]:

_____ Having both parents relocate.

_____ Changing physical custody of the children to the remaining parent.

_____ Allowing a move as long as our children are under age _____ / over age _____.

_____ Time a move with a change in schools.

_____ Allowing our children to chose whether they will move after age _____.

_____ Allowing the parent to relocate as planned.

_____ Finding new ways to meet both parents' needs and goals so that both parents can remain in the area.

_____ We agree that _____ [parent] will move to

_____ [specify] on or after _____ [date],

and after that time, our parenting agreement will be as follows:

_____ It will remain as currently drafted.

_____ It will change as follows [specify]:

_____
_____
_____
_____

_____ We further agree that [specify]:

_____
_____
_____
_____

#_____ **If Our Homes Are Far Apart**

_____ If there is a considerable distance between our homes, we agree as follows [choose all that apply]:

_____ The children will spend the school year with _____ [parent]

and the summers with _____ [other parent].

_____ The children will live with _____ [parent]

for _____ [specify grade or school level] and with _____

_____ [other parent] for _____ [specify grade or school level].

_____ The children will reside at _____ [name of school] and will visit with

each parent as follows [specify; be consistent with the options you choose under holidays and vacations]:

_____
_____
_____

_____ We further agree that [specify]:

_____
_____
_____

#_____ **Holidays**

_____ This agreement covers the following holidays:

_____   _____
_____   _____
_____   _____

_____ Holiday visits will begin at _____ [time] and will end at _____ [time].

_____ We will adopt an odd year/even year plan, as follows:

_____ In odd years, our children will be with _____ [parent] for these holidays:

_____   _____
_____   _____

and with _____ [parent] for these holidays:

_____   _____
_____   _____

In even years, the reverse will be true.

_____ The children will spend one-half of each holiday with each parent as follows:

_____   _____
_____   _____
_____   _____

_____ We will both celebrate the following holidays with our children:

_____   _____

Each parent will celebrate as follows:

_____
_____

_____ We will divide holiday vacation periods as follows:

_____
_____
_____

_____ Our children will always spend the following holidays with _____ [parent]:

_____   _____
_____   _____

and will always spend the following holidays with _____ [other parent]:

_____   _____
_____   _____

_____ We will plan for holidays as they come up. We will decide where the children will spend their holidays at least _____ [specify time, such as two weeks or one month] in advance.

_____ We further agree that [specify]:

_____
_____
_____

#_____ **Vacations**

_____ We will inform each other at least _____ [period of time] in advance of any planned vacation.

_____ We will provide each other with an itinerary of any trip, and contact information.

_____ Our children may accompany one of us on a vacation under the following conditions:

_____ Any time missed from a regularly scheduled visit with the other parent will be made up as follows:

_____
_____

_____ Travel will be restricted to:
_____ local area
_____ in state

_____ in the United States

_____ the following countries: _____

_____ Activities will be limited to _____.

_____ Activities will not include _____.

_____ Our children will not be away for longer than _____.

_____ We further agree that [specify]:

_____

_____

#_____ **Special Occasions and Family Events**

_____ Special occasions and family events are defined as follows:

_____

_____

_____

_____ We will attend special occasions and family events together whenever possible.

_____ We will attend special occasions and family events as our children wish.

_____ We will attend special occasions and family events as we decide.

_____ _____ [parent] will attend the following special occasions and family events:

_____

_____

_____

_____ _____ [parent] will attend the following special occasions and family events:

_____

_____

_____

_____ We further agree that [specify]:

_____

_____

_____

#_____ **Outside Activities**

_____ Our children may participate in [list all appropriate activities]:

_____

_____

_____

_____ Our children may _not_ participate in [list all appropriate activities]:

_____

_____

_____

_____ We will making decisions about which activities our children may participate in as follows:

_____ By consensus agreement.

_____ _____ [parent's name] may make decisions about

[fill in the blank] _____ activities.

_____ _____ [parent's name] may make decisions about

[fill in the blank] _____ activities.

_____ We will use the decision-making process outlined in issue #_____ [fill in the right number from your completed

agreement. This section refers to issue number 11 in Chapter 5 called "Making Decisions"].

_____ We further agree that [specify]: _____

_____

_____

#_____ **Grandparents, Relatives and Important Friends**

_____ Our children will maintain their relationships with grandparents, other relatives and important friends as follows:

_____

_____

_____

_____

#_____ **Transporting the Children**

_____ Transporting our children between our homes will be as follows [choose all that apply]:

_____ We will meet for exchanges at _____ [specify time and location].

_____ We will alternate transporting our children back and forth.

_____ [parent] will actually transport our children

and _____ [other parent] will share in costs as follows:

_____

_____

_____ _____ [parent] will travel to our children for visits.

_____ _____ [parent] will bring our children for visits to the other parent.

_____ Our children may travel on their own by train, bus or airplane when they reach age _____.

_____ We further agree that [specify]:

_____

_____

_____

#_____ **Improving Transition Times**

_____ We will make the transitions between our homes easier for our children by doing as follows [choose all that apply]:

_____ Our children will start visits with _____ [parent]

at _____ [specify time or event, such as after school or after work]. The visits will end at _____ [specify time or event].

_____ When our children are changing homes, we will minimize the contact between us.

_____ We will exchange information regarding our children the night before they change homes.

_____ When our children are changing homes, the parent starting the visit will take time to give each child some undivided attention.

_____ The parent starting a visit will let our children have some quiet time before any scheduled activities or trips.

_____ _____ [parent] will try to establish and maintain a simple ritual to start and end his/her visits with our children.

_____ We will try to be patient regarding any questions that the children wish to ask about the custody and visitation arrangements.

_____ We further agree that [specify]:

_____

_____

_____

#_____ **Treating Each Child as an Individual**

_____ Each of our children will sometimes need separate or special time with each of us. Therefore, we will set up short separate visits as follows [specify]:

_____

_____

_____

_____ Each of our children will sometimes need separate or special time with each of us. Therefore, we will set up separate time for each child while visiting together as follows [specify]:

_____

_____

_____

_____ Each of our children will sometimes need separate or special time with each of us. Therefore, we further agree that [specify]:

_____
_____
_____

#_____ **When Parenting Styles and Values Are Very Different**

_____ Although our parenting styles are very different, we agree to try the following strategies to minimize the effect of those differences on our children [choose all that apply]:

_____ We will focus our attention and conversations on our children, rather than on each other.

_____ We will encourage our children to explore the following aspects of each of our cultural heritages [specify]:

_____
_____
_____

_____ We respect the other's right to establish an independent life with our children, as long as it is not detrimental to our children.

_____ If our living arrangement exacerbates the problems our children experience because of our different styles and values, we will consider modifying that arrangement.

_____ We further agree that [specify]:

_____
_____
_____

#_____ **Consistency in Raising Children**

_____ The standards for discipline in each of our homes will be as follows [choose all that apply]:

_____ We will abide by the same discipline standards.

_____ The following behavior rules will apply in both homes:

_____
_____
_____

_____ If either of us has a discipline issue with our children, that parent will explain the issue and response to the other so we can be consistent in our discipline.

_____ If our children complain about discipline in the other parent's home, we will encourage them to talk about it with the other parent.

_____ If we cannot agree on discipline standards that will apply in both homes, we will make an effort to understand and respect the other's right to establish behavior rules for our children.

_____ We further agree that [specify]:

_____
_____
_____

#_____ **Disparaging Remarks**

_____ We will refrain from making disparaging remarks about the other, his/her partner and his/her chosen life directly to our children or within our children's hearing.

_____ We further agree that [specify]:

_____
_____
_____

#_____ **Undermining the Parent/Child Relationship**

_____ We will encourage and support our children in maintaining a good relationship with the other. If either of us feels that the other is undermining our relationship with our children, we will proceed as follows [choose all that apply]:

_____ We will discuss the matter and try to reach an agreement.

_____ We will resolve the dispute through:

_____ counseling

_____ mediation

_____ arbitration

_____ other: _____ [specify]

_____ We further agree that [specify]:

_____

_____

_____

#_____ **Denying Access to the Children**

_____ If either of us is denied physical access to our children, contact with them or information about them, we will proceed as follows [choose all that apply]:

_____ We will discuss the matter and try to reach an agreement which will involve reinstating a visitation schedule.

_____ We will resolve the dispute through:

_____ counseling

_____ mediation

_____ arbitration

_____ other: _____ [specify]

_____ We further agree that [specify]:

_____

_____

_____

#_____ **When a Parent Needs to Develop Parenting Skills**

_____ _____ [parent] will work on improving his/her parenting skills as follows [choose all that apply]:

_____ Will attend parenting classes through _____.

_____ Will review written materials on parenting.

_____ Will attend counseling with _____ to deal with and resolve these issues.

_____ We further agree that [specify]:

_____

_____

_____

#_____ **When Nonrelatives Live in the Home**

_____ If either of us lives with nonrelatives, our children will have separate sleeping quarters from the adults.

_____ _____ [parent] will be responsible to make sure that no one in the house consumes nonprescription drugs, or becomes a danger to our children because of intoxication.

_____ _____ [parent] will be responsible to make sure the number of other visitors is kept reasonable.

_____ A nonrelative may not care for our children in the parent's absence.

_____ A nonrelative may not discipline our children in the parent's absence.

_____ We further agree that [specify]:

_____

_____

_____

#_____ **When Parents Have New Partners**

_____ We will resolve issues surrounding a parent's new partner as follows [choose all that apply]:

_____ Our children will always know that we are their parents, regardless of their attachment to a parent's new partner.

_____ Our children will refer to new partners as _____.

_____ The adults and the children will have separate sleeping quarters.

_____ Any new partner will participate in decisions regarding the children as follows [specify]:

_____

_____

_____ We further agree that [specify]:

_____

_____

_____

#_____ **Labeling the Custody Arrangement**

_____ The custody of our children will be as follows [choose one]: _(Note: Read Chapter 12 before completing this option._

Your state may require you to differentiate between legal and physical custody.)

_____ sole custody

_____ legal

_____ physical

_____ joint custody

_____ legal

_____ physical

_____ Joint custody to mean that we will make decisions and share time with our children as follows [specify]:

_____

_____

_____ split custody

_____ _____ [parent] will have custody of

_____ [children's name(s)].

_____ _____ [other parent] will have custody of

_____ [children's name(s)].

_____ _____ [other adult] will have custody of our children.

_____ We further agree that [specify]:

_____

_____

_____

_____

#_____ **Separating Adult Relationship Issues From Parenting Issues**

_____ We agree that we will separate our adult relationship issues from the parenting issues as follows

[choose all that apply]:

_____ agree to resolve all parenting decisions first

_____ schedule separate telephone calls

_____ arrange to discuss adult relationship issues when away from our children

_____ discuss adult relationship issues during joint counseling sessions

_____ We further agree that [specify]:

_____

_____   _____
_____   _____
_____   _____
_____

#_____ **Making Changes**

_____ We will regularly review this agreement as follows: _____ [list dates or frequency, as appropriate].

_____ We will review this agreement when problems arise.

_____ Reviews will be:

    _____ by telephone

    _____ in person

    _____ through:

        _____ counseling

        _____ mediation

        _____ arbitration

        _____ other: _____ [specify]

_____ Our children may participate in the discussions.

_____ Our children may participate in the decisions.

#_____ **Making Substantive Changes to This Agreement**

_____ If we negotiate a substantive modification of this agreement, _____ [parent] will prepare (or make sure that someone else prepares) a summary of the agreement so that we may obtain a court order incorporating our changes. Each parent will be responsible to review the agreement prior to its submission to the court, and to seek independent advice on the agreement to ensure that it says what we intend it to say, accomplishes our objectives and is within the general parameters of what a court is likely to approve.

_____ We further agree that [specify]:

_____
_____
_____

#_____ **Explaining the Agreement to Our Children**

_____ _____ [parent] will explain this agreement to our children. _____ [other parent] will be available to answer any questions the children might have.

_____ We further agree that [specify]:

_____
_____
_____

D. Responsibility to Prepare a Final Draft of this Agreement. _____ [parent] will prepare a final draft of this agreement. Both parents will be responsible to review the agreement for completeness and accuracy. By _____ [date], both parents will have made any necessary changes and _____ _____ [parent] will conform this agreement to the specifications of the _____ court for inclusion in an order of the court.

_____   _____
Signature   Date

_____   _____
Signature   Date

Index

CATALOG

...more from Nolo

		PRICE	CODE
BUSINESS			
	Avoid Employee Lawsuits (Quick & Legal Series)	$24.95	AVEL
⊙	The CA Nonprofit Corporation Kit (Binder w/CD-ROM)	$49.95	CNP
▣	Consultant & Independent Contractor Agreements (Book w/Disk—PC)	$24.95	CICA
▣	The Corporate Minutes Book (Book w/Disk—PC)	$69.95	CORMI
	The Employer's Legal Handbook	$39.95	EMPL
	Firing Without Fear (Quick & Legal Series)	$29.95	FEAR
▣	Form Your Own Limited Liability Company (Book w/Disk—PC)	$44.95	LIAB
▣	Hiring Independent Contractors: The Employer's Legal Guide (Book w/Disk—PC)	$34.95	HICI
▣	How to Create a Buy-Sell Agreement & Control the Destiny of your Small Business (Book w/Disk—PC)	$49.95	BSAG
▣	How to Form a California Professional Corporation (Book w/Disk—PC)	$49.95	PROF
▣	How to Form a Nonprofit Corporation (Book w/Disk —PC)—National Edition	$44.95	NNP
⊙	How to Form a Nonprofit Corporation in California (Book w/CD-ROM)	$44.95	NON
▣	How to Form Your Own California Corporation (Binder w/Disk—PC)	$39.95	CACI
▣	How to Form Your Own California Corporation (Book w/Disk—PC)	$39.95	CCOR
▣	How to Form Your Own New York Corporation (Book w/Disk—PC)	$39.95	NYCO
⊙	How to Form Your Own Texas Corporation (Book w/CD-ROM)	$39.95	TCOR
	How to Write a Business Plan	$29.95	SBS
	The Independent Paralegal's Handbook	$29.95	PARA
	Leasing Space for Your Small Business	$34.95	LESP
	Legal Guide for Starting & Running a Small Business, Vol. 1	$29.95	RUNS
▣	Legal Guide for Starting & Running a Small Business, Vol. 2: Legal Forms (Book w/Disk—PC)	$29.95	RUNS2
	Marketing Without Advertising	$22.00	MWAD
▣	Music Law (Book w/Disk—PC)	$29.95	ML

▣ Book with disk
⊙ Book with CD-ROM

	PRICE	CODE
Nolo's California Quick Corp (Quick & Legal Series)	$19.95	QINC
Nolo's Guide to Social Security Disability	$29.95	QSS
Nolo's Quick LLC (Quick & Legal Series)	$24.95	LLCQ
⦿ Open Your California Business in 24 Hours (Book w/CD-ROM)	$24.95	OPEN
▣ The Partnership Book: How to Write a Partnership Agreement (Book w/Disk—PC)	$39.95	PART
Sexual Harassment on the Job	$24.95	HARS
Starting & Running a Successful Newsletter or Magazine	$29.95	MAG
Tax Savvy for Small Business	$34.95	SAVVY
Wage Slave No More: Law & Taxes for the Self-Employed	$24.95	WAGE
▣ Your Limited Liability Company: An Operating Manual (Book w/Disk—PC)	$49.95	LOP
Your Rights in the Workplace	$29.95	YRW

CONSUMER

Fed Up with the Legal System: What's Wrong & How to Fix It	$9.95	LEG
How to Win Your Personal Injury Claim	$29.95	PICL
Nolo's Everyday Law Book	$24.95	EVL
Nolo's Pocket Guide to California Law	$15.95	CLAW
Trouble-Free Travel...And What to Do When Things Go Wrong	$14.95	TRAV

ESTATE PLANNING & PROBATE

8 Ways to Avoid Probate (Quick & Legal Series)	$16.95	PRO8
9 Ways to Avoid Estate Taxes (Quick & Legal Series)	$24.95	ESTX
Estate Planning Basics (Quick & Legal Series)	$18.95	ESPN
How to Probate an Estate in California	$39.95	PAE
⦿ Make Your Own Living Trust (Book w/CD-ROM)	$34.95	LITR
Nolo's Law Form Kit: Wills	$24.95	KWL
▣ Nolo's Will Book (Book w/Disk—PC)	$34.95	SWIL
Plan Your Estate	$39.95	NEST
Quick & Legal Will Book (Quick & Legal Series)	$21.95	QUIC

▣ Book with disk

⦿ Book with CD-ROM

	PRICE	CODE

FAMILY MATTERS

Child Custody: Building Parenting Agreements That Work	$29.95	CUST
Child Support in California: Go to Court to Get More or Pay Less (Quick & Legal Series)	$24.95	CHLD
The Complete IEP Guide	$24.95	IEP
Divorce & Money: How to Make the Best Financial Decisions During Divorce	$34.95	DIMO
Do Your Own Divorce in Oregon	$29.95	ODIV
Get a Life: You Don't Need a Million to Retire Well	$24.95	LIFE
The Guardianship Book for California	$34.95	GB
⊙ How to Adopt Your Stepchild in California (Book w/CD-ROM)	$34.95	ADOP
A Legal Guide for Lesbian and Gay Couples	$25.95	LG
⊙ The Living Together Kit (Book w/CD-ROM)	$34.95	LTK
Nolo's Pocket Guide to Family Law	$14.95	FLD
Using Divorce Mediation: Save Your Money & Your Sanity	$21.95	UDMD

GOING TO COURT

Beat Your Ticket: Go To Court and Win! (National Edition)	$19.95	BEYT
The Criminal Law Handbook: Know Your Rights, Survive the System	$29.95	KYR
Everybody's Guide to Small Claims Court (National Edition)	$18.95	NSCC
Everybody's Guide to Small Claims Court in California	$24.95	CSCC
Fight Your Ticket ... and Win! (California Edition)	$24.95	FYT
How to Change Your Name in California	$34.95	NAME
How to Collect When You Win a Lawsuit (California Edition)	$29.95	JUDG
How to Mediate Your Dispute	$18.95	MEDI
How to Seal Your Juvenile & Criminal Records (California Edition)	$34.95	CRIM
Mad at Your Lawyer	$21.95	MAD
Nolo's Deposition Handbook	$29.95	DEP
Represent Yourself in Court: How to Prepare & Try a Winning Case	$29.95	RYC

▣ Book with disk

⊙ Book with CD-ROM

PRICE CODE

HOMEOWNERS, LANDLORDS & TENANTS

California Tenants' Rights .... $24.95 CTEN

Contractors' and Homeowners' Guide to Mechanics' Liens

(Book w/Disk—PC)—California Edition .... $39.95 MIEN

The Deeds Book (California Edition) .... $24.95 DEED

Dog Law .... $14.95 DOG

Every Landlord's Legal Guide (National Edition, Book w/CD-ROM) .... $44.95 ELLI

Every Tenant's Legal Guide .... $26.95 EVTEN

For Sale by Owner in California .... $29.95 FSBO

How to Buy a House in California .... $29.95 BHCA

The Landlord's Law Book, Vol. 1: Rights & Responsibilities (California Edition) .... $44.95 LBRT

The California Landlord's Law Book, Vol. 2: Evictions (Book w/CD-ROM) .... $44.95 LBEV

Leases & Rental Agreements (Quick & Legal Series) .... $24.95 LEAR

Neighbor Law: Fences, Trees, Boundaries & Noise .... $24.95 NEI

The New York Landlord's Law Book (Book w/CD-ROM) .... $39.95 NYLL

Renters' Rights (National Edition—Quick & Legal Series) .... $19.95 RENT

Stop Foreclosure Now in California .... $34.95 CLOS

HUMOR

29 Reasons Not to Go to Law School $12.95 29R

Poetic Justice .... $9.95 PJ

IMMIGRATION

How to Get a Green Card .... $29.95 GRN

U.S. Immigration Made Easy .... $44.95 IMEZ

Book with disk
Book with CD-ROM

	PRICE	CODE

MONEY MATTERS

	PRICE	CODE
▣ 101 Law Forms for Personal Use (Quick & Legal Series, Book w/Disk—PC)	$29.95	SPOT
Bankruptcy: Is It the Right Solution to Your Debt Problems? (Quick & Legal Series)	$19.95	BRS
Chapter 13 Bankruptcy: Repay Your Debts	$29.95	CH13
▣ Credit Repair (Quick & Legal Series, Book w/Disk—PC)	$18.95	CREP
▣ The Financial Power of Attorney Workbook (Book w/Disk—PC)	$29.95	FINPOA
How to File for Chapter 7 Bankruptcy	$29.95	HFB
IRAs, 401(k)s & Other Retirement Plans: Taking Your Money Out	$24.95	RET
Money Troubles: Legal Strategies to Cope With Your Debts	$24.95	MT
Nolo's Law Form Kit: Personal Bankruptcy	$16.95	KBNK
Stand Up to the IRS	$29.95	SIRS
Surviving an IRS Tax Audit (Quick & Legal Series)	$24.95	SAUD
Take Control of Your Student Loan Debt	$24.95	SLOAN

PATENTS AND COPYRIGHTS

	PRICE	CODE
⊙ The Copyright Handbook: How to Protect and Use Written Works (Book w/CD-ROM)	$34.95	COHA
Copyright Your Software	$24.95	CYS
Domain Names	$24.95	DOM
▣ Getting Permission: How to License and Clear Copyrighted Materials		
Online and Off (Book w/Disk—PC)	$34.95	RIPER
How to Make Patent Drawings Yourself	$29.95	DRAW
The Inventor's Notebook	$34.95	INOT
Nolo's Patents for Beginners (Quick & Legal Series)	$29.95	QPAT
▣ License Your Invention (Book w/Disk—PC)	$39.95	LICE
Patent, Copyright & Trademark	$29.95	PCTM
Patent It Yourself	$49.95	PAT
Patent Searching Made Easy	$29.95	PATSE
The Public Domain	$34.95	PUBL
⊙ Software Development: A Legal Guide (Book w/ CD-ROM)	$44.95	SFT
Trademark: Legal Care for Your Business and Product Name	$39.95	TRD
The Trademark Registration Kit (Quick & Legal Series)	$19.95	TREG

▣ Book with disk
⊙ Book with CD-ROM

▣ Book with disk

⊙ Book with CD-ROM

Special Upgrade Offer

Save 35% on the latest edition of your Nolo book

Because laws and legal procedures change often, we update our books regularly. To help keep you up-to-date, we are extending this special upgrade offer. Cut out and mail the title portion of the cover of your old Nolo book and we'll give you **35% off** the retail price of the NEW EDITION of that book when you purchase directly from Nolo. This offer is to individuals only.

Call us today at 1-800-992-6656

Prices and offer subject to change without notice.

Order Form

Name _____

Address _____

City _____

State, Zip _____

Daytime Phone _____

E-mail _____

Item Code	Quantity	Item	Unit Price	Total Price

Subtotal	
Add your local sales tax (California only)	
Shipping: RUSH $8, Basic $3.95 (See below)	
"I bought 3, ship it to me FREE!"(Ground shipping only)	
TOTAL	

Method of payment

☐ Check   ☐ VISA   ☐ MasterCard
☐ Discover Card   ☐ American Express

Account Number _____

Expiration Date _____

Signature _____

Shipping and Handling

Rush Delivery—Only $8

We'll ship any order to any street address in the U.S. by UPS 2nd Day Air* for only $8!

* Order by noon Pacific Time and get your order in 2 business days. Orders placed after noon Pacific Time will arrive in 3 business days. P.O. boxes and S.F. Bay Area use basic shipping. Alaska and Hawaii use 2nd Day Air or Priority Mail.

Basic Shipping—$3.95

Use for P.O. Boxes, Northern California and Ground Service.

Allow 1-2 weeks for delivery. U.S. addresses only.

For faster service, use your credit card and our toll-free numbers

Order 24 hours a day

Online	www.nolo.com
Phone	1-800-992-6656
Fax	1-800-645-0895
Mail	Nolo.com 950 Parker St. Berkeley, CA 94710

Visit us online at
www.nolo.com

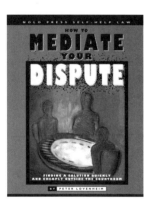

Take 2 Minutes
& Give Us Your 2 cents

Your comments make a big difference in the development and revision of Nolo books and software. Please take a few minutes and register your Nolo product—and your comments—with us. Not only will your input make a difference, you'll receive special offers available only to registered owners of Nolo products on our newest books and software. Register now by:

PHONE
1-800-992-6656

FAX
1-800-645-0895

EMAIL
cs@nolo.com

or **MAIL** us
this registration card

REMEMBER:
Little publishers have big ears. We really listen to you.

fold here

- -

REGISTRATION CARD

NAME	DATE

ADDRESS

CITY	STATE	ZIP

PHONE	E-MAIL

WHERE DID YOU HEAR ABOUT THIS PRODUCT?

WHERE DID YOU PURCHASE THIS PRODUCT?

DID YOU CONSULT A LAWYER? (PLEASE CIRCLE ONE)   YES   NO   NOT APPLICABLE

DID YOU FIND THIS BOOK HELPFUL?   (VERY)   5   4   3   2   1   (NOT AT ALL)

COMMENTS

WAS IT EASY TO USE?   (VERY EASY)   5   4   3   2   1   (VERY DIFFICULT)

DO YOU OWN A COMPUTER? IF SO, WHICH FORMAT? (PLEASE CIRCLE ONE)   WINDOWS   DOS   MAC

We occasionally make our mailing list available to carefully selected companies whose products may be of interest to you.

❏ If you do not wish to receive mailings from these companies, please check this box.

❏ You can quote me in future Nolo promotional materials. Daytime phone number _____.

CUST 3.0

NOLO IN THE NEWS

"Nolo helps lay people perform legal tasks without the aid—or fees—of lawyers."

—**USA TODAY**

Nolo books are …"written in plain language, free of legal mumbo jumbo, and spiced with witty personal observations."

—**ASSOCIATED PRESS**

"…Nolo publications…guide people simply through the how, when, where and why of law."

—**WASHINGTON POST**

"Increasingly, people who are not lawyers are performing tasks usually regarded as legal work… And consumers, using books like Nolo's, do routine legal work themselves."

—**NEW YORK TIMES**

"…All of [Nolo's] books are easy-to-understand, are updated regularly, provide pull-out forms…and are often quite moving in their sense of compassion for the struggles of the lay reader."

—**SAN FRANCISCO CHRONICLE**

fold here

Place
stamp here

nolo
950 Parker Street
Berkeley, CA 94710-9867

Attn: CUST 3.0